The Ultimate UKCAT Guide

UniAdmissions

ISBN 978-0-9932311-1-7

Revised Version

Published by *RAR Medical Services Limited*
www.uniadmissions.co.uk
info@uniadmissions.co.uk
Tel: 0203 375 6294

The Ultimate UKCAT Guide

1000 Practice Questions

Dr. David Salt

Dr. Rohan Agarwal

UniAdmissions

The Basics

What is the UKCAT?

The United Kingdom Clinical Aptitude Test (UKCAT) is a two hour computer based exam that is taken by applicants to medical and dental schools. The questions are randomly selected from a huge question bank. Since every UKCAT test is unique, candidates can sit the UKCAT at different times.

You register to sit the test online and book a time slot. On the day, bring along a printout of your test booking confirmation and arrive in good time. Your identity will be checked against a photographic ID that you'll need to bring. You then leave your personal belongings in a locker and enter the test room. Make sure you go to the toilet and have a drink before going in, to save wasting time during the test.

Test Structure:

SECTION	WHAT DOES IT TEST?	QUESTIONS	TIMING
ONE	**Verbal reasoning**: Essentially a reading comprehension test, with questions based on passages. This is a test of accuracy and speed of reading.	44	22 minutes
TWO	**Quantitative reasoning**: The maths is usually intellectually straightforward but can involve complex or multi stage calculations against the clock. Assesses your understanding of numbers.	36	25 minutes
THREE	**Abstract reasoning**: Matching shapes to which set they belong in. This tests your pattern recognition skills and rewards those who have clear and logical organisation of thought.	55	14 minutes
FOUR	**Decision analysis**: This is the code translation section. It tests your decision making ability when provided with complex information.	28	32 minutes
FIVE	**Situational Judgement**: This tests your ability to make decisions in a clinical environment. To perform well, you must understand the role and responsibilities of a medical student.	67	27 minutes

Who has to sit the UKCAT?

You have to sit UKCAT if you are applying for any of the universities that ask for it in the current application cycle. You are strongly advised to check this list in May to see if the universities you are considering require it. The following is a list of the universities and courses requiring UKCAT for 2015 entry. As it is subject to change, it is included for guidance only:

University Name	Courses requiring UKCAT
University of Aberdeen	A100, A201
University of Birmingham	A100, A200
Cardiff University	A100, A101, A104, A200, A204
University of Central Lancashire	8J68
University of Dundee	A100, A104, A200, A204
Durham University	A100
University of East Anglia	A100, A104
University of Edinburgh	A100
University of Exeter	A100
University of Glasgow	A100, A200
Hull York Medical School	A100
Keele University	A100, A104
King's College London	A100, A101, A102, A202, A205, A206
University of Leicester	A100, A101
University of Manchester	A104, A106, A204, A206
University of Newcastle	A100, A101, A206
University of Nottingham	A100, A108
Plymouth University	A100, A206, B750
Queen Mary, University of London	A100, A101, A200
Queen's University Belfast	A100, A200
University of Sheffield	A100, A104, A200
University of Southampton	A100, A101, A102
University of St Andrews	A100, A990, B900
St George's, University of London	A100, A900
University of Warwick	A101

The following table gives the subject area for each of the course codes that require UKCAT.

Course Code	Course Details
A100	Undergraduate medicine, full time
A101	Graduate-entry medicine, full time
A102	Graduate-entry medicine, full time
A104	Undergraduate medicine with preliminary year, full time
A200	Undergraduate dentistry, full time
A202	Graduate-entry dentistry, full time
A204	Undergraduate dentistry with preliminary year, full time
A205	Undergraduate dentistry, full time
A206	Undergraduate dentistry, full time
(St. George's) A900	Undergraduate medicine for international, full time
(St. Andrew's) A990	Undergraduate medicine Canadian programme, full time
B750	Dental hygiene and therapy
B900	Biomedical sciences
(UCLAN) 8J68	Undergraduate medicine, full time

Why is the UKCAT used?

For medical schools, choosing the best applicants is hard. Every year, medical schools are flooded with talented applicants, all of whom have top grades and great personal statements. They felt they needed extra information to help them find the very best from the pool of very talented applicants they always had. That's why admissions tests were created.

The UKCAT was first introduced in 2006 to help medical schools make their choices. The test examines skills in different areas, all of which are related to critical thinking and decision making. The idea was to create a pure aptitude test, something which cannot be prepared for. However this is certainly not the case with the UKCAT, and this is even acknowledged by UKCAT itself based on their research. In our experience, you can improve your UKCAT score with only a small amount of work, and with proper organised preparation the results can be fantastic. In the UKCAT, timing is everything.

When do I sit the UKCAT?

When you register to sit UKCAT online, you choose your date and time slot and also the test centre. The UKCAT can be sat from 1st July through to early October. Registration for the test opens in early May – we recommend you book your test early so you have the best choice of possible dates.

Many students find it helpful to sit UKCAT in mid-late August – this gives you time in the summer to prepare, but gets the test complete before you go back to school, so you have one less thing to worry about at that busy time. Remember that you may want to modify your university choices based on your UKCAT score to maximise your chances.

How much does it cost?

In the EU, tests sat between 1 July and 31 August cost £65. Tests sat between 1 September and 6 October cost £80. Tests outside the EU cost £100 throughout the testing period.

Some candidates who might struggle to fund the UKCAT fee are eligible for a bursary. If eligible to apply for one, you need to apply with supporting evidence by the deadline of 22 September 2015.

Bursary Eligibility Criteria

> ➤ Receipt of 16–19 bursary or EMA.
> ➤ Receipt of discretionary learner support.
> ➤ Receipt of full maintenance grant or special support grant.
> ➤ Receipt of income support, job seeker's allowance or employment support allowance.
> ➤ Receipt of universal credit.
> ➤ Receipt of child tax credit.
> ➤ Living with a family member in support of income support, job seeker's allowance or child tax credit.

Can I resit the UKCAT?

You can't resit UKCAT in the same application cycle – whatever score you get is with you for the year. That's why it's so important to make sure you're well prepared and ready to perform at your very best on test day.

If I reapply, do I have to resit the UKCAT?

If you choose to re-apply the following year, you need to sit UKCAT again. You take your new score with you for the new applications cycle. UKCAT scores are only valid for one year from the test date.

When do I get my results?

Because the test is computerised, results are generated immediately and you will be given your score on the day of the test. You will be given a printed sheet with your details and your score to take away. Knowing your score is useful as it can help you choose your universities tactically to maximise your chances of success. Note that you don't put your UKCAT score anywhere on your UCAS form, nor do you contact any universities to inform them. Universities that request UKCAT are sent your scores directly by UKCAT, so you don't need to do anything besides apply through UCAS.

Where do I sit the UKCAT?

UKCAT is a computerised exam and is sat at computer test centres, similar to the driving theory test. When you book the test, you choose the most convenient test centre to sit it at.

How is the UKCAT Scored?

When you finish the test, the computer works out your raw score by adding up your correct responses. There are no mark deductions for incomplete or incorrect answers, so it's a good idea to answer every question even if it's a guess. For the first four sections, this is then scaled onto a scale from 300 – 900. The totals from each of the four sections are added together to give your overall score out of 3,600.

For section 5 (the situational judgement test, SJT) the scoring is slightly different. Here the appropriateness of your responses is used to generate a banding, from band 1 (being the best) to band 4 (being the worst). This is presented separately to the numerical score, such that every candidate's score contains a numerical score out of 3,600 and an SJT banding.

How does my score compare?

This is always a tough question to answer, but it makes sense to refer to the average scores. The scaling is such that around 600 represents the average score in any section, with the majority of candidates scoring between 500 and 700. Thus a score higher than 700 is very good and a score less than 500 is very weak.

For reference, in the 2015 entry cycle the mean scores at the end of testing were 571, 684, 636 and 614 for sections 1 – 4 respectively, giving an overall mean score of 2505. An overall score of 2180 or below was the bottom 10% of candidates and a score above 2820 was the top 10% of candidates.

How is the UKCAT used?

Different universities use your UKCAT score in different ways. Firstly, universities that do not explicitly subscribe to UKCAT cannot see your UKCAT score and are unaware whether or not you sat UKCAT. Universities that use UKCAT can use it in a variety of ways – some universities use it as a major component of the assessment such as selecting candidates for interview based upon the score. Others use it as a smaller component, for example to settle tie-breaks between similar candidates. Each university publishes guidance on how they use the UKCAT, so you should check this out for the universities you are considering.

It's important to know how UKCAT is used in order to maximise your chances. If you score highly in UKCAT, you might decide to choose universities that select for interview based on a high UKCAT score cut-off. That way, you help to stack the odds in your favour – you might, for instance, convert a one in eight chance to a one in three chance. If your score isn't so good, consider choosing universities that don't use UKCAT in that way, otherwise you risk falling at the first hurdle and never getting the chance to show them how great you actually are.

By this logic, **it makes sense for all medical applicants to sit UKCAT** – if you score well it opens doors, and if you don't you don't even have to apply to UKCAT universities. It makes sense not to place all your eggs in one basket. If you were to, for example, apply to only BMAT universities, you risk jeopardising your entire application if you are unlucky on test day.

Can I qualify for extra time?

Yes – some people qualify for extra time in the UKCAT, sitting what is known as UKCAT SEN. If you usually have extra time in public exams at school, you are likely to be eligible to sit the UKCAT SEN. The overall time extension is 30 minutes, bringing the total test time up from 120 to 150 minutes; this is allocated proportionately across the different sections. If you have any medical condition or disability that may affect the test, requiring any special provision, or requiring you to take any medical equipment or medication into the test you should contact customer services to discuss how to best proceed.

General Advice

Practice

Preparing for the UKCAT will almost certainly improve your UKCAT score. You are unlikely to be familiar with the style of questions in sections 3, 4 and 5 of the UKCAT when you first encounter them. With practice, you'll become much quicker at interpreting the data and your speed will increase greatly. Practising questions will put you at ease and make you more comfortable with the exam format, and you will learn and hone techniques to improve your accuracy. This will make you calm and composed on test day, allowing you to perform at your best.

Initially, **work through the questions at your own pace**, and spend time carefully reading the questions and looking at the additional data. The purpose of this is to gain familiarity with the question styles and to start to learn good techniques for solving them. Then closer to test day, make sure you practice the questions under exam conditions and at the correct pace.

Start Early

It is much easier to prepare if you practice little and often. Start your preparation well in advance, ideally by early July but you are advised to start no later than early August. This way, you will have plenty of time to work through practice questions, to build up your speed and to incorporate time-saving techniques into your approach. How to start – well by reading this you're obviously on track!

How to Work

Although this obviously depends on your learning style, it can be helpful to split your preparation into two stages. Early on, it's often best to focus on only one section per day. Firstly read about the section, then maybe follow through a fully worked example, then try some practice questions, stop and mark them and work out anywhere you've gone wrong. By working on only one section per day, you focus your thoughts and allow yourself to get deeper into understanding the question type you're working on. The aim of early preparation is to *learn* about the test and the question styles. Don't worry so much about timing as you do about accuracy and technique. It is a good idea to start on the verbal reasoning and quantitative reasoning as these take the greatest amount of time to improve.

Nearer to test day, you'll need to work on multiple sections per day to help train your thinking to switch quickly from one mode to another. Start to attempt questions with strict timing. The aim now is that you're comfortable in answering the questions, so the next step is to work on exam technique to ensure you know what to expect on the day. Attempt the online UKCAT practice questions – although there are not very many of these, they are set out as the computer will be on the day with the official UKCAT calculator, so getting familiar with this is important.

Repeat tough questions

When checking through answers, pay particular attention to questions you have got wrong. Look closely through the worked answers in this book until you're confident you understand the reasoning- then repeat the question later without help to check you can now do it. If you use other resources where only the answer is given, have another look at the question and consider showing it to a friend or teacher for their opinion.

Statistics show that without consolidating and reviewing your mistakes, you're likely to make the same mistakes again. Don't be a statistic. Look back over your mistakes and address the cause to make sure you don't make similar mistakes when it comes to the test. You should avoid guessing in early practice. Highlight any questions you struggled with so you can go back and improve.

Positive Marking

When it comes to the test, the marking scheme is only positive – you won't lose points for wrong answers. You gain a mark for each correct answer and do not gain one for each wrong or unanswered one. Therefore if you aren't able to answer a question fully, you should guess. Since each question provides you with 3 to 4 possible answers, you have a 33% or 25% chance of guessing correctly – something which is likely to translate to a number of points across the test as a whole.

If you do need to guess, try to make it an educated one. By giving the question a moment's thought or making a basic estimation, you may be able to eliminate a couple of options, greatly increasing your chances of a successful guess. This is discussed more fully in the subsections.

Booking your Test

Unless there are strong reasons otherwise, you should try to **book your test during August**. This is because in the summer, you should have plenty of time to work on the UKCAT and not be tied up with schoolwork or your personal statement deadline. If you book it any earlier, you'll have less time for your all-important preparation; if you book any later, you might get distracted with schoolwork, your personal statement deadline and the rest of your UCAS application. In addition, you pay £15 more to sit the test on or after 1 September.

Mock Papers

There are 2 full UKCAT papers freely available online at www.ukcat.ac.uk and once you've worked your way through the questions in this book, you are highly advised to attempt both of them and check your answers afterwards. There are also a further 2 full mock papers available at www.uniadmissions.co.uk/ukcat-mock-papers.

Prioritising Sections

Many students find sections 3 and 4 the easiest to improve on. Initially, they can often be the hardest sections, but with a bit of familiarity and practice their score can increase greatly. If you start your preparation late or have limited time for any reason, it would be wise to concentrate most on these sections in order to achieve the best gains.

A word on timing...

"If you had all day to do your UKCAT, you would get 100%, 3600 points. But you don't."
Whilst this isn't completely true, it illustrates a very important point. Once you've practiced and know how to answer the questions, the clock is your biggest enemy. This seemingly obvious statement has one very important consequence. **The way to improve your UKCAT score is to improve your speed.** There is no magic bullet. But there are a great number of techniques that, with practice, will give you significant time gains, allowing you to answer more questions and score more marks.

Timing is tight throughout the UKCAT – mastering timing is the first key to success. Some candidates choose to work as quickly as possible to save up time at the end to check back, but this is generally not the best way to do it. UKCAT questions have a lot of information in them – each time you start answering a question it takes time to get familiar with the instructions and information. By splitting the question into two sessions (the first run-through and the return-to-check) you double the amount of time you spend on familiarising yourself with the data, as you have to do it twice instead of only once. This costs valuable time. In addition, candidates who do check back may spend 2–3 minutes doing so and yet not make any actual changes. Whilst this can be reassuring, it is a false reassurance as it has no effect on your actual score. Therefore it is usually best to pace yourself very steadily, aiming to spend the same amount of time on each question and finish the final question in a section just as time runs out. This reduces the time spent on re-familiarising with questions and maximises the time spent on the first attempt, gaining more marks.

There is an option to flag questions for review, making it easier to check back if you have time at the end of the section. There is absolutely no disadvantage to using this. If you've guessed a question then it makes sense to mark it, so you know where to best spend your spare time if you do finish the section early. Always select an answer first time round (even if it's a guess), as there is no negative marking – you may not have time to turn back later on.

It is essential that you don't get stuck with the hardest questions – no doubt there will be some. In the time spent answering only one of these you may miss out on answering three easier questions. If a question is taking too long, choose a sensible answer and move on. Never see this as giving up or in any way failing, rather it is the smart way to approach a test with a tight time limit. With practice and discipline, you can get very good at this and learn to maximise your efficiency. It is not about being a hero and aiming for full marks – this is essentially impossible and in any case completely unnecessary. It is about maximising your efficiency and gaining the maximum possible number of marks within the time you have.

Verbal Reasoning

The Basics

Section 1 of the UKCAT is the verbal reasoning subtest. It tests your ability to quickly read a passage, find information that is relevant and then analyse statements related to the passage. There are 44 questions to answer and the time allowed is 22 minutes, so you have exactly 30 seconds per question. The idea is that this tests both your language ability and your ability to make decisions, traits which are important in a good doctor.

You are presented with a passage, upon which you answer questions. Typically, there are 11 separate passages, each with 4 questions about it. There are two styles of question in section 1, and each requires a slightly different approach. All questions start with a statement relating to something in the passage.

In the first type of question, you are asked if the statement is true or false based on the passage. There is also the option to answer "cannot tell". Choose "true" if the statement either matches the passage or can be directly inferred from it. Choose "false" if the statement either contradicts the passage or exaggerates a claim the passage makes to an extent that it becomes untrue.

Choosing the "cannot tell" option can be harder. Remember that you are answering based *ONLY* on the passage and not on any of your own knowledge – so you choose the "cannot tell" option if there is not enough information to make up your mind one way or the other. Try to choose this option actively. "Cannot tell" isn't something to conclude too quickly, it can often be the hardest answer to select. Choose it when you're actively looking for a certain piece of information to help you answer a question, and you cannot find it.

In the other type of question, you are given a stem and have to select the most appropriate response based on the question. There is only one right answer – if more than one answer seems appropriate, the task is to choose the *best* response. Remember that there is no negative marking in the UKCAT. There will be questions where you aren't certain. If that is the case, then choose an option that seems sensible to you and move on. A clear thought process is key to doing well in section 1 – you will have the opportunity to build that up through the worked examples and practice questions until you're answering like a pro!

This is the first section of the UKCAT, so you're bound to have some nerves. Ensure that you have been to the toilet because once the exam starts you can't pause and go. Take a few deep breaths and calm yourself down. Try to shut out distractions and get yourself into your exam mindset. If you're well prepared, you can remind yourself of that to help keep calm. See it as a job to do and look at the test as an opportunity. If you perform well it will boost your chances of getting into good medical schools. If the worst happens, there are plenty of good medical schools that do not use UKCAT, so all is not lost.

How to Approach This Section

Time pressure is a recurring theme throughout the UKCAT, but it is especially important in Section 1, where you have only 30 seconds per question and a lot of information to take in.

> ***Top tip!*** Though it might initially sound counter-intuitive, it is often best to read the question ***before*** reading the passage. When read the passage knowing what you're looking for, you're likely to find the information you need much more quickly.

You should look carefully to see what the question is asking. Sometimes the question will simply need you to find a phrase in the text. In other instances, your critical thinking skills will be needed and you'll have to carefully analyse the information presented to you.

Extreme Words

Words like "extremely", "always" and "never" can give you useful clues for your answer. Statements which make particularly bold claims are less likely to be true, but remember you need a direct contradiction to be able to conclude that they are false.

To answer an "always" question, you're looking for a definition. Always be a bit suspicious of "never" – make sure you're certain before saying true, as most things are possible.

Prioritise

With UKCAT, you can leave and come back to any question. **By flagging for review**, you make this easier. Since time is tight, you don't want to waste time on long passages when you could be scoring easier marks. Score the easy marks first, then come back to the harder ones if time allows. If time runs too short, at least take enough time to guess the answers as there's a good chance you could pick up some marks anyway.

Be a Lawyer

Put on your most critical and analytical hat for section A! Carefully analyse the statements like you're in a court room. Then look for the evidence! **Examine the passage closely, looking for evidence** that either supports or contradicts the statement. Remember **you're making decisions based on ONLY the passage**, not using any prior knowledge. Does the passage agree or disagree? If there isn't enough evidence to decide, don't be afraid to say "cannot tell".

Read the Question First

Follow our top tip and read the question before the passage. There is simply not enough time to read all the passages thoroughly and still have time to complete everything in 22 minutes. By reading the statement or question first, you can understand what it is that is required of you and can then pick out the appropriate area in the passage. Do not fall into the trap of trying to read all of the passage, you will not score highly enough if you do this.

When skim reading through the passage, it is inevitable that you will lose accuracy. However you can reduce this effect by doing plenty of practice so your ability to glean what you need improves. A good tip is to practice reading short sections of complicated texts, such as quality newspapers or novels, at high pace. Then test yourself to see how much you can recall from the passage.

Find the keywords

The keyword is the most important word to help you relate the question to the passage; sometimes there might be two keywords in a question. When you read the passage, focus in on the keywords straight away. This gives you something to look for in the passage to identify the right place to work from.

It is usually easy to find the keyword/s, and you'll become even better with practice. When you find it, go back a line and read from the line before through the keyword to the end of the line after. Usually, this contains enough relevant information to give you the answer.

If this is not successful, you need to consider your next steps. Time is very tight in the UKCAT and especially so in section 1. There are other passages that need your attention, and there may be much easier marks waiting for you. If reading around the keyword has not given you the right answer it may well be time to move on. It might be that there is a more subtle reference somewhere else, that you need to read the whole passage to reach the answer or indeed that the answer cannot be deduced from the passage. Either way, if it's difficult to find your time could be better spent gaining marks elsewhere. Make a sensible guess and move on.

Use only the Passage

Your answer *must* only be based on the information available in the passage. Do not try and guess the answer based on your general knowledge as this can be a trap. For example, if the question asks who the first person was to walk on the moon, then states "the three crew members of the first lunar mission were Edwin Aldrin, Neil Armstrong and Michael Collins". The correct answer is "cannot tell" – even though you know it was Neil Armstrong and see his name, the passage itself does not tell you who left the landing craft first. Likewise if there is a quotation or an extract from a book which is factually inaccurate, you should answer based on the information available to you rather than what you know to be true.

If you have not been able to select the correct answer, eliminate as many of the statements as possible and guess – you have a 25 – 33% chance of guessing correctly in this section even without eliminating any answers, and if you've read around some keywords in the text you may well have at least some idea as to what the answer is. These odds can add a few easy marks onto your score.

Flagging for review

There is an additional option to flag a question for review. **Flagging for review has absolutely no effect on the overall score.** All it does is mark the question in an easy way for it to be revisited if you have time later in the section. Once the section is complete, you cannot return to any questions, flagged or unflagged.

Coming back to questions can be inefficient – you have to read the instructions and data each time you work on the question to know what to do, so by coming back again you double the amount of time spent on doing this, leaving less time for actually answering questions. We feel the best strategy is to work steadily through the questions at a consistent and even pace.

That said, flagging for review has one great utility in Section 1. If you come across a particularly long or technical passage, you may want to flag for review immediately and skip on to the next passage. By coming back to the passage at the end, you allow yourself the remaining time on the hardest question. This has an advantage in each of two scenarios. If you're really tight for time, at least you maximised the time you did have answering the easier questions, thereby maximising your marks. If it turns out you have extra time to spare, you can spend it on the hardest question, allowing you a better chance to get marks you otherwise would have struggled to obtain. Thus flagging for review can be useful in Section 1, but its usefulness is probably greatest when you flag questions very soon after seeing them rather than when you have already spent time trying to find the answer.

Remember to find the right balance: if you flag too many questions you will be overloaded and won't have time to focus on them all; if you flag too few, you risk under-utilising this valuable resource. You should flag only a few questions per section to allow you to properly focus on them if you have spare time.

Worked Examples

Example 1:

In 287 BC, in the city of Athens, there lived a man named Archimedes who was a royal servant to the King. One day, the King received a crown as a birthday gift and wanted to know whether it was made of pure gold. He ordered Archimedes to find out whether the crown was indeed pure gold or an alloy. For many days, Archimedes pondered over the solution to this problem. He knew the density of gold, but could not calculate the volume of the crown.

One day, as he was bathing, he realised as he got into the bath that the volume of water displaced must be exactly equal to the volume of his own body. Upon this realisation he ran across the streets naked, yelling eureka! He weighed the crown and found its volume by immersing it in water and then calculated its density. He discovered that the density did not match that of pure gold. The crown was impure, and the blacksmith responsible for its manufacture suffered the consequences.

1. Archimedes knew the volume of the crown but could not calculate its weight
    a. True
    b. False
    c. Cannot tell

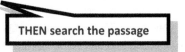

Look for the keyword!

THEN search the passage

2. Archimedes gave the crown as a birthday gift to the King
    a. True
    b. False
    c. Cannot tell
3. The crown had silver impurities
    a. True
    b. False
    c. Cannot tell
4. Archimedes found the weight of the crown using a balance scale
    a. True
    b. False
    c. Cannot tell

Answers

1. **False** – The keywords are volume and weight. Check these against the text and you will find that Archimedes could calculate the weight, but not the volume.
2. **False** – Whilst it does not explicitly state the giver of the gift, the description of Archimedes as a servant and his role in investigating the crown is wholly incompatible with him being the giver of the gift.
3. **Cannot tell** – The word silver does not appear anywhere in the passage so this statement cannot be true. But this statement is not false either because nowhere does it say that silver was not the impurity.
4. **Cannot tell** – Through your own logic, you probably guessed that this is how Archimedes weighed the crown, but remember to only use the information within the passage and use of a balance scale is not mentioned.

Example 2:

Gregor Mendel was an Austrian-Hungarian monk who is regarded to be the father of genetics. Mendel was born in poverty and was often believed to suffer from autism. He studied mathematics and physics at university, but subsequently dropped out as he could not fund his studies. He joined a monastery to escape a life of poverty. He loved to collect biological specimens and from this he noticed the different traits that animals and plants possessed. Curiosity led him to experiment with plants in a greenhouse at the monastery, as experiments using animals was forbidden.

He collected pure bred pea plants of different colours (green and yellow) and bred them together. He collected the seeds and planted them, noting that all the plants of this second generation produced green peas. He cross bred this second generation of peas and replanted the seeds. Surprisingly, of the third generation, most of the peas produced were green, and a few plants produced yellow peas. From this he deduced that the pea colour was determined by a gene that had different forms, called alleles. Using mathematics he found that the ratio of green peas to yellow peas came to 9:3:3:1, now called the classical Mendelian ratio. This work led to the development of the theory of genetics and how some alleles were dominant over the other and thus deduces the phenotype of the organism in question.

1. Gregor Mendel was a scientist
    a. True
    b. False
    c. Cannot tell

> Don't waste time! Remember to read the questions before the passage!

2. The facilities of the monastery enabled him to carry out his experiments
    a. True
    b. False
    c. Cannot tell
3. The genotype of the organism is influenced by alleles
    a. True
    b. False
    c. Cannot tell
4. The monastery allowed Mendel to carry out experiments on animals
    a. True
    b. False
    c. Cannot tell

Answers
1. **True** – This is a slightly tricky question. Mendel studied mathematics and physics, and used these skills and scientific method to produce groundbreaking scientific results. Therefore, though not explicitly stated, he is by any reasonable definition a scientist – so the statement is true.
2. **True** – It says clearly that the monastery had a greenhouse that he utilised to perform experiments on plants.
3. **Cannot tell** – Although you know this to be true from your own knowledge, it cannot be inferred from the passage.
4. **False** – This is a direct contradiction to the passage which states that experimenting on animals was forbidden at the monastery.

Example 3:
Before the 20ᵗʰ century, relatively little was known about the atom. The concept that objects were made of smaller particles that could not become any smaller was theorised by two Greek philosophers; Leucippus and Democritus. They believed that if you keep cutting an object consistently, there will come a point where it will not be able to be cut any further. Therefore, the theory of the atom was established but it was not possible to explore it further.

In 1897, JJ Thompson discovered the electron. He subjected a hot metal coil into an electric field, thereby producing the first cathode ray. Importantly, he noticed that the cathode ray could be deflected by a magnetic field, when viewed under a cloud chamber, and realised that it was negatively charged. As the atom is neutral, he proposed that there must be positively charged particles that give the atom an overall neutrality. JJ Thompson put forward the plum pudding model theory of the atom; that positively charged particles and negatively charged particles are mixed together in an infinitely small region of space.

In 1911, Ernest Rutherford carried out the gold leaf experiment. He fired alpha particles at a gold leaf and found that although most of the alpha particles went through, some were deflected. Occasionally, he also saw a small spark upon collision. From this, he theorised that the atom cannot be a mixture of negatively and positively charged particles, but rather has a dense core of positively charged particles. He called these particles protons. He also realised that most of the atom is empty space.

In 1932, James Chadwick performed an experiment that discovered the final component of the atom. On observation of alpha decay, he noticed that one of the particles being emitted was not deflected by a magnetic field, hence being neutrally charged. He called this particle the neutron.

Thus, the Rutherford Model of the Atom was born; the protons and neutrons form the nucleus of the atom, which electrons in spinning in orbit.

> This is a long passage. Consider flagging for review and coming back later if you have time

1. The passage supports which of the following conclusions?
A. The experiments of the previous scientist led to the development and guidance of the other.
B. The Rutherford Atomic Model cannot be further improved.
C. Rutherford had the help of other scientists to put forward his theory.
D. The deflection of the cathode ray by magnetism was the phenomenon that led JJ Thompson to develop the Plum Pudding model.

2. Based on the passage, each of these statements is true except
A. Earnest Rutherford is from New Zealand.
B. James Chadwick named the neutron.
C. The direction of particle deflection was determined using the cloud chamber.
D. Most of the atom is empty space.

3. Using the information in the passage, it can be inferred that:
A. Previous to Leucippus and Democritus, no one had thought of the idea of the atom.
B. Rutherford is the father of nuclear physics.
C. The gold leaf experiment was key in discovering the atomic nucleus.
D. The positron also exists.

4. Which of the following statements about the work of Earnest Rutherford is true?
A. He never carried out his own experiments without assistance from others.
B. The experimental data from the gold leaf experiment led to the development of the Geiger counter.
C. He discovered that most of the atom is empty space.
D. The foundation of nuclear fission was built from the gold leaf experiment.

Answers
1. **D** – D is the only conclusion supported by the passage, none of the other statements are mentioned in the passage. You may know from your general knowledge or simply from common sense that Rutherford had the help of other scientists, but because the passage does not mention this, it is not the answer.
2. **A** – Earnest Rutherford was indeed from New Zealand, but this is not mentioned in the passage.
3. **C** – There is no way that you know that A is true. The passage does not suggest that Rutherford is considered to be the father of nuclear physics. Finally, although the positron does indeed exist, this is not mentioned in the passage!
4. **C** – A and B are also true but not supported in the passage. D is not mentioned in the passage and also not scientifically correct.

Verbal Reasoning Questions

For questions 1 – 106 decide if each of the statements is true, false or can't tell:

SET 1

The Kyoto Protocol is an international agreement written by the United Nations in order to reduce the effects of climate change. This agreement sets targets for countries in order for them to reduce their greenhouse gas emissions. These gases are believed to be responsible for causing global warming as a result of recent industrialisation.

The Protocol was written in 1997 and each country that signed the protocol agreed to reduce their emissions to their own specific target. This agreement could only become legally binding when two conditions had been fulfilled: When 55 countries agreed to be legally bound by the agreement and when 55% of emissions from industrialised countries had been accounted for.

The first condition was met in 2002 however countries such as Australia and the United States refused to be bound by the agreement so the minimum of 55% of emissions from industrialised countries was not met. It was only after Russia joined in 2004 that allowed the protocol to come into force in 2005.
Some climate scientists have argued that the target combined reduction of 5.2% emissions from industrialised nations would not be enough to avoid the worst consequences of global warming. In order to have a significant impact, we would need to aim at reducing emissions by 60% and to get larger countries such as the US to support the agreement.

1.   The Kyoto Protocol is legally binding in all industrialised countries.
2.   The greenhouse gas emissions from Australia and the United States represent 45% of emissions from industrialised countries.
3.   Each country chose the amount by which they would reduce their own emissions.
4.   The global emission of greenhouse gases has reduced since 2005.
5.   The harmful effects of climate change would be avoided if all countries reduced their emissions by 60%.

SET 2

The space race was a competition between the Soviet Union and the United States to show off their technological superiority and economic power. It took place during the Cold War when there was a tense relationship between these nations. As the technology used in space exploration could also have military applications, both nations had many scientists and technicians involved.

In 1957, the USSR launched the first artificial satellite into the Earth's orbit, named Sputnik. The launch of this satellite was one of the first steps towards space exploration. The Americans were worried that the Soviets could use similar technology to launch nuclear warheads. This prompted urgency within the Americans, leading President Eisenhower to found NASA, and so began the space race.

The Soviets took another step forward in April 1961 when they sent the first person into space, a cosmonaut named Yuri Gagarin. This prompted President John F. Kennedy to make the unexpected claim that the US would beat the Soviets to land a man on the moon and that they would do so before the end of the decade. This led to the foundation of Project Apollo, a programme designed to do this.

In 1969, Neil Armstrong and Buzz Aldrin set off for the moon on the Apollo 11 space mission and became the first astronauts to walk on the moon. Neil Armstrong famously said "one small step for man, one giant leap for mankind." This lunar landing led the US to win the space race that started with Sputnik's launch in 1957.

6. The Soviet Union were mainly concerned with launching satellites into space for a military advantage over the United States.
7. Project Apollo was founded in order for the United States to defeat the Soviet Union in the Cold War.
8. Yuri Gagarin did not become the first man on the moon because the Soviet technology could not handle the conditions on the moon.
9. The United States began their attempts at space exploration when the Soviets launched Sputnik.
10. The United States were losing the space race when John F. Kennedy said they would land a man on the moon.

SET 3

A marathon is a long distance running event that is 26.2 miles long. This race was named after the famous Battle of Marathon. The first Persian invasion of Greece took place in 490 BC. The Greek soldiers did not expect to defeat the Persian army, which had greater numbers and superior cavalry. The Greek commander utilised a tactical flank to defeat the Persians forcing them to retreat back to Asia. According to legend, the fastest Greek runner, Pheidippides, was ordered to run from Marathon to Athens to announce the Greek victory over the Persians, but then collapsed and died of exhaustion. This legendary 25 mile journey from Marathon to Athens is the basis for modern marathons.

The initial organisers of the Olympic Games in 1896 wanted an event that would celebrate the glory of Ancient Greece. They therefore chose to use the same course that Pheidippides ran. In subsequent Olympic Games, the exact length of the route depended on the location but was roughly similar to the 25 mile distance. The current standardised distance of 26.2 miles has been chosen by the IAAF and used since 1921, and has been taken from the distance used at the 1908 Olympics in London. Nowadays, more than 500 marathons are organised each year.

11. Pheidippides was chosen as he was the only Greek runner determined enough to make the journey to Athens
12. Marathon distances have been standardised since the 1908 Olympics
13. The Persian commander believed he would defeat the Greeks in the Battle of Marathon.
14. The original route from Marathon to Athens is used for IAAF marathons today.
15. The Persian soldiers were trained better than the Greek soldiers.

SET 4

Many species of bird migrate northwards in the spring to take advantage of the abundance of nesting locations and insects to eat. As the availability of food resources decreases during the winter to the point where the birds cannot survive, the birds migrate south again. Some species are capable of flying all the way around the earth. The act of migration itself can be risky for birds due to the amount of energy required to sustain flight over these long distances. Many juvenile birds can die from exhaustion during their first migration. Due to this inherent risk of migration, many species of birds have acquired different adaptations to increase the efficiency of flight. Flying with other birds in certain formations can allow their flight patterns to be more energy efficient.

The Northern bald ibis migrates from Austria to Italy. The behaviour of these birds is such that they migrate together within a flock and each individual bird continuously changes its position within the flock. Each individual bird benefits by spending some time flying in the updraft produced by the leading birds and a proportional amount of time leading the formation. Although it would theoretically be possible for an individual bird to take advantage of this energy-efficient flight without leading the formation itself, no Northern bald ibis has been shown to do this.

16. As migration is risky and dangerous, it would be better for birds not to migrate.
17. All migrating birds do so in flocks to increase their efficiency
18. All the birds within a flock of Northern bald ibis benefit from flocking behaviour
19. A bird within a Northern bald ibis flock that does not lead will be forbidden from flying with the rest of the flock
20. The migration timing depends on different seasons

SET 5

The dramatic decline of the bee population in the UK has been attributed to a number of causes such as the loss of wild flowers in the countryside. Bees require these wildflowers for food and it has been estimated that 97% of the flower-rich grassland has been lost since the 1930s. Other causes include climate change and pesticides that are toxic to bees. This is particularly problematic in the UK, which has had a 50% reduction in the honey bee population between 1985 and 2005 whilst the rest of Europe has only averaged a 20% reduction during the same time period.

This loss of flowers from the British countryside has been caused by agricultural pressures. In order to increase food production, traditional farming methods have been abandoned in favour of techniques that increase productivity. These techniques, however, involve the reduction of wild flowers.

Bumblebees are required to pollinate wildflowers and commercial crops. A reduction of wildflower pollination will result in their decline, which will ultimately affect other wildlife as they can be involved in a complex food chain. The commercial crops will need to be pollinated artificially using expensive methods that will ultimately drive up the price of fruits and vegetables. The global economic value of pollination from bees has been estimated at €265 billion annually.

21. The bee population in the UK has decreased by 97% since the 1930s.
22. The UK is the country with the largest decline in bee population
23. Reverting back to traditional farming methods will decrease the overall production of food
24. Artificial pollination will be capable of replacing bees if it becomes cheap enough
25. Increasing pesticide-free fruit and vegetable growth will slow the decline in bee population

SET 6

Driving in snowy and icy conditions can be dangerous as it increases stopping distances. The stopping distance represents how far a car will travel before slowing down to a halt. It is made up of the thinking distance, which is how long it takes for a driver to react, and the braking distance, which represents the time taken for the brakes to fully stop the car.

It is advised to fit winter tyres during the winter season as these have much better grip on snow and ice. These tyres are made out of a softer material than regular tyres, allowing them to have more traction at colder temperatures. This ultimately reduces the braking distance.

As the brakes are not very effective at stopping a vehicle on icy roads, it is recommended to steer out of trouble if possible rather than applying the brakes. It is therefore important to be travelling at slower speeds to avoid the need to suddenly brake.

If the car is stuck and cannot move, the driver can stay warm by running the engine to generate heat. However, if the exhaust pipe becomes blocked by snow and the fumes cannot escape then the engine must be turned off. This is because the engine produces carbon monoxide, which is extremely toxic and odourless.

26. Driving whilst tired increases the braking distance.
27. Regular tyres are more dangerous than winter tyres in cold conditions as they are harder
28. It is always safe to run the engine for heat in cold conditions
29. It is dangerous to use winter tyres in hot summer conditions.
30. To avoid a collision on icy surfaces, it is important to gently apply the brakes.

SET 7

The Socratic method is a form of philosophical questioning named after the Greek philosopher Socrates. It takes place as a dialogue between Socrates and another individual and attempts to investigate difficult concepts such as justice and ethics. In this dialogue, Socrates' partner puts forward an opinion or a thesis. Socrates then proposes extra premises that will attempt to disprove the original thesis. If there is an opposition, this shows that the original thesis is false and that the opposite is true.

In this dialogue, Socrates often showed other philosophers and thinkers how their reasoning was wrong. Some respected him for doing so as he was aware of the fact that his knowledge was limited and that he was merely questioning everything critically. However, many people were angered by him asking questions without providing any answers to these difficult questions himself. This led to him making a number of enemies in Greece.

In 399 BC, Socrates was accused of heresy and corruption of the youth by three of his enemies. He was then trialled and found guilty by the jury and so sentenced to death by drinking the poison hemlock. One of his friends, Crito, bribed the guards to allow Socrates to escape; however he chose not to flee away. Many have referred to him as a martyr as he chose to die standing for knowledge and wisdom.

31. Socrates was the first person to use this method of questioning.
32. The Socratic method questions the wisdom of the person forming the opinions.
33. As described in the passage, the Socratic method involved corrupting the youth and heresy.
34. Socrates chose not to escape from prison because he was afraid his enemies would find him again.
35. Socrates was able to define concepts such as justice and ethics himself.

SCHULER BOOKS
&MUSIC

Schuler Books
1982 Grand River Ave.
Okemos MI, 48864

QTY	SKU	PRICE
1 T	The Ultimate Ukcat Gu	19.99

Total Sale	$19.99
Sales Tax	$1.20
Net Sale	$21.19

Special Order Deposi	$21.19
Account # 17769	

daniel jennings -
1688 e grand river ave
east lansing, MI 49923
Phone: 517-775-3539
email:
Account: jennings, daniel

Sale Date: 5/27/2016
Register: 6
Store: 2
Cashier: ZML
Items: 1 Quantity: 1

Schuler Books and Music Gift Cards
are available in any denomination and
can be used online at:

www.schulerbooks.com
****

5/27/2016 3:11:50 PM

0008560242

SCHULER BOOKS
&MUSIC

Schuler Books
1982 Grand River Ave.
Okemos, MI, 48864

QTY	SKU	PRICE
1	T The Ultimate Ukcat Gu	19.99

	Total Sale	$19.99
	Sales Tax	$1.20
	Net Sale	$21.19

Special Order Deposit		$21.19
Account # 17765		

daniel jennings -
1588 e grand river ave
east lansing, MI 49923
Phone: 517-775-3539
email:
Account: jennings, daniel

Sale Date: 5/27/2016
Register: 6
Store: 2
Cashier: ZMU
Items: 1 Quantity: 1

Schuler Books and Music Gift Cards
are available in any denomination and
can be used online at:

www.schulerbooks.com

****
Refunds - 30 days with receipt.
Sealed items must be returned unaltered
CD's & DVD's must be unopened.
Used, seasonal, dated, special orders
and markdown items are non-returnable.

5/27/2016 3:1:50 PM

0008580242

SET 8

The Anglo-Saxons were the group of people who lived in England between the 5th Century and the Norman conquest in 1066 AD. When the Germanic tribes of the Saxons, Angles and Jutes came to Britain in 449 AD, they pushed the Celtic Britons who were there before them up into Wales. The combination of the Germanic dialects of these different tribes became Anglo-Saxon or Old English.

Old English is very different from Modern English and uses more Germanic words and its grammar is closer to Old German. If English speakers were to read a passage of Old English, they would struggle to understand any more than a few words. It is thought that this Old English is most similar to the Dutch dialect spoken in Friesland, a province in the north of the Netherlands. One of the famous literary works written in Old English was the poem Beowulf. It is not known who wrote this poem and only one original manuscript of the poem still exists today. The story involves the hero Beowulf who fights and kills the giant Grendel. All the people celebrate the death of Grendel however Grendel's mother comes to the town and attempts to kill as many people for revenge. Beowulf then fights Grendel's mother and kills her as well.

36. The Jute tribe did not contribute to the Anglo-Saxon language.
37. German speakers would be able to read Beowulf in its original language.
38. Beowulf was the strongest warrior at that time.
39. A dialect of Old English is currently spoken in the Netherlands.
40. The Celts lived in England in 449 AD

SET 9

A constellation is a group of stars that are often visible forming a pattern in the sky. The constellation's visibility depends on a number of factors. The biggest factor is your position on the Earth, for example the constellation Cassiopeia is only visible in the northern hemisphere. As the Earth orbits the Sun, another significant factor affecting constellation visibility is the season on Earth.

As the Earth rotates on its own axis, certain stars and constellations can appear to rise and fall in the night sky. Constellations that do not move in this manner are called circumpolar. This factor can allow people to navigate on the Earth using the positioning of the stars. This is especially useful during marine navigation as there are no visible landmarks. The most commonly used star for navigation is the North Star Polaris, as its position is constant within the night sky.

There are 12 constellations that take the form of animals or humans known as the zodiac signs. This is the basis for the origin of star signs in astrology, which suggests that human behaviour is influenced by the celestial phenomena. The star sign of a person represents the position of the sun at the moment of their birth. The zodiac sign which shares the same position as the sun in the sky becomes their star sign.

41. Certain stars are not visible from the southern hemisphere
42. The constellation Cassiopeia is circumpolar
43. Star signs are chosen by the constellations visible at birth
44. Polaris is used for navigation as it is the brightest star in the sky
45. Different constellations are visible from London and Sydney.

SET 10

Maple syrup is a sweet syrup made from maple trees. The sap from the trees is harvested during March. It is then boiled to evaporate water, making it denser and sweeter. It takes roughly 40 litres of maple sap to produce 1 litre of maple syrup. This current process is very similar to that used by the Native Americans except it uses more advanced equipment.

According to American Indian legend, the maple trees originally made life free from hardship. They produced a thick syrup all year round which the people would drink. A mythological creature named Glooskap saw that the people of a village were strangely silent. The men were not getting ready to hunt and the women were not minding the fires. He found the villagers sitting near the maple trees letting its syrup drip into their mouth.

Glooskap was angered by their laziness and used his powers to fill the trees with water so that they would only produce a dilute, watery sap. This meant that the people had to boil the sap to produce the sweet syrup. Although it wasn't very difficult to do this, it meant that they had to look after their fires and gather firewood. Furthermore, it meant that the trees were not able to produce enough sap to sustain the people all year so they would be forced to hunt and forage during the spring and summer.

46. Sweet syrup can be made from the sap from other trees.
47. Glooskap was angered because there was no syrup left for him to drink.
48. The technique for making maple syrup is similar to that used in the time of the American Indian legends.
49. Sap is only harvested from maple trees for one month a year.
50. Hunting animals was more difficult than drinking maple syrup.

SET 11

Stockholm syndrome is an interesting phenomenon that sometimes happens to people who have been kidnapped or held hostage. They may feel some loyalty or attraction towards the person that has kidnapped them.

This phenomenon was named after a bank robbery in Stockholm, Sweden in 1973. Four bank workers were kept hostage by two criminals who wanted to rob the bank. After being held against their will for six days, they showed that they had formed a positive relationship with their captors. The hostages were seen to be hugging and kissing the men who had kidnapped them.

It can be hard to explain why this might be the case as it involves the captor putting the hostage in a terrifying situation. In the mind of the hostage it is this person who can ultimately decide if the hostage is going to die. As a result of this fear of death, any small act of kindness prompts them to be thankful for the gift of life. This can ultimately lead to them developing Stockholm syndrome.

It is important to understand the interaction between victims and captors in cases of Stockholm syndrome as this knowledge can improve the chances of hostage survival. As such, the FBI is willing to devote resources in order to improve crisis negotiation.

51. People who get kidnapped will eventually develop positive emotions towards their kidnapper.
52. The bank workers hugged and kissed their kidnappers because the criminals forced them to.
53. Stockholm syndrome is useful to understand for crisis negotiation.
54. According to the passage, it is the victims that fear for their life that tend to develop Stockholm Syndrome.
55. The bank robbery in 1973 was the first recorded instance of a positive relationship developing between captors and hostages.

SET 12

Clownfish are a type of fish that live in salt water. They are orange fish that have white stripes. They are capable of growing up to 10-18 cm. They have also been called anemone fish as they have a symbiotic relationship with certain sea anemones.

The tentacles of sea anemone are capable of stinging fish that come near them, which the anemone then eat. The clownfish have a special mucous covering that protects them from this sting. As a result of this, clownfish that live inside sea anemone are safe from other predators but do not get stung themselves. The sea anemone benefit from the clownfish as the clownfish eat the algae that grows on the anemone. The bright colour of the clownfish lures in small fish to the anemone which ultimately get stung. They also receive better water circulation from the action of the clownfish fins.

Many people like keeping clownfish in aquariums because of their bright orange colour and how easy they are to look after. This can be dangerous as the clownfish lifespan is greatly increased by living within an anemone. Even if an anemone is added to the aquarium, only certain species of clownfish are capable of living within certain species of anemone.

56. A clownfish that loses its mucous layer can live inside sea anemone.
57. Clownfish help sea anemone to eat fish.
58. Clownfish will die if they do not have an anemone to live in.
59. Clownfish have a mutually beneficial relationship with all anemone.
60. Anemone protect clownfish from predators.

SET 13

The guillotine was a machine used to kill people by chopping off their head. It consists of a heavy blade attached to a frame. When the blade was released, it would fall down under its own weight and chop off the victim's head, killing them instantly. It was commonly used in France during the French Revolution as it was the only legal method of execution in order to enact the death penalty.

The guillotine was named after a French doctor called Joseph Guillotin. He decided that a more humane way of executing someone was needed as he realised he was unable to get rid of the death penalty. He decided that using an automatic mechanical device for decapitation would be more humane than by a person with an axe. The first guillotine built was then tested on animals to see if the axe would have enough force to decapitate its victim.

Before the guillotine was used in execution, the criminal would be hanged. This was seen to be less humane as the victim was supposed to die from the impact of the rope snapping their necks, however this did not happen all the time. The victim could be in agony for up to forty minutes before eventually dying from asphyxiation.

61. Joseph Guillotin agreed with the death penalty.
62. According to the passage, the guillotine was used for execution before the French Revolution.
63. Hanging usually causes death by asphyxiation.
64. The guillotine was seen as being more humane as it was automatic with the blade falling through its own weight.
65. During the French Revolution, hanging was the common form of execution.

SET 14

"The Gherkin" is a building in the City of London named after and famous for its distinctive shape. Its modern architecture was designed by Norman Foster and was built between 2001 and 2003. Norman Foster is famous for utilising the laws of physics in designing many of his buildings. The walls of the Gherkin would allow air to enter the building for passive cooling. As this air warms up, it rises and is then let out of the building.

The site where the Gherkin is built used to belong to the Baltic Exchange, the headquarters of the global marketplace for ship sales. In 1992, the site was damaged by bombs placed by the Provisional IRA. As there were many historic buildings in the area and only a few were damaged, the City of London governing body was insistent that any redevelopment must restore the old historic look. They later discovered that the amount of damage caused was too severe and so removed this restriction.

The building was sold in 2007 for a sum of £630 million, making it the most expensive office building in the UK. The building was then put up for sale in 2014, initially at a lower price as its owners could not afford to pay loan repayments due to high interest rates and the devaluing of the British pound. It was bought by a Brazilian billionaire for £700 million.

66. According to the passage, The Gherkin is famous because of its passive cooling system.
67. The Baltic Exchange was built with a modern architectural design.
68. The Gherkin was sold in 2014 at a loss.
69. The Provisional IRA intended to destroy the Baltic Exchange.
70. Norman Foster has designed many buildings that incorporated physics in their design.

SET 15

The living wage represents the minimum hourly rate for employment which allows an individual to cover their basic costs of living. This wage is set at £9.15 per hour in London and £7.85 per hour in the rest of the UK. This difference in living wage between London and the rest of the UK is explained by the significant costs associated with living in London.

The minimum wage is currently £6.50 for employees aged over 21 and £5.13 for employees aged between 18 and 20. This is lower than the living wage values quoted above and represents the legal minimum wage. It would be illegal for an employer to pay less than these values. Although many employers have agreed to pay a living wage, they are not legally obliged to do so.

The introduction of the living wage in companies has been argued to be beneficial for these companies. Many employers found that employees who were paid the living wage were able to work harder with better quality. It has also improved the quality of life for the families of employees as it has allowed those who are parents to spend more time with their children. However, some employers have argued that the introduction of the living wage would force them to fire some workers, forcing others to work harder.

71. The living cost across UK cities is approximately equal.
72. Companies introduce the living wage to avoid the legal complications of underpaying their employees.
73. A 24 year old working at minimum wage would be able to live comfortably in Manchester
74. Introducing a living wage would be beneficial for all employees.
75. Paying someone a living wage will only benefit that individual

SET 16

The ecological footprint is a simple way to look at how sustainable people are being. It is based on the idea that all the resources taken from the Earth are finite. It is defined by how much land and water would be required to produce the resources that the population consumes within a year. It has been calculated that there are currently 11.2 billion bio-productive hectares available on the Earth.

A study in 2004 has suggested that our ecological footprint is 13.5 billion hectares, meaning that we are using the Earth's resources 20% faster than they are being renewed. This will ultimately result in the loss of all the Earth's resources.

Individual countries can look at their own ecological footprint and compare it to the size of their bio-productive capacity. Some countries are in an ecological deficit - they require more land than their bio-productive capacity to sustain them. Other countries have an ecological reserve, meaning that their bio-productive capacity is greater than their footprint.

It can be difficult for individual countries to reduce their ecological footprint. This can either be performed by reducing that countries reliance on unsustainable resources or by increasing the amount of bio-productive land available. It is important, however, that a global effort is made to increase our sustainability.

76. The ecological footprint of a country directly depends on its population.
77. The combined area of the Earth's land and water mass is 11.2 billion hectares
78. The ecological footprint can be reduced by using sustainable resources.
79. Only the countries with an ecological deficit are able to tackle the global problem of sustainability.
80. The bio-productive capacity of the Earth is fixed.

SET 17

English punk rock band The Sex Pistols formed in 1975, and sparked off the British punk movement, leading to the subsequent creation of multiple punk and alternative rock acts. They produced only one album - 'Never Mind the Bollocks, Here's the Sex Pistols' – in their brief existence. However, despite these, some state The Sex Pistols are one of the most important bands in the history of popular music.

Originally, the band was made up of Johnny Rotten (the singer), Paul Cook (the drummer) and Glen Matlock (the bassist), however the latter was subsequently replaced by Sid Vicious. The band was involved in numerous controversies, due to their lyrics, performances and public appearances. One may argue the band was asking for trouble when they created songs attacking the music industry (such 'EMI') and commenting on controversial topics like consumerism, the Berlin wall, the Holocaust and abortion ('Bodies'). The band did not take kindly to local figureheads, as demonstrated with the release of 'God Save the Queen' in 1977, which was an attack on both conforming to societal norms and also blindly accepting the royalty as an authority.

81. It is believed by some that pop music's most influential act is The Sex Pistols.
82. The Sex Pistols kick-started the punk movement.
83. The Sex Pistols' lyrics denounced abortion.
84. The Sex Pistols controversially equated the music industry with the Holocaust.
85. The Sex Pistols' songs showed they were staunch royalists.
86. The Sex Pistols had two bassists.

SET 18

Cancer is a disease of the tissues of the body which occurs when cells begin to grow and replicate rapidly. These cells are capable of becoming masses called tumours which can obstruct the parts of the body in which they are found. Some of these tumours are also able to spread to other parts of the body in a process known as metastasis.

The incidence of cancer has significantly increased recently in the Western developed world. The most common form of cancer in the UK is breast cancer, even though it very rarely affects men. Most cancers seem to have no obvious cause whilst a few are known to have a specific cause. Mesothelioma, for example, is a type of lung cancer that is caused by exposure to asbestos. People who have worked with asbestos without adequate protection in the past are eligible for compensation from the government.

Before the 19th century, the only way to treat a cancer was to physically remove the tumour from the body. This usually involved amputation or removing a lot of tissue. It was only in the 19th century when improvements in surgical hygiene enhanced the success rates of tumour removal. At this time, Marie and Pierre Curie discovered the first non-surgical treatment, which involved irradiating the tumour.

87. Everyone exposed to asbestos will eventually suffer from mesothelioma.
88. Breast cancer is the most common type of cancer in British women.
89. The surgical success rate for tumour removal in the 19th century was improved by irradiating the tumour.
90. Irradiation is more effective than surgery in removing tumours.
91. Only cells that are capable of spreading cause tumours.

SET 19

The indigenous Australians are the native people of Australia, also known as the Aborigines. It is believed that they arrived in Australia 50,000 years ago from South-east Asia. They lived a traditional life, which involved living in wooded areas and hunting animals with spears and boomerangs. This lifestyle would not harm the environment of Australia as they believe that the land, with all of its animals and plants, is sacred.

When the British people came to Australia in 1788, there were not many people living in Australia. According to British law, any land could be claimed for the monarchy if they believed that nobody owned it and so they claimed all of the land. It was later agreed by the Australian government in 1976 that the aboriginal people would have the rights to the land where they were originally located if they could prove that they have been living there.

Nowadays, many of the 517,000 aboriginal people in Australia have chosen to integrate with the modern ways of life. They live in cities and towns and some of them have acquired professional jobs. Others have decided to maintain their traditional aboriginal way of living. Few have been unfortunate in that they haven't been educated enough to benefit from Australian society but have also lost their traditional aboriginal ways.

92. The British people claimed the Australian land because the Aborigines only lived in the wooded areas.
93. There are 517,000 Aborigines currently living in the cities and towns of Australia.
94. The aboriginal people were able to reclaim all their land in 1976.
95. Most Aborigines have received enough education to integrate with Australian culture.
96. The Aborigine lifestyle is similar to that of the south-east Asians from 50,000 years ago.

SET 20

Chilli peppers are a type of fruit grown all over the world. Most of these peppers are spicy and used in cooking. These peppers are believed to initially originate from Bolivia. As they spread throughout Europe, it was found that their spiciness had a similar taste to black peppercorns, which were incredibly valuable in the 15th century. As such, many people began to grow chilli peppers, which spread rapidly to India and China.

These chilli peppers began to be incorporated into the cooking of different cultures, being used more commonly in hotter countries. There are a number of reasons suggested for why these countries would prefer spicy food. One suggestion is that spicy food would help people to sweat in hot conditions, allowing them to cool down. This however, is unlikely to explain the prevalence of chilli peppers as it is possible to sweat without eating them. Adding spice to food was also found to be a convenient method of preserving food as it discouraged the growth of bacteria.

The peppers are spicy because they produce the chemical capsaicin. This chemical binds to receptors in the mouth and throat and cause the sensation of heat. This receptor is also capable of responding to heat directly. This is an example of labelled line coding which suggests that the perception of a stimulus is determined by which receptor it activates, not the nature of the stimulus itself.

97. Chilli peppers became more valuable in the 15th century.
98. Eating chilli peppers in hot conditions causes sweating.
99. All chilli peppers are spicy.
100. An individual lacking the capsaicin receptor would be able to eat the spiciest chillies without any pain.
101. Different methods of activating the capsaicin receptor (TRPV1) cause different sensations.

SET 21

The social determinants of health are factors in which people are born, grow, live, work and age. These factors depend on the social distribution of resources and can affect the life expectancy and quality of life that people have. These factors refer to the social context that people live in and include characteristics such as level of education, culture, stress and socioeconomic conditions as well as many others. It can be difficult to see how some of these factors may affect somebody's health but it is likely to involve a combination of multiple factors.

A number of mechanisms acting together have been described to explain why someone with a poor diet would have a lower life expectancy. One such mechanism is as follows: This individual would be more likely to be malnourished which would weaken their immune system. This would ultimately increase their likelihood of suffering from infections. Recurrent infections would place strain on the body, which could eventually result in organ failure. On average, the life expectancy in the most deprived areas can be up to 10 years lower than in the least deprived areas.

Many of these health inequalities are avoidable. Understanding how these social determinants affect the health of a population will allow us to improve its care. Knowledge of how social policies impact health can better allow us to monitor changes in health care, and is allowing us to reduce the gaps between those with a more disadvantaged social background from those with a privileged background.

102. Dropping out of school can have an effect on an individual's health.
103. The effects of the social determinants of health are principally measured by life expectancy.
104. The health impact of poor diet can be avoided completely by using multivitamins that supplement the immune system.
105. Nothing can be done to improve the health care of the poor in comparison to the rich.
106. Alan lives in a less deprived area than Henry so Alan will live longer than Henry.

SET 22

J.S. Mill describes his ethical theory and the reception of this in his book, 'Utilitarianism', and states:

'The creed which accepts as the foundation of morals, Utility, or the Greatest Happiness Principle, holds that actions are right in proportion as they tend to promote happiness, wrong as they tend to produce the reverse of happiness. By happiness is intended pleasure, and the absence of pain; by unhappiness, pain, and the privation of pleasure. To give a clear view of the moral standard set up by the theory, much more requires to be said; in particular, what things it includes in the ideas of pain and pleasure; and to what extent this is left an open question. But these supplementary explanations do not affect the theory of life on which this theory of morality is grounded—namely, that pleasure, and freedom from pain, are the only things desirable as ends; and that all desirable things are desirable either for the pleasure inherent in themselves, or as means to the promotion of pleasure and the prevention of pain.

Now, such a theory of life provokes in many minds, and among them in some of the most estimable in feeling and purpose, dislike. To suppose that life has (as they express it) no higher end than pleasure—no better and nobler object of desire and pursuit—they designate as utterly mean and grovelling; as a doctrine worthy only of swine, to whom the followers of Epicurus were, at a very early period, contemptuously likened; and modern holders of the doctrine are occasionally made the subject of equally polite comparisons by its German, French, and English assailants.

When thus attacked, the Epicureans have always answered, that it is not they, but their accusers, who represent human nature in a degrading light; since the accusation supposes human beings to be capable of no pleasures except those of which swine are capable.'

107. How do the Epicureans answer their critics?
A. By claiming the critics are miserable, in their refusal to embrace pleasure.
B. That the critics do not understand the multiplicity of things contained in the word 'pleasure'.
C. By calling their critics degraded.
D. By suggesting their critics are more susceptible to animalistic pleasures than they.

108. Which of the following actions are NOT in keeping with the theory of utility?
A. Providing a crash mat for a gymnast, to prevent him or her hurting him or herself.
B. Getting a crash mat for yourself, to prevent hurting yourself when performing gymnastics.
C. Not eating a chocolate bar because social pressures deem it wrong.
D. Eating a chocolate bar because it is delicious.

109. Which of the following does the passage suggest about critics of utilitarianism?
A. They are Christians.
B. They are European.
C. They are unintelligent.
D. They are reactionary.

110. Utilitarianism is only concerned with ends.
A. True
B. False
C. Can't tell

111. The above passage defines:

A. What is included by the term pleasure
B. What is included by the term pain
C. What is meant by Epicureanism
D. What is meant by utility

SET 23

Geology deals with the rocks of the earth's crust. It learns from their composition and structure how the rocks were made and how they have been modified. It ascertains how they have been brought to their present places and wrought to their various topographic forms, such as hills and valleys, plains and mountains. It studies the vestiges, which the rocks preserve, of ancient organisms that once inhabited our planet. Geology is the history of the earth and its inhabitants, as read in the rocks of the earth's crust.

To obtain a general idea of the nature and method of our science before beginning its study in detail, we may visit some valley, on whose sides are rocky ledges. Here the rocks lie in horizontal layers. Although only their edges are exposed, we may infer that these layers run into the upland on either side and underlie the entire district; they are part of the foundation of solid rock found beneath the loose materials of the surface everywhere.

Take the sandstones ledge of a valley. Looking closely at the rock we see that it is composed of myriads of grains of sand cemented together. These grains have been worn and rounded. They are sorted also, those of each layer being about of a size. By some means they have been brought hither from some more ancient source. Surely these grains have had a history before they here found a resting place—a history which we are to learn to read.

The successive layers of the rock suggest that they were built one after another from the bottom upward. We may be as sure that each layer was formed before those above it as that the bottom courses of stone in a wall were laid before the courses which rest upon them.

112. Based on the passage, each of these statements can be verified, EXCEPT?
A.   We can learn about earth's inhabitants through its crust.
B.   Individual layers of sandstone form one after another.
C.   Rocks are made of sand.
D.   Geology does not always demand explicit evidence.

113. Wall-building is used in this passage to help us understand:
A.   Mountains
B.   Valleys
C.   Hills
D.   Plains

114. The sand mentioned in the passage comes from:
A.   An ancient beach
B.   The sea
C.   The earth's crust
D.   It is undisclosed

115. A foundation of rock is **NOT** found underneath:
A.   Upland
B.   Lowland
C.   Nowhere
D.   Water

116. 'Grains of sand' are described as sorted by:
A.   Shape
B.   Texture
C.   Age
D.   Measurements

SET 24

The genus of plants called Narcissus, many of the species of which are highly esteemed by the floriculturist and lover of cultivated plants, belongs to the Amaryllis family (Amaryllidaceæ.) This family includes about seventy genera and over eight hundred species that are mostly native in tropical or semi-tropical countries, though a few are found in temperate climates.

Many of the species are sought for ornamental purposes and, on account of their beauty and remarkable odour, they are more prized by many than are the species of the Lily family. In this group is classed the American Aloe (Agave Americana) valued not only for cultivation, but also by the Mexicans on account of the sweet fluid which is yielded by its central bud. This liquid, after fermentation, forms an intoxicating liquor known as pulque. By distillation, this yields a liquid, very similar to rum, called by the Mexicans mescal. The leaves furnish a strong fibre, known as vegetable silk, from which, since remote times, paper has been manufactured. The popular opinion is that this plant flowers but once in a century; hence the name 'Century Plant' is often applied to it, though under proper culture it will blossom more frequently.

117. Which of the following are **NOT** mentioned as potential uses for a narcissus plant:

A. Perfume production
B. Alcohol production
C. Visual decoration
D. Stationary production

118. Why is the plant known as 'the century plant'?

A. It is sown only once every hundred years.
B. It can only able to be fertilised once a century.
C. It is perceived as blooming centennially.
D. It can only able to flower once within a hundred years.

119. Which of the following statements is most supported by the above passage:

A. Lilies are generally valued less than members of the Narcissus genus.
B. Lilies are famously not as attractive as members of the Narcissus genus.
C. A number are people prefer members of the Narcissus genus over Lilies.
D. Members of the Narcissus genus are a welcome addition to any household.

120. Which of the following statements is NOT true:

A. American Aloe can be used to make rum.
B. The Amaryllis family contains more than six hundred species of Narcissus.
C. Members of the Narcissus genus can be found in all climates.
D. The members of the Narcissus genus have a distinctive smell.

121. Which of the following statements can be verified by the passage:

A. The 'Narcissus' genus is named after the mythical character, famed for his beauty.
B. Agave syrup can be collected by American Aloe.
C. A genus belongs to a family.
D. Members of the Narcissus genus are used for their soothing properties.

SET 25

The following passage is found in a book on nature published in 1899:

Five women out of every ten who walk the streets of Chicago and other Illinois cities, says a prominent journal, by wearing dead birds upon their hats proclaim themselves as lawbreakers. For the first time in the history of Illinois laws it has been made an offense punishable by fine and imprisonment, or both, to have in possession any dead, harmless bird except game birds, which may be possessed in their proper season. The wearing of a tern, or a gull, a woodpecker, or a jay is an offense against the law's majesty, and any policeman with a mind rigidly bent upon enforcing the law could round up, without a written warrant, a wagon load of the offenders any hour in the day, and carry them off to the lockup. What moral suasion cannot do, a crusade of this sort undoubtedly would.

Thanks to the personal influence of the Princess of Wales, the osprey plume, so long a feature of the uniforms of a number of the cavalry regiments of the British army, has been abolished. After Dec. 31, 1899, the osprey plume, by order of Field Marshal Lord Wolseley, is to be replaced by one of ostrich feathers. It was the wearing of these plumes by the officers of all the hussar and rifle regiments, as well as of the Royal Horse Artillery, which so sadly interfered with the crusade inaugurated by the Princess against the use of osprey plumes. The fact that these plumes, to be of any marketable value, have to be torn from the living bird during the nesting season induced the Queen, the Princess of Wales, and other ladies of the royal family to set their faces against the use of both the osprey plume and the aigrette as articles of fashionable wear.

122. In 1899:
A. Women across the USA could be prosecuted for owning ornamental dead birds.
B. There was a significant rise of female arrests in America.
C. Possession of a dead gull could lead to trouble.
D. Americans responded to law by citing the use of jays as ornamentation unfashionable.

123. Ostrich feathers were seen as preferable to osprey plums because:
A. Ostriches are less intelligent birds.
B. Ostriches are killed for their meat, so one might as well use their feathers.
C. Queen Elizabeth has an especial love of ospreys.
D. Harvesting osprey feathers was seen as an inhumane process.

124. Games birds could be possessed by citizens of Illinois all year round.
A. True
B. False
C. Can't tell

125. Banning Osprey feathers in the UK's army was difficult because:
A. Many uniforms required them.
B. The Princess did not have the authority to implement the ban.
C. Her ultimate support was predominately female, and thus their concerns seemed to have no relevance from the male domain of the army.
D. It would be hard to differentiate between other regiments within the army, who were already wearing ostrich feathers.

126. Which of the following could NOT be legally owned in Illinois, according to the passage:
A. A live bird intended for personal ornamentation.
B. A dead bird of prey that had violently attacked you.
C. Feathered garments.
D. None of the above.

SET 26

Indie game developer Lucas Pope created 'Papers Please', a video game where the player is an immigration officer processing people attempting to enter Arstotzka, a fictional dystopia. Released in 2013, the game was originally made for Microsoft Windows and OS X platforms. It was subsequently released for Linux and the iPad in 2014.

The game is set in 1982, and gameplay involves the player processing large numbers of applicants attempting to enter the country, through checking various pieces of paperwork. This is intended to keep criminals out, whether they are terrorists or drug smugglers. When looking through the applicant's 'papers', discrepancies may be discovered: the player must then enquire about these and may go on to use other tools, such as a body scanner and finger printing to discover the truth of the candidate's motives. Applicants may attempt to bribe the officer in order to get through. Ultimately, the game player must stamp candidates passports, either accepting into or rejecting them from the country. Their work is being monitored, however: after two false acceptances/rejections, the player will be pecuniarily punished, with their day's wages being decreased in response to their administrative sloppiness. They have a limited amount of time, representing each 'day', to work, during which they will be paid in accordance to the number of people processed.

127. Which of the following statements is best supported by the above passage:

A.   Lucas Pope created the Papers Please for a small games company.
B.   Papers Please is a multi-platform game.
C.   Arstotzka is a fictionalised version of an ex-Soviet block state.
D.   The game gained significant media attention in 2014.

128. Which of the following statements best sums up the official job of the player's character:

A.   To accept as many applicants into Artstotzka as possible.
B.   To reject as many new applicants entering Arstotzka as possible.
C.   To avoid making mistakes in processing people.
D.   To stamp passports.

129.   Discrepancies in information provided by applicants lead to the player:

A.   Interrogating and performing a fingerprint check on the suspicious individual.
B.   Interrogating and performing a full body scan on the suspicious individual.
C.   Asking the suspicious individual for further information.
D.   Performing one or multiple physical assessments of the individual.

130.   Which of the following statements is true:

A.   The game-player solely makes money through processing applicants.
B.   The game-player will ultimately be responsible for multiple arrests.
C.   The game-player will not be forgiven for their mistakes.
D.   The game-player may be subject to fiscal penalisation.

SET 27

Emerging in 1970s USA, Blaxploitation, or 'blacksploitation', gives homage to many other genres: within it, there are western, martial arts films, musicals, coming-of-age dramas and comedies, and the genre has even parodied itself with films like 'Black Dynamite'. Blaxploitation movies may take place in the South, and focus on issues like slavery, or be set in the poor neighbourhoods of the Northeast or West coast, but in any case they will feature a predominately black cast. It is also known to feature soundtracks comprised of soul and funk music, and the common feature of character's using the words 'honky', 'cracker' and other slurs against white people.

Originally, the genre's exports were aimed at city-dwelling black Americans, but their appeal has since grown and is not exclusive to any race. Despite the negative sound of the title 'blaxploitation', the term was coined by ex-film publicist Junius Griffin, the then head of LA's NAACP, National Association for the Advancement of Coloured People. He came up with the name through a play on the word 'sexploitation' describing films which featured pornographic scenes.

The film 'Shaft' and 'Sweet Sweetback's Baadasssss Song' are two of the forerunners of this genre, both released in 1971. The latter has been said, by Variety, to have created the genre

131. Which of the following statements is supported by the information in the above passage:

A.   'Blaxploitation' was a term coined by porn directors moving into a new genre.
B.   'Blaxploitation' was a term made popular by black audiences.
C.   'Blaxploitation' was a term coined by a civil rights activist.
D.   'Blaxploitation' was a term criticised by white sympathisers.

132. Which of the following statements best describes the most common element of a Blaxploitation film:
A.   Characters performing funk songs.
B.   Characters coming to terms with the legacy of slavery.
C.   Characters performing martial arts.
D.   Characters using racial slurs.

133. Which of these statements best describes casting in Blaxploitation films:

A.   Primarily white
B.   Primarily black
C.   Exclusively white
D.   Exclusively black

134. Which of the following best describes the audiences of Blaxploitation films:

A.   Originally for all middle-class African-Americans.
B.   Originally for all urban-dwellers.
C.   Multi-ethnic.
D.   Shrinking since the mid-1970s.

135. The legacy of films including soft-core porn is knowingly acknowledged in the name of two Blaxploitation titles, 'Shaft' and 'Sweet Sweetback's Baadasssss song', both of which suggest body parts associated with sex films.
A.   True
B.   False
C.   Can't tell

SET 28

When discussing his famous character Rorschach, the antihero of 'Watchmen', Moore explains, 'I originally intended Rorschach to be a warning about the possible outcome of vigilante thinking. But an awful lot of comic readers felt his remorseless, frightening, psychotic toughness was his most appealing characteristic – not quite what I was going for.' Moore misunderstands his own hero's appeal within this quotation: it is not that Rorschach is willing to break little fingers to extract information, or that he is happy to use violence, that makes him laudable. The Comedian, another 'superhero' within the alternative world of Watchmen, is a thug who has won no great fan base; his remorselessness (killing a pregnant Vietnamese woman), frightening (attempt at rape), psychotic toughness (one only has to look at the panels of him shooting out into a crowd to witness this) is repulsive, not winning. This is because The Comedian has no purpose: he is a nihilist, and as a nihilist, denies any potential meaning to his fellow man, and so to the comic's reader. Everything to him is a 'joke', including his self, and consequently his own death could be seen as just another gag.

Rorschach, on the other hand, does believe in something: he questions if his fight for justice 'is futile?' then instantly corrects himself, stating 'there is good and evil, and evil must be punished. Even in the face of Armageddon I shall not compromise in this.' Jacob Held, in his essay comparing Rorschach's motivation with Kantian ethics, put forward the postulation 'perhaps our dignity is found in acting as if the world were just, even when it is clearly not.' Rorschach then causes pain in others not because he is a sadist, but because he feels the need to punish wrong and to uphold the good, and though he cannot make the world just, he can act according to his sense of justice - through the use of violence.

136. Which of the following best describes 'Watchmen':
A. A book that contains only vicious characters.
B. An expression of despair when contemplating an imperfect world.
C. An example of how an author's intentions are not always realised.
D. A book that accidentally glamorises violence.

137. 'The Comedian' is a misnomer - the character that goes by this title should not, logically, be called this.
A. True
B. False
C. Can't tell

138. Which of the following best articulates the view put forward by Jacob Held?
A. We find dignity through just actions.
B. If one decides to behave as though the world is fair, this may lead to a discovery of self-worth.
C. It is shameful to view the world as corrupt.
D. Self-value can only be found in madness.

139. What does the passage above argue?
A. Rorschach breaking little fingers is preferable to the Comedian attempting rape somebody.
B. The Comedian's depressing sense of humour has made him unpopular.
C. Rorschach is not actually violent.
D. Rorschach is popular because his aggressive behaviour has a moral intent, and is not just violence.

140. What does the word 'nihilist' mean in the context of the passage?
A. Someone who believes there is no meaning to life.
B. Someone who is full of anger at the corruption of society.
C. Someone who is narcissistic.
D. Someone who hates other people.

SET 29

'The Bechdel Test', also known as the 'Mo Movie Measure' and 'The Bechdel Rule' is named after cartoonist Alison Bechdel, who in 1985 wrote a cartoon containing the original proposal of the 'test'. It depicts one woman telling another that she has 'a rule' that she will only see a film if it satisfies three basic requirements: that it contains at least two women, that they talk to each other and that their conversation is on something other than a man. The second woman states that this is 'pretty strict, but a good idea', to which the first responds the last film she saw that complied with this was 'Alien'. The original notion described in the strip has been attributed to Liz Wallace, and the test is sometimes referred to as the Bechdel/Wallace Test.

Following this, a website entitled 'The Bechdel Test Movie List' has formed an extensive list of cinematic output, showing movies that pass and do not pass the test. One may be surprised at the number of movies that would not be watched by first woman in the Bechdel comic: many blockbusters do not make the mark, and such titles as 'Godzilla', 'The Imitation Game' and 'Robocop' all feature on the list of 'failed' films.

141. According to The Bechdel Test, 'The Imitation Game' is a sexist film.

A. True
B. False
C. Can't tell

142. Which of the following films would pass the Bechdel test:

A. One where the only conversation between two women is on woman A's brother.
B. One where there are two conversations, one on woman A's son and another on woman B's boss, Mr Smith.
C. One where there are five women, in which at one point they all have a chat about how to lose weight and the best hair removal techniques.
D. One where there is one woman who chats about all manner of things with her male colleagues, including her USA presidential campaign.

143. 50% of horror films, according to the above extract, pass the Bechdel test.

A. True
B. False
C. Can't tell

144. Which of the following phrases best describes the reaction of the second woman within the comic strip:

A. Ecstatically approving
B. Condemning
C. Cautiously approving
D. Apathetic

145. The two women in the comic strip are manifestations of Bechdel and Wallace, with the piece of art being a recreation of their original conversation on this matter.

A. True
B. False
C. Can't tell

SET 30

There are many comic tropes a comedian or group of comedians may want to employ in their set or act, but for the purpose of this extract we shall focus on the device of the 'call-back'. A call-back is a reference made to a previous joke, in a different context: for example, a comedian may make the joke 'why did the chicken cross the road? To get to the other side' early on in his or her set, and then later on may reference this again by telling an anecdote and saying 'so then I crossed the road - oh, look, there's a chicken! Strange, I could have sworn he was over there a moment ago'. Though the call-back may appear to simply rely on the idea that repetition is inherently funny, it actually has several desirable effects. Firstly, it means that one joke can provide more than one laugh, as the memory of the previous joke encourages renewed chuckling, and so the original quip's comic potential is increased. It also builds up a relationship between comedian and audience, as it builds up a sense of familiarity with the speaker and his or her subject matter, and this bond also may encourage more laughter - the second joke creates the same feeling as an 'in-joke'. If used at the end of a set - as a call-back often is - it gives a sense of completion, and also may lead to the ending of the act culminating in the largest laugh.

In TV, a call-back often refers to a joke made in a previous episode.

146. Repetition is inherently funny.

A. True
B. False
C. Can't tell

147. Which of the following best explains how a call-back works:

A. Previous understanding of a subject makes it potentially more comic.
B. Doubling a joke makes it potentially twice as funny.
C. Making the audience feel comfortable is more likely to make them laugh.
D. We find people we have a relationship with funny.

148. For a call-back to work, the original joke has to be significantly funny.

A. True
B. False
C. Can't tell

149. A call-back cannot be used in an un-comic setting.

A. True
B. False
C. Can't tell

150. Which of the following statements is best supported by the above passage:

A. A call-back is used to create a sense of the circle having fully come to pass.
B. A call-back can be a useful addition to an individual comedian's set.
C. A call-back creates unity through disparate TV episodes.
D. A call-back is an especially important trope to consider.

SET 31

Harriet Beecher (Stowe) was born June 14, 1811, in the characteristic New England town of Litchfield, Connecticut. Her father was the Rev. Dr. Lyman Beecher, a distinguished Calvinistic divine, her mother Roxanna Foote, his first wife. Harriet Beecher was ushered into a household of happy, healthy children, and found five brothers and sisters awaiting her. The eldest was Catherine, born September 6, 1800. Following her were two sturdy boys, William and Edward; then came Mary, then George, and at last Harriet. Another little Harriet was actually born three years before, but died when aged only one month old; the fourth daughter, the subject of this passage, was named in memory of this sister Harriet Elizabeth. Just two years after Harriet was born, in the same month, another brother, Henry Ward, was welcomed to the family circle, and after him came Charles, the last of Roxanna Beecher's children.

The first memorable incident of Harriet's life was the death of her mother, which occurred when she was four years old, and which ever afterwards remained with her as the most tender, sad and sacred memory of her childhood. Mrs Stowe's recollections of her mother are found in a letter to her brother Charles, afterwards published in the 'Autobiography and Correspondence of Lyman Beecher.' She says: —

"I was between three and four years of age when our mother died, and my personal recollections of her are therefore but few. But the deep interest and veneration that she inspired in all who knew her were such that during all my childhood I was constantly hearing her spoken of, and from one friend or another some incident or anecdote of her life was constantly being impressed upon me.

151. Harriet, the main character in the article, was the third daughter of Roxanna Beecher:
A.   True
B.   False
C.   Can't tell

152. Which of the following statements, according to the passage, are true:
A.   Harriet Beecher had a religious father.
B.   Harriet Beecher was born in the English town Litchfield.
C.   Harriet Beecher was born in the 18th century.
D.   Harriet Beecher was born in an average American town.

153. Roxanna Beecher was an admired woman.
A.   True
B.   False
C.   Can't tell

154. Harriet Beecher Stowe's mother's death is described as:
A.   Her saddest memory of her life.
B.   The earliest significant event in her life.
C.   Her most tender memory of her life.
D.   All of the above.

155. Which of the following statements is supported by the above passage:
A.   Harriet Beecher was between three and four when her mother died.
B.   Harriet Beecher had five brothers waiting for her when she was born.
C.   Harriet Beecher was a letter-writer.
D.   Harriet Beecher was an autobiographer.

SET 32

Gutenberg's father was a man of good family. Very likely the boy was taught to read. But the books from which he learned were not like ours; they were written by hand. A better name for them than books is 'manuscripts,' which means handwritings.

While Gutenberg was growing up a new way of making books came into use, which was a great deal better than copying by hand. It was what is called block printing. The printer first cut a block of hard wood the size of the page that he was going to print. Then he cut out every word of the written page upon the smooth face of his block. This had to be very carefully done. When it was finished the printer had to cut away the wood from the sides of every letter. This left the letters raised, as the letters are in books now printed for the blind.
The block was now ready to be used. The letters were inked, paper was laid upon them and pressed down. With blocks the printer could make copies of a book a great deal faster than a man could write them by hand. But the making of the blocks took a long time, and each block would print only one page.

Gutenberg enjoyed reading the manuscripts and block books that his parents and their wealthy friends had; and he often said it was a pity that only rich people could own books. Finally he determined to contrive some easy and quick way of printing.

156. Which of the following reasons can be inferred from the above passage to explain Gutenberg's desire to create a new way of printing was:
A.   It was a lucrative business to go into.
B.   He wanted to make text more accessible.
C.   He was tired of waiting for each book to be hand written or block pressed, and wanted quicker access to literature.
D.   He found the current books too costly for him to continue his reading habit.

157. Which of the following of the following is **NOT** mentioned as a concern of block printing?
A.   It exhausts the carver.
B.   It is intricate and demands attention to detail.
C.   It is a lengthy process.
D.   An individual block has limited utility.

158. Which of the following statements is definitely true according to the above passage?
A.   Gutenberg was taught to read as a boy.
B.   Gutenberg's father belonged to the aristocracy.
C.   Block printing was the predominant book manufacturing process whilst Gutenberg was growing up.
D.   Gutenberg's family was somewhat sociable.

159. Printing with the block process was a simple task of inking up the prepared block and pressing it down on a piece of paper, to make one page of the text.
A.   True
B.   False
C.   Can't tell

160. Which of the following statements are **NOT** supported by the above passage:
A.   Manuscripts were beautifully crafted.
B.   'Manuscripts' is an appropriate name for what it describes.
C.   Block printing is an appropriate name for what it describes.
D.   Having well off friends was a good way to expand your reading.

SET 33

Cassandra may be considered an odd name to give your daughter, when you consider the mythical significance of it. Cassandra was a figure in ancient Greek mythology, a Trojan girl born to King Priam, who had been cursed: she had the gift of prophecy, but no one would believe in her words. She ultimately ends up taken from her homeland, as the sexual slave of Agamemnon. Agamemnon's wife then slaughters the girl, and one might wonder why any parent would name their daughter after such an ill-fated figure.

There are several stories that explain how Cassandra gained her gift and her curse. One narrative states that the god Apollo gave the girl the ability to tell the future, in an attempt to seduce her. When she refused him, he corrupted her gift. Another version tells us that Cassandra originally told Apollo she would have sex with him, in exchange for the gift of prophecy. When she subsequently refused him, having attained this power, he then spat in her mouth during a kiss, and this action made her ever after doomed to be disbelieved.

The figure of Cassandra has been presented in various pieces of classical literature, including Homer's epic poem 'The Iliad', Euripides' 'Trojan Women' and Aeschylus' 'The Agamemnon'. Although the presentation of her character alters in the different manifestation, the tragic fate of the woman is known within the different texts, as it would be known by the different authors and audiences of these works.

161. Throughout mythology, Apollo is always presented as the figure who gives Cassandra prophecy.

A.   True
B.   False
C.   Can't tell

162. Which of the following statements is best supported by the passage:

A.   Parents who call their daughter Cassandra must hate their children.
B.   Cassandra prizes chastity higher than her personal comfort.
C.   Cassandra had supernatural powers.
D.   Cassandra is often seen as a home wrecker.

163. Which of the following statements is **NOT** supported by the passage:

A.   Cassandra comes from a royal line.
B.   Cassandra had a happy childhood before her horrible fate.
C.   Cassandra has been written about for the stage.
D.   Homer has been inspired by Cassandra.

164. Cassandra's personality is consistently presented in the different pieces of literature she is included in.

A.   True
B.   False
C.   Can't tell

165. Which of the following is offered in the above passage to explain Apollo's ire:

A.   Cassandra breaking her promise.
B.   Cassandra not accepting his gift.
C.   Cassandra demanding more gifts.
D.   Cassandra not acknowledging his gifts.

SET 34

Despite the fact that some associate musicals with cheesy joy, the genre is not limited to gleeful stories, as can be demonstrated by the macabre musical, 'Sweeney Todd'. The original story of the murderous barber appears in a Victorian penny dreadful, 'The String of Pearls: A Romance'. The penny dreadful material was adapted for the 19th century stage, and in the 20th century was adapted into two separate melodramas, before the story was taken up by Stephen Sondheim and Hugh Wheeler. The pair turned it into a new musical, which has since been performed across the globe and been adapted into a film starring Johnny Depp.

Sondheim and Wheeler's drama tells a disturbing narrative: the protagonist, falsely accused of a crime by a crooked judge, escapes from Australia to be told that his wife was raped by that same man of the court. In response, she has committed suicide, and her daughter - Todd's daughter - has been made the ward of the judge. The eponymous figure ultimately goes on a killing spree, vowing vengeance for the people who have wronged him but also declaring 'we all deserve to die', and acting on this belief by killing many of his clients, men who come to his barbershop. His new partner in crime, Mrs Lovett, comes up with the idea of turning the bodies of his victims into the filling of pies, as a way of sourcing affordable meat - after all, she claims, 'times is hard'.

Cannibalism, vengeance, murder and corruption - these are all themes that demonstrate that this show does not conform to a happy-clappy preconception of its genre.

166. Which of the following statements are best supported by the above passage:
A.   Sondheim is a brilliant musician and lyricist.
B.   Most musicals deal with morbid themes.
C.   Wheeler is an avid penny dreadful fan.
D.   Generalisations can be misleading.

167. All the adjectives below are explicitly supported by the passage as ways of describing the crimes described within it, except:
A.   Comic
B.   Culinary
C.   Vengeful
D.   Sexual

168. Mrs Lovett and Sweeney Todd are in a romantic relationship.
A.   True
B.   False
C.   Can't tell

169. The best way to describe the belief of Todd as mentioned in the above passage:
A.   Bad people should die so good can live and prosper.
B.   Good people should die because the bad have basically taken over.
C.   All men should die.
D.   All humans merit death.

170. Which of the following statements is best supported in the above passage:
A.   There are four themes in 'Sweeney Todd'.
B.   Legal corruption is the predominate theme of 'Sweeney Todd'.
C.   Several 'Sweeney Todd' themes are morbid.
D.   There is nothing positive in 'Sweeney Todd'.

SET 35

The United States released the following as part of a pamphlet titled 'If Your Baby Must Travel in Wartime', released during the Second World War:

'Have you been on a train lately? The railroads have a hard job to do these days, but one that they are doing well. But before you decide on a trip with a baby, you should realise what a wartime train is like. So let's look into one.

This train is crowded. At every stop more people get on—more and still more. Soldiers and sailors on furloughs, men on business trips, women—young and not so young—and babies, lots of them, mostly small.

The seats are full. People stand and jostle one another in the aisle. Mothers sit crowded into single seats with toddlers or with babies in their laps. Three sailors occupy space meant for two. A soldier sits on his tipped-up suitcase. A marine leans against the back of the seat. Some people stand in line for 2 hours waiting to get into the diner, some munch sandwiches obtained from the porter or taken out of a paper bag, and some go hungry. And those who get to the diner have had to push their way through five or six moving cars.

You will want to think twice before taking your baby into such a crowded, uncomfortable place as a train. And having thought twice, you'd better decide to stay home unless your trip is absolutely necessary.

But suppose you and your baby must travel. Well then, you will have to plan for the dozens of small but essential things incidental to travelling with a baby and equip yourself to handle them.'

171. First World War passenger trains were exceptionally crowded.
A.   True
B.   False
C.   Can't tell

172. Which of the following phrases is described by the above passage:
A.   A soldier responds to the situation by creating his own seat.
B.   A sailor rest against a seat's back.
C.   Many people queue for over an hour to get to the diner car.
D.   Many go without eating for the duration of a train journey.

173. The pamphlet wishes to increase the number of passengers on trains.
       True
A.   False
B.   Can't tell

174. Every station the described train passes through has passengers wanting to get onto the vehicle.
A.   True
B.   False
C.   Can't tell

175. Which of the following does the above passage do:
A.   Compliment the railroads.
B.   Insult passengers who are mothers.
C.   Insult passengers who work for the navy.
D.   Compliment soldiers.

SET 36

The following extract is from 'Foods That Will Win the War', published in the USA during the First World War:

'A slice of bread seems an unimportant thing. Yet one good-sized slice of bread weighs an ounce. It contains almost three-fourths of an ounce of flour. If every one of the country's 20,000,000 homes wastes on the average only one such slice of bread a day, the country is throwing away daily over 14,000,000 ounces of flour—over 875,000 pounds, or enough flour for over a million one-pound loaves a day. For a full year at this rate there would be a waste of over 319,000,000 pounds of flour—1,500,000 barrels—enough flour to make 365,000,000 loaves.

As it takes four and one-half bushels of wheat to make a barrel of ordinary flour, this waste would represent the flour from over 7,000,000 bushels of wheat. Fourteen and nine-tenths bushels of wheat on the average are raised per acre. It would take the product of some 470,000 acres just to provide a single slice of bread to be wasted daily in every home.

But someone says, 'a full slice of bread is not wasted in every home.' Very well, make it a daily slice for every four or every ten or every thirty homes—make it a weekly or monthly slice in every home—or make the wasted slice thinner. The waste of flour involved is still appalling. These are figures compiled by government experts, and they should give pause to every housekeeper who permits a slice of bread to be wasted in her home.'

176. According to the above passage, a slice of bread:

A.   Contains 1/6 lb. of flour
B.   Contains a 1/4-ounce of air
C.   Is 75% flour
D.   Is one fourth salt, butter and yeast

177. The passage denies that 20,000,000 homes at the point of writing wasted at least a slice of bread a day.

A.   True
B.   False
C.   Can't tell

178. If 20,000,000 homes wasted a slice of bread, this waste would be equal to:

A.   One million loaves of bread a day.
B.   Over 319,000,000 bushels of flour in 365 days.
C.   1.5 million barrels per annum.
D.   Over 365,000 loaves a year.

179. According to the above passage, a slice of bread is an unimportant thing.

A.   True
B.   False
C.   Can't tell

180. Which of the following statements are supported by the above passage:

A.   The writer has received much criticism for his views.
B.   The government should do more to inform the public about waste.
C.   The government has taken responsibility for public waste.
D.   Responsibility lies with the person who keeps the house.

SET 37

At the election of President and Vice President of the United States, and members of Congress, in November, 1872, Susan B. Anthony, and several other women, offered their votes to the inspectors of election, claiming the right to vote, as among the privileges and immunities secured to them as citizens by the fourteenth amendment to the Constitution of the United States. The inspectors, Jones, Hall, and Marsh, by a majority, decided in favour of receiving the offered votes, against the dissent of Hall, and they were received and deposited in the ballot box. For this act, the women, fourteen in number, were arrested and held to bail, and indictments were found against them, under the 19th Section of the Act of Congress of May 30th, 1870, (16 St. at L. 144.) independently charging them with the offense of knowingly voting without having a lawful right to vote. The three inspectors were also arrested, but only two of them were held to bail, Hall having been discharged by the Commissioner on whose warrant they were arrested. All three, however were jointly indicted under the same statute—for having knowingly and wilfully received the votes of persons not entitled to vote.

Of the women voters, the case of Miss Anthony alone was brought to trial, a nolle prosequi having been entered upon the other indictments. Upon the trial of Miss Anthony before the U.S. Circuit Court for the Northern District of New York, at Canandaigua, in June, 1873, it was proved that before offering her vote she was advised by her counsel that she had a right to vote; and that she entertained no doubt, at the time of voting, that she was entitled to vote.

181. According to the above passage, how many people in total were arrested due to the group of women voting?

A.   Fourteen
B.   Three
C.   Seventeen
D.   Sixteen

182. Susan B. Anthony was the only person brought to trial because of the incident.

A.   True
B.   False
C.   Can't tell

183. Which of the following best describes initial opinions of the election officers:

A.   United by each member's personal support of the women's votes.
B.   Divided in response to the women's actions.
C.   Apathetic about the women's actions.
D.   United by general disapproval of the women's actions.

184. Which defence for Susan B. Anthony is mentioned above?

A.   She did not realise she was not allowed to vote.
B.   That all people born in the USA should be able to vote for their president.
C.   That gender should not prevent her vote.
D.   The election officers accepted her vote, showing the responsibility is not with her.

185. The women were charged jointly under the same indictment.
A.   True
B.   False
C.   Can't tell

SET 38

The following is taken from a book about Norway published in 1909:

'In a country like Norway, with its vast forests and waste moorlands, it is only natural to find a considerable variety of animals and birds. Some of these are peculiar to Scandinavia. Some, though only occasionally found in the British Isles, are not rare in Norway; whilst others (more especially among the birds) are equally common in both countries.

There was a time when the people of England lived in a state of fear and dread of the ravages of wolves and bears, and the Norwegians of the country districts even now have to guard their flocks and herds from these destroyers. Except in the forest tracts of the Far North, however, bears are not numerous, but in some parts, even in the South, they are sufficiently so to be a nuisance, and are ruthlessly hunted down by the farmers. As far as wolves are concerned civilization is, fortunately, driving them farther afield each year, and only in the most out-of-the-way parts are they ever encountered nowadays. Stories of packs of hungry wolves following in the wake of a sleigh are still told to the children in Norway, but they relate to bygone times—half a century or more ago, and such wild excitements no longer enter into the Norsemen's lives.'

186. Which of the following is best supported by the above passage:

A.   The variety of birds and animals to be found in Norway is unique to that country.
B.   The variety of birds and animals to be found in Norway is common to all European countries.
C.   By having forests, a country is more likely to have a variety of birds and animals.
D.   England and Norway have similar geographical features.

187. English people are described as:

A.   Having been anxious of certain animals.
B.   Sceptical of bears.
C.   Living in fear of wolves.
D.   Developmentally behind the Norwegians.

188. Bears are described as:

A.   Hunting
B.   Scavenging
C.   Damaging
D.   Man-eating

189. Bears are also:

A.   Numerous in all forest tracts.
B.   Numerous throughout the North.
C.   Numerous throughout the South.
D.   At risk in parts of Norway.

190. The passage suggests:

A.   The movement of wolves to the out-of-reach parts of Norway is beneficial.
B.   Wildlife currently threats Norwegian children.
C.   Regret at the loss of adventures.
D.   Norsemen particularly respect their natural surroundings.

SET 39

The following extract is taken from Freud's book 'Dream Psychology: Psychoanalysis for Beginners'

In what we may term pre-scientific days, people were in no uncertainty about the interpretation of dreams. When they were recalled after awakening they were regarded as either the friendly or hostile manifestation of some higher powers, demoniacal and divine. With the rise of scientific thought the whole of this expressive mythology was transferred to psychology; today there is but a small minority among educated persons who doubt that the dream is the dreamer's own psychical act.

But since the downfall of the mythological hypothesis an interpretation of the dream has been wanting. The conditions of its origin; its relationship to our psychical life when we are awake; its independence of disturbances which, during the state of sleep, seem to compel notice; its many peculiarities repugnant to our waking thought; the incongruence between its images and the feelings they engender; then the dream's evanescence, the way in which, on awakening, our thoughts thrust it aside as something bizarre, and our reminiscences mutilating or rejecting it—all these and many other problems have for many hundred years demanded answers which up till now could never have been satisfactory. Before all there is the question as to the meaning of the dream, a question that is in itself double-sided. There is, firstly, the psychical significance of the dream, its position with regard to the psychical processes, as to a possible biological function; secondly, has the dream a meaning—can sense be made of each single dream as of other mental syntheses?

191. Dreams used to be regarded as having a potentially religious quality.
A. True
B. False
C. Can't tell

192. According to the passage, at this point of time, amongst the educated:
A. A vocal majority believe that dreams come from somewhere outside the dreamer.
B. A small minority believes that dreams come from the dreamer alone.
C. The majority accepts that a dreamer's dream is his or her own psychical act.
D. A vocal minority believes dreams are the direct products of angels and devils.

193. With a dream:
A. Images seemingly logically dictate feelings.
B. Events happen which are pleasant to waking thought.
C. Only boring things occur that are often too dull to be remembered.
D. There are relationships between images and feelings that would appear illogical to the awake mind.

194. The passage wonders about the significance of individual dreams.
A. True
B. False
C. Can't tell

195. Which of the following statements is supported by the above passage:
A. There is a definite link between the waking and dreaming self.
B. Human society has never had a hypothesis to explain dreams that has satisfied them.
C. A memory of a dream may be untrustworthy.
D. The origin of the dream has been scientifically sourced.

SET 40

Most of the colonists who lived along the American seaboard in 1750 were the descendants of immigrants who had come in fully a century before; after the first settlements there had been much less fresh immigration than many latter-day writers have assumed. According to Prescott F. Hall, "the population of New England … at the date of the Revolutionary War … was produced out of an immigration of about 20,000 persons who arrived before 1640," and we have Franklin's authority for the statement that the total population of the colonies in 1751, then about 1,000,000, had been produced from an original immigration of less than 80,000. Even at that early day, indeed, the colonists had begun to feel that they were distinctly separated, in culture and customs, from the mother-country and there were signs of the rise of a new native aristocracy, entirely distinct from the older aristocracy of the royal governors' courts. The enormous difficulties of communication with England helped to foster this sense of separation. The round trip across the ocean occupied the better part of a year, and was hazardous and expensive; a colonist who had made it was a marked man—as Hawthorne said, "the petit maître of the colonies." Nor was there any very extensive exchange of ideas, for though most of the books read in the colonies came from England, the great majority of the colonists, down to the middle of the century, seem to have read little save the Bible and biblical commentaries, and in the native literature of the time one seldom comes upon any reference to the English authors who were glorifying the period of the Restoration and the reign of Anne.

196. Over half of the 1750 colonists that lived on the American seaboard had genetic links to immigrants who had arrived a century ago.

A. True
B. False
C. Can't tell

197. Which of the following statements is supported by the above passage:

A. According to Hall, America's population at the date of the Revolutionary war could be entirely traced back to 20,000 immigrants.
B. The population in the 1751 colonies was over ten times the original immigration that moved there.
C. According to Hall, in 1751 the population in the American colonies was one million.
D. According to Hall, 80,000 people led to a population of 1,000,000.

198. According to the passage, the new aristocracy that existed in the colonies was:

A. Similar to the England's.
B. Similar to European aristocratic systems in general.
C. Not based in royal governors' courts.
D. Not based on genetic lines.

199. Most of the books on board ships were Bibles and Biblical commentaries.
A. True
B. False
C. Can't tell

200. Which of these is **NOT** given as a reason for poor communications with England:

A. Travel between America and England was costly.
B. The English saw the early colonists as backwards.
C. Travel between America and England was slow.
D. Travel between America and England was dangerous.

Quantitative Reasoning

The Basics

The Quantitative Reasoning subtest tests your ability to quickly interpret data and perform relevant calculations upon them. Section 2 contains 36 questions and you have 24 minutes to answer them, giving a total of 40 seconds per question – slightly more generous than in Section 1.

There are different types of question you can be asked in Section 2, but all involve interpreting a numerical data source and performing calculations. This is all about testing your natural ability with numbers, how easily you understand numbers and how well you can make calculations based upon new data. You won't find advanced mathematics, so you are at absolutely no disadvantage by not taking A-level maths. Common sources include food menus, timetables, sales figures, surveys, conversion tables and more. All questions have 5 options of which only one is correct.

In this section, the whiteboard you are provided can be useful – use it to scribble down working and intermediate numbers as required.

There is an on screen calculator – a basic calculator for performing arithmetic. You should ideally **practice with a non-scientific calculator** when working through this book, as that will give the closest simulation to what you will get on the day. When you move on to trying the online UKCAT practice papers, the calculator is available on screen as you will see it in the test. In addition to using it to solve questions, practice different calculations to build your speed using it – though this sounds boring, it will save you valuable time on the day. Something many candidates do not realise is that the calculator can be operated using the keyboard controls. Try this out for yourself in practice, and if it works for you it is yet another way to boost your speed when you come to the UKCAT for real. If not then it's fine, it can be used with the mouse too and you will at least be properly prepared, knowing the best approach for you.

Preparation

Be comfortable using the on-screen calculator
As discussed, it's important to know exactly how the calculator works so that you use it quickly and most effectively during the test. Also make sure you know which functions the calculator has, and does not have. Practice using the calculator until you're really familiar with it to ensure you waste no time on the day. Use the automated practice section of the UKCAT website for this – that way, you practice using the same software you will use on the day.

Practice common question styles
Be especially comfortable with things like bus and rail timetables, sales figures, surveys, converting units and working with percentage changes in both directions. These are commonplace in the UKCAT –, but could prove awkward if you're rusty. Likewise be sharp on your simple arithmetic – it might seem basic, but a good knowledge of times tables will save you a lot of time. Even if you're not answering questions, you can hone your skills by practicing reading charts, graphs and tables quickly.

Familiarise yourself with the format of diagrams

Working through plenty of practice questions will help here, as you'll see similar questions coming up again and again. Commonly you will need to use timetables, data tables and different types of graphs to answer Section 2 questions. Make sure you are comfortable with all of these styles of questions.

When looking at an unfamiliar diagram, a clear approach will help you quickly grasp what it shows. Candidates who let the time pressure stop them from properly interpreting the data are much more likely to lose marks. Avoid this common pitfall by following our approach below to quickly read complex data.

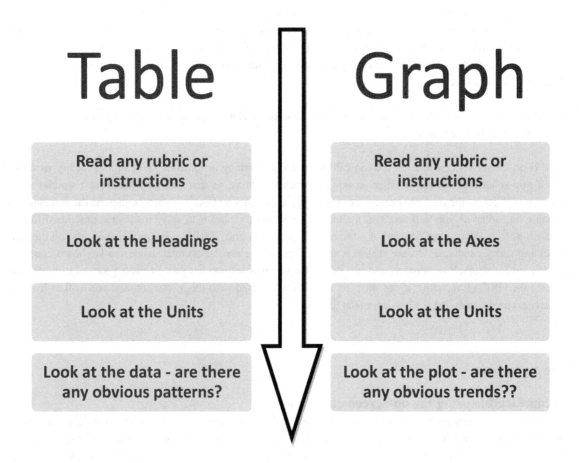

Mental Speed

The main challenge in most questions is finding the right data and selecting the appropriate calculation to perform, rather than the actual calculation itself. However, time is tight so you should be confident with addition, subtraction, multiplication, division, as well as working out percentages, fractions and ratios. Although there is an on-screen calculator in the test, you can save time by doing the basic sums in your head – being confident in your mental arithmetic ability will help you use the time most effectively.

Answering Questions

Estimation

Estimation can be very helpful, particularly when the answers are significantly different. If, for instance, answers are an order of magnitude or more away from each other, you can ignore the fine print of the numbers and still get the right answer. If it's a particularly complicated calculation, quickly ask yourself roughly what answer you are expecting. With the simple UKCAT calculator it can be easy to slip up – but if you've already made a quick estimation then you may be alerted to your mistake before you put the wrong answer down. Another important use of estimation is to generate educated guesses if you're short on time. In Section 2 there are five answers per question, so your odds of blindly guessing correctly are low. But here a simple estimation can help. A quick glance or simplified sum might help you eliminate a few answers in only seconds, boosting the chance your guess is correct.

Flagging for review

Flagging for review is so quick and easy, it can always be a useful tool. If you're finding a question difficult, or you've decided it is likely to take too long to solve, put a guess (or quick estimation if possible), flag for review and move on. This allows you to revisit the question at the end if there's time whilst using your time more efficiently elsewhere. When doing this you should make an initial guess, as this ensures you have at least a chance of being correct if you don't have enough time to come back again.

Pace yourself

In this section you have an average of 40 seconds per question, and this is a very useful guide to have. Of course some questions will take more or less time, but you should aim to work steadily forwards at roughly that pace. So after 6 minutes you should be about 9 questions in, and after 12 minutes should have completed about 18 questions and so on. By keeping a regular rhythm to your work, you ensure you don't leave lots of potentially easy questions at the end untouched. It's far better to skip a few tricky questions with a guess to make sure you make a decent effort at all questions, rather than wasting time with the hardest questions and missing out on easier marks.

Read the question first

If the data looks complex, it makes sense to look at the question first before beginning to interpret the data. Just like data-heavy questions in section 1, it can take a few moments to interpret the data provided. By reading the question first, you focus your mind, giving you a better focus to approach the data with and ensuring you only spend time analysing data you actually need to work from.

Top tip! Don't spend too long on any one question. In the time it takes to answer one hard question, you could gain three times the marks by answering three easier questions. *Make the most of every second!*

Example Questions

Example 1

An online company provides personalised sports kit with discounts for bulk purchases. Shipping rates are £4.99. All prices are quoted in pounds and are per item.

No of items	Plain T-shirt	Polo Shirt	Long sleeve T-shirt
1-10	4.99	5.59	5.99
11-50	4.49	5.09	5.49
51+	3.99	4.49	4.99

> Having read the instructions you know what the table will show. Now look straight at the question below so you know what to do with the data.

No of Items	Monotone Print	Multi-tone Print	Embroidered Logo
1-6	0.99	1.99	3.99
7-25	0.49	1.29	3.49
26+	0.29	0.89	2.99

A local hockey team requires 26 polo shirts with embroidered logo on the front and printed monotone number on the back. How much will this cost?

A. £194.01
B. £217.62
C. £222.61
D. £225.21
E. £240.81

> This is a typical question. Find the right data in the table and start adding it up

Answer: C

This question highlights the need to read the question carefully as to use the correct data from the tables and is a relatively common type of question. If you look closely at the tables, you will realise that the number of items bracketed together changes between the tables. Watch out for this, or similar changes in unit, in the test. If you only skim over the tables you are in danger of missing this and will therefore get the question wrong. However, the calculation required is simple as is often the case, the question is more looking at your ability to pick out relevant data.

Price per polo shirt = 5.09 (base price) + 2.99 (embroidered logo) + 0.29 (monotone print) = £8.37
Price for 26 polo shirts as specified = 8.37 x 26 (number of items required) = £217.62
Total Price = 217.62 + 4.99 (shipping) = £222.61

Example 2

Sarah's route to work consists of an 8 minute walk followed by the 200 bus from Styal centre to Wilmslow station, the train from Wilmslow to Manchester Piccadilly and finally a 6 minute walk to her offices.

200 Bus Timetable				
Manchester Airport	07.05	07.21	07.36	07.49
Styal centre	07.14	07.30	07.45	07.57
Green road	07.18	07.34	07.49	08.01
Wilmslow Leisure centre	07.23	07.39	07.54	08.05
Wilmslow Station	07.31	07.47	08.02	08.13
Wilmslow Centre	07.36	07.52	08.07	08.22
Train Times				
Macclesfield	07.26	07.42	07.58	08.14
Alderley Edge	07.32	07.48	08.04	08.20
Wilmslow	07.40	07.56	08.12	08.28
Stockport	07.54	08.10	08.26	08.42
Manchester Piccadilly	08.14	08.30	08.46	09.02
Manchester Oxford Road	08.23	08.39	08.55	09.11

If Sarah needs to arrive at her offices by 9.00, what time must she leave her house?

A. 07.08
B. 07.24
C. 07.30
D. 07.37
E. 07.49

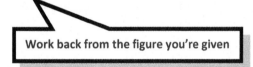

Work back from the figure you're given

Answer: D

Bus and train timetables are common questions and it is worth being comfortable working through them logically. On first glance of the question, there appears to be a lot of information. However, if you read the question carefully, you can simply work through the timetables from the end of the question. Split Sally's journey down into stages and consider each in turn – this splits the question so it is easily manageable and makes it less likely to make mistakes.

Sally must be at the offices for 09.00, therefore she must get into Manchester Piccadilly by 08.54 (6 minute walk). The latest train that gets into Manchester Piccadilly by 08.54 arrives in at 08.46. This train leaves Wilmslow Station at 08.12. The latest 200 bus that gets to Wilmslow Station by 08.12 arrives at 08.02. The 08.02 bus to Wilmslow Station leaves Styal Centre at 07.45. It takes Sally 8 minutes to walk to the bus stop therefore she must leave her house at 07.37.

Example 3

The following table shows the rates of income tax per annual income amount. The rates shown apply to James, who earns £10,156 per quarter before tax. Tax is applied to annual income bands as shown:

Annual Income / £	% pay as Income Tax
0 – 10,000	0
10,001 – 25,000	15
25,001 – 41,200	25
41,201 – 50,000	34
50,001 +	40

How much does James earn, to the nearest pound, annually after tax has been deducted?

A. £10,127

B. £30,468

C. £34,468

D. £34,469

E. £40,624

> **Firstly convert James' quarterly income to an annual income to simplify the sums**

Answer: C

Notice the bands of income are not of equal width, and that the question supplies James' income per quarter, but the answer asks for his annual income. Tax is calculated individually per band – no one will pay tax on the first £10,000 earned, the next £15,000 earned is taxed at a rate of 15%, the next £16,200 at 25% and so on.

Firstly you should make life easier for yourself by converting his quarterly income into an annual income. In this question, it is most sensible to work out all calculations as annual income, and annual tax, as this is what the answer requires.

Annual income before tax: 10156 x 4 = £40,624

Tax: income within band x tax rate for that band

Band (0-10000): £0

Band (10001-25000): (25000-10000) x 0.15 = £2250

Band (25001 – 41200): (40624-25000) x 0.25 = £3,906

Total tax: 2250 + 3906 = 6156

Final income after tax deducted: 40624 (total income) – 6156 (tax) = £34,468

Example 4

The following table shows a bank's currency conversion rates between different currencies, with the purchasing currency being listed on the left and the purchased currency being listed across the top. The bank charges a flat fee commission rate of £2.50 on all transactions.

	EUR	AUD	USD	GBP	JPY	INR
EUR	1.00	1.41	1.12	0.75	133	69
USD	0.89	1.26	1.00	0.67	118	62
GBP	1.33	1.88	1.48	1.00	177	92
AUD	0.71	1.00	0.80	0.53	94	49

Peter is travelling to Australia next summer and requires AUD. Using the given currency conversion rates, how much will it cost him in GBP, to the nearest pound, to purchase 650 AUD?

A. £343
B. £346
C. £348
D. £1,220
E. £1,224

> **These answers are in two very different ranges. A quick estimation will narrow down from five to either two or three possible options**

Answer: C

This question is assessing your ability to convert, in this case using currency, but may be using different units of area or such like. Again, it is important to read the question closely to ensure you use the correct currencies, and do not miss the commission rate. Find the row which states the currencies per 1GBP, in this case this is the third row. These are the conversion rates you should be using for your calculation. In this question it is worth simply noting that the amount in GBP will be less than the amount in AUD, as each 1GBP buys you towards 2AUD. This will be useful to check you have converted with the figures in the correct order, as the final answer you get should be less than 650AUD. It is also necessary to look at what currency the commission rate is in. As it is stated in GBP, the easiest way is to convert and then take off the commission rate. This will save you time as it is not necessary to make a further calculation of converting the commission rate to AUD.

When writing your working it is essential to write the currency each value is in as to not get confused. This is the case for any question which requires conversion between different units.

Convert 650 AUD to GBP: 650 ÷1.88 (conversion rate GBP to AUD) = £345.74
Price after commission fee 345.74 + 2.50 (commission fee) = £348.24
The question asks for the answer to the nearest pound, therefore final answer = £348

Quantitative Reasoning Questions

SET 1

The country of Ecunemia has a somewhat complicated tax code. There are four states that make up Ecunemia: Asteria, Bolovia, Casova and Derivia. Each state has its own tax code, including different tax rates on different items. The table below represents the tax a **customer** has to pay when they purchase an item from a store. E.g. a £100 coat in Asteria would cost £110.

	Asteria	Bolovia	Casova	Derivia
Clothes	10%	15%	10%	10%
Food	5%	0%	10%	0%
Imports from other states	20%	5%	10%	15%

The customer must add the tax onto the advertised purchase price. In the case of an item falling into multiple categories (for example, in the case of Imported Food) the higher tax rate is paid and the lower rate is ignored.

Question 1:

A shopper visits a certain supermarket. Without tax, the shopper spends $50 on food, $30 on clothes and nothing on imported items. She spends $88 in total. Which state is this supermarket in?
A. Asteria
B. Bolovia
C. Casova
D. Derivia

Question 2:

Someone runs a supplier in Bolovia, supplying supermarkets in each state in Ecumenia. Each year they supply each state with 250 items of clothing, which the supermarket sells for $40 (including tax), and the supplier gets all of this revenue, minus the tax paid. A competitor in Asteria goes out of business, and this supplier has the opportunity to buy the manufacturing plant for $20,000, and transfer to this state.

If the supplier purchases the site, and moves to Asteria, how many years will it take to make back the cost of purchasing the site?
A. 5 years
B. 12 years
C. 23 years
D. 26 years

Question 3:

John goes into a store and spends $100. Of this, $12 is tax. Which of the following is possible?
A. He shopped in Asteria and bought no imported goods.
B. He shopped in Casova.
C. He shopped in Derivia and bought at least $50 of food (excluding tax).
D. He shopped in Bolovia and spent $10 on imported goods (excluding tax).

Question 4:

Sibella is on a road trip through Ecunemia, driving through different states. On the journey she buys $100 of the finest Asterian ham, $30 of the finest Bolovian caviar, a $10 case of Casovan orange juice and spends $100 on a Derivian dress (all of these prices without tax). Which of the following cannot have been the total amount Sibella spent, including tax?
A. $256
B. $264
C. $273
D. $288

SET 2

As a probe drops through the ocean, the pressure it experiences increases. For every 10 metres the probe drops down, the pressure it experiences increases by 10,000 Pascals (Pa).

Question 5:

A particular probe can survive 200 pounds per square inch without incurring damage. Given that the conversion factor between these units is 7000 Pa = 1 pound per square inch and assuming that pressure at sea level is 0 Pascals, how deep can the probe drop into the ocean without incurring damage?

A.   14 m
B.   140 m
C.   1.4 km
D.   14 km

Question 6:

A different probe is dropped into the ocean and falls downward. This probe can withstand 300,000 Pa of pressure without breaking. A model of the effect of the fluid states that the object's depth in the fluid is $d = \frac{1}{2}\sqrt{(t^3)}$, where d is depth in metres and t is time in seconds. How long will it take for this probe to break?

A.   65 seconds
B.   71 seconds
C.   75 seconds
D.   78 seconds.

SET 3

The fictional drug Cordrazine is used to treat four separate conditions. The following table gives the amount of drug used in each case to treat each condition, written in the form x mg/kg: i.e. for every kilogram you weigh, you take x mg of the drug. The recommended course for the drug is also listed, in the form of number of times a day and how many weeks you need to take the drug.

Condition	Dosage	Course
Black Trump Virus	4 mg/kg	3 times daily for 4 weeks
Swamp Fever	3 mg/kg	Once daily, 1 week
Yellow Tick	1 mg/kg	2 times daily for 12 weeks
Red Rage	5 mg/kg	2 times daily, 3 weeks

Question 7:

Over the course of treatment, John, an 80 kg male, takes 26.88 grams of the drug. Which disease was he prescribed the drug for?

A. Black Trump Virus
B. Swamp Fever

C. Yellow Tick
D. Red Rage

Question 8:

Carol is a 60 kg female who is prescribed the drug (precisely and at different times) three times in one year. Two of the cases are for Yellow Tick. In total she takes 40.32 grams of the drug. Which was the third disease she was prescribed the drug for?

A. Black Trump Virus
B. Swamp Fever

C. Yellow Tick
D. Red Rage

Question 9:

Clarence takes the drug twice in his life. Once he takes it for Swamp Fever at age 18, when he weighs 80 kg, and he takes it later in life at age 40 for Black Trump Virus, when he weighs 110 kg. What is the ratio of the amount he takes each time?

A. 1:23
B. 1:22

C. 1:21
D. 1:20

Question 10:

Danny has liver disease. His system cannot cope with more than 15.5 grams of Cordrazine every 4 weeks. Danny has a medical condition usually treated with Cordrazine, but doctors have advised him to not complete a course of the treatment, as he would exceed the dose that his system is able to cope with. Which of the following statements is possible?

A. Danny suffers from Red Rage and weighs 75 kg.
B. Danny suffers from Swamp Fever and weighs 100 kg.
C. Danny suffers from Black Trump and weighs 45 kg.
D. Danny suffers from Yellow Tick and weighs 75 kg.

Question 11:

Eileen has kidney failure. Her system cannot cope with more than 10 grams of Cordrazine every 4 weeks. She suffers from Red Rage, but doctors have recommended she does not use Cordrazine to treat it, as this would exceed the 10 g dosage her system can cope with. Which of the following weights is the minimum that would support this recommendation?

A. 40.34 kg
B. 42.53 kg

C. 45.81 kg
D. 47.62 kg

SET 4

A bakery sells four varieties of cakes. The cakes contain the following ingredients:

	Sponge (520g)	Madeira (825g)	Pound (710g)	Chocolate (885g)
Flour (g)	125	250	150	200
Butter (g)	125	175	185	175
Egg (g)	120	180	180	120
Milk (g)	25	45	45	150
Sugar (g)	125	175	150	200
Cocoa (g)	-	-	-	40

Question 12:

Which cake contains the highest proportion of flour?

A. Sponge

B. Madeira

C. Pound

D. Chocolate.

Question 13:

The cake recipes are scaled up for a large order. One cake weighs 2.6 kg and contains 625 g of flour. What variety of cake is it?

A. Sponge

B. Madeira

C. Pound

D. Chocolate

Question 14:

Eliza is having a wedding and wants to produce a 4-tiered wedding cake. She wishes each tier to be of different size, and scaled such that that the bottom cake is 50% heavier than normal (e.g. the cake contains 50% more ingredients), the second cake is 25% heavier than normal, the third cake is 10% heavier than normal and the top cake is normal-sized, where each cake is of the same type.

Which of the following is a possible weight of sugar for the cake (rounded to 2 s.f.)?

A. 940 g

B. 970 g

C. 1,000 g

D. 1,030 g

Question 15:

It is known that flour costs £0.55 per 1.5 kg and sugar costs £0.70 per 1 kg. Which of the following is the closest to the cost ratio of flour to sugar in a Madeira cake?

A. 1:2

B. 3:4

C. 4:5

D. 5:6

Question 16:

Milk costs £0.44 per kilogram and flour costs £0.55 per 1.5 kg. What is the cost ratio of flour to milk in a chocolate cake?

A. 1:1

B. 2:3

C. 8:7

D. 10:9

SET 5

The Kryptos Virus is particularly virulent. The infection rate is dependent upon the gender of the recipient. A random sample of 100 men and 100 women are taken from a population and tested for the Kryptos virus using Test A. The results of Test A are displayed below:

	Men	Women
Have virus	45	63
Do not have virus	55	37

Question 17:

What percentage of people tested have the virus?

A. 45%

B. 54%

C. 55%

D. 63%

Question 18:

A population of 231,768 is divided: 53% women, 47% men. Use the data in the table to estimate the number of people in the population that have the Kryptos virus. Assume that the infection rates in each gender will be the same as for the sample population in Test A. Which of the following is the number of people expected to be infected with Kryptos virus in this population?

A. 123,587

B. 123,589

C. 125,541

D. 126,406

Question: 19

3/9 of the men and 5/7 of the women testing positive for Kryptos in Test A have visited the city of Atlantis. Which of the following is the correct percentage of people in the test group testing positive for Kryptos who have **NOT** visited Atlantis?

A. 40%

B. 44%

C. 50%

D. 55%

Question 20:

It is known that Test A is not always correct. Test B is a more accurate test. The 45 men who tested positive for the Kryptos virus using Test A were then re-tested with Test B - only 20 tested positive. Assuming the same proportion of men and women experienced false positive results with Test A, how many women in the test group do we expect to actually have the Kryptos virus?

A. 20

B. 28

C. 35

D. 42

Question 21:

It is decided the women who tested positive under test A should be retested using test B. This time 29 women test positive for the Kryptos Virus. Considering both the men and women tested, what percentage of people who tested positive in Test A also tested positive in Test B (to the nearest whole number)?

A. 40%

B. 45%

C. 50%

D. 55%

SET 6

A business has 3 manufacturing plants and 3 stores. Each plant can ship to each store, and the following table shows the flat rate cost, in pounds sterling (£), of the business sending a truck from the plant to the store.

	Store 1	Store 2	Store 3
Plant A	100	190	530
Plant B	120	180	600
Plant C	140	200	450

Question 22:
Currently the businesses strategy is to send material from Plant A to store 2, from Plant B to store 3 and from Plant C to store 1. One truck is sufficient for a day's delivery. What is the daily cost of this plan?

A. £850
B. £930
C. £970
D. £1,030

Question 23:
The store wishes to optimize their shipping costs by sending material from Plant C to store 3, noticing that the delivery cost is lower. They then choose the two other options that save the most money. What percentage saving is achieved by this strategy relative to the strategy in the previous question (to the nearest whole number)?

A. 18%
B. 20%
C. 22%
D. 24%

SET 7

The table below shows the number of books sold by a bookshop in one day:

	Below 18	Above 18
Non-Fiction	12	30
Horror	50	45
Sci-Fi/Fantasy	23	90
Other Fiction	103	159

Question 24:

The shop also ran an author's visit event in the evening in which 106 people purchased the author's book. These books are **NOT** counted in the above table. What proportion of the books sold on this particular day were sold at the author's visit event (to the nearest whole number)?

A. 13%
B. 17%
C. 21%
D. 25%

Question 25:

Non-fiction books cost, on average, £10, and fiction books cost, on average, £6. What percentage of the shop's revenue (excluding the author's visit event) came from non-fiction books?

A. 10%
B. 13%
C. 19%
D. 23%

Question 26:

Assume that the shop makes this number of sales of each type of book every day. One week, the shop adopts a new marketing strategy and markets non-fiction books more heavily. The result is that the number of non-fiction sales double during this week, but all of the other book sales stay in line with previous sales. How much does the shop earn this week?

A. £24,250
B. £25,620
C. £26,950
D. £27,890

Question 27:

The following week, the shop decides to market the horror books more heavily, resulting in the sales of horror books doubling, and the sales of non-fiction books returning to the normal level. How much does the shop's income increase this week compared to the non-fiction marketing week? Sales of all other books can be assumed to be the same as un-marketed weeks.

A. 1%
B. 2%
C. 3%
D. 4%

SET 8

The following table shows the taxing structure for Italian city hotels:

City	Tax
Venice	1 euro per star per room per night. Rooms with children under 16 are tax exempt.
Rome	Per person, per night: 5 euros for 3 star, 6 euros for 4 star, 7 euros for 5 star, up to a maximum of ten nights worth, after which no tax is charged. Rooms with children under age 10 are tax exempt.
Padua	Per person, per night: 2 euros for 3 star or below, 3 euros for 4 star or above. Rooms with children under 16 are tax exempt.
Siena	2 euros per person per night in high season, 1 euro per person per night in low season. Rooms with children under 12 are tax exempt.

Unless specifically mentioned, assume that all of the people below are aged 18 or over.

Question 28:

A family goes on a tour of Italy in the High season. They are 2 adults and 2 children, aged 9 and 13. They spend two nights in each of Venice, Rome, Padua and Siena. They stay in 3 star hotels for the entire trip, and have two rooms (an adult room and a child room). How much tax do they pay for their trip?

A. EUR 35
B. EUR 56
C. EUR 60
D. EUR 65

Question 29:

Claude is comparing cities. He can either spend 7 nights in Rome in a 4 star hotel, or 8 nights in Padua in a 5 star hotel. Which of the following is the ratio between the tax he pays in Rome and the tax he pays in Padua?

A. 8:3
B. 7:4
C. 6:2
D. 1:4

Question 30:

Alice goes on a trip for 2 days to Venice in a 3 star hotel and for 3 days to Padua in a 4 star hotel. What is the percentage more tax she pays in Padua relative to Venice?

A. 25%
B. 50%
C. 75%
D. 100%

Question: 31

How long does Reuben have to stay in a 4 star hotel in Rome so that the tax would be less than or equal to the tax he incurs if staying the same length of time in a 4 star hotel in Padua?

A. 10 days
B. 15 days
C. 20 days
D. 25 days

SET 9

Peter is building a house that contains rooms of different sizes. The sitting room is 10m x 20m, the hallway is 3m x 10m, and the master bedroom is 15m x 15m. In addition, the house has another square-shaped bedroom, a kitchen and a bathroom.

Question 32:

Assuming that the second bedroom walls are 60% of the length of the master bedroom, what is the area of the second bedroom?

A. 64 m^2
B. 81 m^2
C. 100 m^2
D. 121 m^2

Question 33:

Suppose the kitchen has a floor area of 100 m^2 and the bathroom has a floor area of 4 m^2, and the second bedroom has the floor area calculated in the previous question. What percentage of the area of the house is taken up by the master bedroom?

A. 30%
B. 35%
C. 40%
D. 45%

Question 34:

After building the house, Peter decides to add an extension to the sitting room, turning it into a combined lounge and dining room. He extends the room by increasing the length of the longer wall by 5 metres. The lounge is 3 metres high. How much extra wall (in m^2) does Peter have to build, assuming that he is extending directly outwards and cannot move or re-use any wall?

A. 15m^2
B. 30m^2
C. 45m^2
D. 60m^2

Question 35:

A larger extension is considered, and two builders offer Peter separate quotes. The first builder offers to build wall at a cost of £15 per m^2, but there is also a flat fee of £200 just for starting the job. The second builder offers to build wall at a cost of £16 per m^2 but with no flat fee at the start. If Peter builds 300 m^2 of wall, what is the ratio of builder 1 cost to builder 2 cost (to 3 s.f.)

A. 1.00:1.00
B. 1.00:1.02
C. 1.02:1.00
D. 2.00:3.00

SET 10

The table below shows the service prices for competing mobile phone plans A-D. Any SMSs or call minutes beyond those free with the plan are charged individually at listed price.

	A	B	C	D
Monthly fee	£0	£5	£10	£15
# Free SMSs	0	200	1000	Unlimited
# Free call minutes	0	0	100	Unlimited
Price/SMS	10p	20p	20p	-
Price/call minute	10p	20p	20p	-

Question 36:

John buys Plan B for one month and calls for 15 minutes and sends 207 SMSs. How much does he pay this month?

A. £5.00
B. £6.60
C. £7.80

D. £9.40
E. £11.20

Question 37:

Robin buys Plan A, and makes no calls. How many SMSs can Robin send before Plan B would have been cheaper?

A. 6
B. 21
C. 51

D. 101
E. 121

Question 38:

Mary wants to call for 5 minutes and send 5 SMSs every day in September. Which plan should she choose for the lowest cost?

A. A
B. B
C. C

D. D
E. A and B are both the lowest

Question 39:

Evan buys Plan B but Chris buys Plan C. Which of these options is cheaper for Evan than Chris per month?

A. They each call for 29 minutes and send no SMSs.
B. They each call for 26 minutes and send 174 SMSs
C. They each send 351 SMSs and call for 8 minutes.
D. They each call for 4 minutes every day of the month.
E. They each send 223 SMSs and make no calls.

Question 40:

Rachel doesn't send any SMSs and buys Plan C. What is the maximum percentage by which she can exceed her free call minutes allowance without Plan D being cheaper?

A. 5 %
B. 10 %
C. 25 %
D. 50 %
E. 75 %

SET 11

A muffin recipe calls for ingredients in the amounts listed in the table below:

Ingredient	Density	Amount
Flour	600 gram/dm^3	2 cups
Sugar	850 gram/dm^3	1 cup
Milk	1050 gram/dm^3	½ cup
Butter	950 gram/dm^3	4 tablespoons

1 cup = 2.5 decilitres (dl); 1 tablespoon = 15 millilitres (ml); 1 cubic decimetre (dm^3) = 1 litre

Question 41:

How many cups of ingredients are called for overall by the recipe (to 2 decimal places)?

A. 3.54

B. 3.66

C. 3.74

D. 3.82

E. 3.86

Question 42:

What weight ratio of milk to butter does the recipe call for (to 1 decimal place)?

A. 2.3:1

B. 2.7:1

C. 3.1:1

D. 3.4:1

E. 3.9:1

Question 43:

Jane wants to use only a ½ cup measure for baking. What is the smallest number of cups of flour she would need for it to be possible to measure all required ingredients in ½ cups?

A. 2

B. 10

C. 25

D. 30

E. 50

Question 44:

To make pancakes, the amount of flour and milk are reversed. What is the average density of pancake batter, assuming that there are no interactions that change the densities of the individual ingredients when they are mixed?

A. 930 grams/dm^3

B. 970 grams/dm^3

C. 1,050 grams/dm^3

D. 1,070 grams/dm^3

E. 1,100 grams/dm^3

Question 45:

If Peter wanted to make 10 muffins weighing 100 grams each, how much butter would he need to 1 decimal place? Assume that the finished product weighs the same as the initial dough.

A. 55.1 grams

B. 62.3 grams

E. 81.3 grams

C. 70.7 grams

D. 76.4 grams

Question 46:

When Peter's ten 100 gram muffins are done, assuming no losses to cooking, what percentage of the weight will be made up by flour, to the nearest whole number?

A. 35 %

B. 39 %

C. 43 %

D. 46 %

E. 52 %

SET 12

New ocean crust is formed at spreading ridges. The area of the crust formed is dependent on temperature. The volume of crust formed in a given time interval depends on the **crust cross sectional area** and on the spreading rate (the rate at which newly formed crust moves away from the spreading ridge, an independent variable).

The relationship between **crust volume** formed in a time interval, **cross sectional area** and **spreading rate** is:

Crust volume per time = cross sectional area x spreading rate

The table below gives the crustal cross sectional area, spreading rate and temperature at Locations A-D:

	A	B	C	D
Cross Sectional Area (km²)	10	20	30	40
Spreading rate (mm/year)	150	20	100	50
Temperature (°C)	1300	1400	1500	1600

Question 47:

Assuming that the trends in this table can be reliably extrapolated, at which temperature would the crust volume formed in a year be expected to be 0 km³?

A. 1,200 °C
B. 1,400 °C
C. 1,600 °C

D. 1.800 °C
E. 2,000 °C

Question 48:

If the temperature at Location A increased by 50%, what would be the spreading rate?

A. 25 mm/year
B. 50 mm/year
C. 100 mm/year

D. 150 mm/year
E. 225 mm/year

Question 49:

What volume of crust is formed in a year at Location B?

A. 400 m³
B. 400 °C km³
C. 40,000 km³

D. 400,000 m³
E. 560,000 °C km³

Question 50:

If the spreading rates of Locations A and C were exchanged, what would be the ratio of crust volume formed at the two locations each year (to 1 decimal place)?

A. 1:1.0
B. 1:3.3
C. 1:4.5

D. 1:5.6
E. 1:6.0

Question 51:

If the same crustal volume was produced in the same amount of time at 2 locations, E with temperature 1300 °C and F with temperature 1450 °C, how many percent faster/slower was the spreading rate at location E than F?

A. 250 % faster
B. 25 % slower
C. 400 % faster

D. 40 % slower
E. 500 % faster

Question 52:

If the temperature at Location D was decreased by 10%, what would be the crustal volume formed in 3 years?

A. 2,000 m³
B. 2,000 °C km³
C. 3,200 km³

D. 3, 200,000 m³
E. 3, 600,000,000,000,000 mm³

~ 63 ~

SET 13

A new drug to treat vision problems in diabetics is tested on volunteers. It is also tested on control groups of diabetics without vision problems and healthy volunteers with or without vision problems. Some volunteers are given one inactive placebo pill which they are told is the drug. There are the same number of people in each group testing either the drug or placebo, as indicated below.

The table below shows the number of volunteers in Groups A-D who self-reported improved vision and their measured average accuracy reading letters before and after taking the drug or a placebo.

Group		Drug	Placebo
A	Number Improved	15	9
	Accuracy Before (%)	27 %	27 %
	Accuracy After (%)	36 %	31 %
B	Number Improved	8	6
	Accuracy Before (%)	60 %	60 %
	Accuracy After (%)	66 %	61 %
C	Number Improved	9	7
	Accuracy Before (%)	29 %	29 %
	Accuracy After (%)	31 %	32 %
D	Number Improved	7	8
	Accuracy Before (%)	68 %	68 %
	Accuracy After (%)	70 %	70 %

Group A: 50 diabetics with vision problems (25 in each group)
Group B: 46 diabetics without vision problems (23 in each group)
Group C: 44 healthy volunteers with vision problems (22 in each group)
Group D: 48 healthy volunteers without vision problems (24 in each group)

Question 53:
What is the average percentage of participants who self-report vision improvements after receiving an inactive pill to the nearest percent?
A. 26 %
B. 31 %
C. 32 %
D. 33 %
E. 36 %

Question 54:
By what ratio is visual accuracy in reading letters increased by the drug in diabetics with poor sight relative to healthy volunteers with poor sight (to 2 decimal places)?
A. 1:0.78
B. 3.50:1
C. 4.21:1
D. 4.50:1
E. 4.83:1

Question 55:

If there are 10 women in Group A and their average accuracy was 45 % after receiving the drug, what was the average accuracy of the men in the group after receiving the drug?

A. 16 %
B. 27 %
C. 30 %
D. 36 %
E. 41 %

Question 56:

If the general population has 100 000 diabetics with vision problems, how many of these people would be expected to self-report improvements in their vision because of the effects of the drug?

A. 24,000 people
B. 32,000 people
C. 36,000 people
D. 60,000 people
E. 96,000 people

Question 57:

When the drug dose was doubled, the placebo groups showed no change in numbers or accuracy, but the number of Group A volunteers who reported improved vision jumped to 18. Assuming that drug effectiveness is dose dependent, what percent of volunteers in Group A taking the drug would be expected to self-report improved vision if the dose was tripled?

A. 54.0 %
B. 72.0 %
C. 84.0 %
D. 90.0 %
E. 100.0 %

Question 58:

Which of the following statements is supported by the data in the table?

A. The placebo is more effective than the drug.
B. The drug acts to improve vision in diabetics and healthy volunteers.
C. Volunteers who see well are more motivated to improve vision than those with vision problems.
D. Thinking you have taken a drug to improve vision improves your vision.
E. The data are inconclusive.

SET 14

Dave weighs 200 pounds and has a Basal Metabolic Rate (BMR) of 2000 calories. Elizabeth weighs 140 pounds and has a BMR of 1500 calories. The table below shows the calorific value of the foods they eat:

	Cereal	Sandwich	Apple	Chocolate	Lasagna	Chicken	Vegetables
Calories	400	500	100	350	700	250	200

To lose one pound of fat requires a 3500 calorie deficit, obtained by eating fewer calories than the BMR or burning calories by exercising. Running burns 5 calories per hour per pound you weigh at any running speed. Cycling burns calories according to the following relationship, where M is mph cycling speed:

Calories burned per mile = 50 calories + (5 calories x (M-10))

Question 59:

Dave wants his workout to take one hour on a 5 mile track. What is the maximum number of calories he can burn by running or cycling?

A. Burn 125 calories running
B. Burn 125 calories cycling
C. Burn 1,000 calories running
D. Burn 1,000 calories cycling
E. Burn 1,250 calories running

Question 60:

Dave doesn't want to eat less than his BMR and can only run for 30 minutes a day, but cycles 20 miles every day in an hour. How long will it take him to lose 10 pounds?

A. 5 days
B. 7 days
C. 10 days
D. 14 days
E. 30 days

Question 61:

Elizabeth and Dave both want to lose 10% of their body weight without dieting or cycling. What is the ratio of minutes a day Elizabeth would have to run to those Dave would have to run to achieve their goal at the same time to 1 decimal place?

A. 1:0.5
B. 1:0.7
C. 1:1.0
D. 1.1.4
E. 1:2.0

Question 62:

If Elizabeth eats cereal for breakfast, a sandwich for lunch, chicken and vegetables for dinner and does no exercise, in how many full days will she have reached her goal of 10% weight-loss?

A. 327 days
B. 354 days
C. 372 days
D. 416 days
E. 435 days

Question 63:

If Elizabeth also began cycling 10 miles in 1 hour every day, how much faster would she reach her goal than in question 62?

A. 1.00
B. 2.50
C. 3.00
D. 3.33
E. 4.33

Question 64:

Elizabeth eats one chocolate everyday; 3 times as much chicken as chocolate and twice as much cereal as chicken. If she exchanged these foods with 3 different foods in the table in the same proportions, what is the ratio of her rate of weight change before and after the switch, assuming she is trying to obtain the lowest weight she can?

A. 1:1   B. 1:2   C. 1:5   D. 2:1   E. 5:1

SET 15

Visitors to an amusement park pay for food, rides and games with coupons. Coupons can be bought individually for £1 each or in multipacks at a discounted price. A £70 wristband can gives free entry and access to all rides (but not games or food) without using coupons. The table below shows the cost in coupons for each activity:

	Entrance	Rollercoaster	Fun House	Swings	Carnival Games	Candy Floss
All Day	10	4	2	3	1	2
Night	5	3	2	2	1	2

Question 65:

Susan buys a 20 coupon multi-pack at 10 % off single coupon price. She rides the rollercoaster five times at night. What percent off did she get on the first rollercoaster ride compared to buying single day tickets (to 1 decimal place)?

A. 10.0 %

B. 22.5 %

C. 25.0 %

D. 32.5 %

E. 33.3 %

Question 66:

One weekend the single coupon prices are raised 20 %. Greg wants to ride the rollercoaster 10 times, buy 3 candy floss, play a carnival game, go through the fun house 2 times and ride the swings during the day. What is the ratio of the cost with a wristband to the cost without a wristband to 2 decimal places?

A. 1:0.93

B. 1:0.98

C. 1:1.02

D. 1:1.10

E. 1:1.12

Question 67:

Andy went to the amusement park one night. He rode the rollercoaster 50 % more times than he rode the swings, and rode the swings 20 % more times than he played carnival games. He used a whole number of coupons that were cheaper than getting a wristband. How much did Andy pay?

A. £31

B. £44

C. £49

D. £56

E. £70

Question 68:

Anna and James each spent one pound less than the cost of a wristband on single coupons one day at the amusement park. Anna went on the rollercoaster for half of her rides and the fun house for the rest. James went on the swings every odd ride and in the fun house every even ride. Neither of them went on any other rides or bought any food. What is the ratio of the number of rides Anna went on to the number James went on?

A. 1:0.78

B. 1:0.81

C. 1:1.23

D. 1:1.28

E. 1:2.56

Question 69:

A 10-weekend season pass covers all costs in the park and is available for £1,000. Erik goes to the park one day every weekend and buys a wristband each time. On the first weekend he buys one candyfloss, and the next four weekends increases the number of candyfloss he buys by 100%, relative to the previous weekend. The four weekends after that he increases the number of candyfloss he buys by 50% each weekend, relative to the previous weekend. On the 10th weekend he is sick of candyfloss and buys none.

What is the ratio of the cost without and with a season pass (to 2 decimal places)?

A. 0. 7 : 1

B. 0.92 : 1

C. 1 : 0.92

D. 1 : 1.15

E. 1.15 : 1

SET 16

The table shows the prices a pizzeria charges for their pizza:

Type	Italian		Pan Pizza		
	Cheese	Toppings	Cheese	Topping	Stuffed Crust
Price Small	£6.00	+50p/topping	£10.00	+50p/topping	+£1.00
Price Medium	£8.00	+£1.00/topping	£12.00	+£1.00/topping	+£1.50
Price Large	£10.00	+£1.50/topping	£14.00	+£2.00/topping	+£2.00

The pizzeria also offers three discount deals: 20% off orders from £20 - £29.99, 30% off orders from £30 - £49.99, and 50% off orders over £50. Small pizzas have 6 slices, medium pizzas have 8 slices, and large pizzas have 10 slices

Question 70:
Josh gets 2 large stuffed-crust 2 topping pan pizzas, 1 medium 3 topping Italian pizza and 3 small cheese pan pizzas. How much does he pay?

A. £31.00
B. £40.50
C. £52.50

D. £81.00
E. £96.00

Question 71:
Janet bought cheese pan pizzas for the cheapest cost per slice and got £35 off as a discount deal. How many slices did she buy?

A. 35
B. 48
C. 50

D. 64
E. 70

Question 72:
Joey bought some plain cheese pizzas for a total price of £60 post-discount. All the plain cheese pizzas were the same. What is the price of the one type of pizza he could **NOT** have bought?

A. £6.00
B. £8.00
C. £10.00

D. £12.00
E. £14.00

Question 73:
Lea always buys 30 slices of cheese pan pizza with 2 toppings and stuffed crust. What is the ratio of the cost of buying all large to all small pizzas (to 2 decimal places)?

A. 1:0.50
B. 1:0.75
C. 1:0.80

D. 1:1.00
E. 1:1.25

Question 74:
Kate and two friends each order cheese pan pizzas (with no toppings) and get 30% off their order. They ordered the pizzas to pay the smallest price which gets this discount, but ended up with 25% more slices than they could eat. How many slices did they manage to eat?

A. 16
B. 18
C. 20

D. 25
E. 32

SET 17

Sarah has three journalist jobs she splits her time across. The table shows a breakdown of what she earns at each job. Her salary is composed of a fixed starter wage she earns for showing up and an hourly wage on top of that. Her hourly wage increases in each job the more hours she works at that job. She must pay for her own travel expenses. Each travel cost occurs once per job she completes, and is not affected by the length of the job in hours.

	Travel Cost	Fixed Starter Wage	Hourly Wage	Average Job Length	Hourly Wage Growth
Job A	£5	£10	£10 per hour	2 hours	£5 per 50 worked
Job B	-	£5	£15 per hour	1 hours	£10 per 100 worked
Job C	£10	£5	£20 per hour	4 hours	£5 per 100 worked

Question 75:

If Sarah works for 1 hour at each job, what will be the ratio of the earnings expressed as [Job A Earnings:Job B Earnings:Job C Earnings] (to 2 decimal places)?

A. 1.00:0.75:1.00

B. 1.00:1.00:0.75

C. 1.00:1.25:1.00

D. 1.00:1.33:0.75

E. 1.00:1.33:1.00

Question 76:

Sarah worked 25 2-hour jobs, 4 1-hour jobs and 1 4-hour job for Job A in her first month. How much did she earn?

A. £625.00

B. £730.00

C. £770.00

D. £980.00

E. £1,020.00

Question 77:

Sarah can work 50 2-hour jobs per month. For which single job should she work these hours to earn the most from 2 hour jobs at the end of the month?

A. A

B. B

C. C

D. A and B are the same

E. B and C are the same

Question 78:

Sarah pays 10% income tax if her monthly salary exceeds £1275. How many hours should she work in her first month for Job C, if all jobs are the average job length, to earn the highest amount possible whilst not paying tax, to the nearest half-hour?

A. 60.0 hours

B. 62.5 hours

C. 65.0 hours

D. 68.0 hours

E. 75.0 hours

Question 79:

At the start of her third month, Sarah has worked 200 hours at Job C. She works 100 hours at average job length this month. How much of her month's earnings go to 10% income tax?

A. £150.00   B. £187.50   C. £200.00   D. £287.50   E. £300.00

Question 80:

Job B wants her to work a minimum of 50 hours a month for them, and Job A and Job C require that she works at least the same hours for them as she does at any other jobs she has, or no hours at all. Assuming all jobs are the average job length, which arrangement would give her maximum earnings in her first 100-hour work month?

A. 50 hours for A and 50 hours for B

B. 50 hours for A and 50 hours for B

C. 50 hours for B and 50 hours for C

D. 100 hours for B

E. None of the above.

SET 18

The table below shows the number of cars passing a toll booth going into the town centre and how many passengers the cars carried, including the drivers. It also shows the number of passengers who got off at the town's central underground station each day.

	Mon	Tue	Wed	Thu	Fri	Saturday
Number of cars	1,517	1,632	987	1,465	2,024	478
Total car passengers (incl. Drivers)	1,873	2,421	1,116	2,101	2,822	1,339
Underground passengers	2,346	1,798	3,103	2,118	1,397	576

Question 81:

Taking the underground costs £5. On Wednesdays this fare is reduced 15% and it is cheaper for some drivers to leave the car at home. How much more revenue is generated on Wednesday than the next highest grossing day?

A. £1,457.75

B. £3,537.25

C. £5,275.75

D. £1,1730.00

E. £1,3187.75

Question 82:

On weekdays, what is the ratio of the average number of people being driven (not driving) in cars to the average number of people riding on the underground (to 2 decimal places)?

A. 1:0.25

B. 1:0.78

C. 1:3.97

D. 1:7.60

E. 1:9.60

Question 83:

What is the ratio of the average number of people per car on Tuesday compared to the average number of people per car on Saturday?

A. 1:0.67

B. 1:0.85

C. 1:1.27

D. 1:1.33

E. 1:1.89

Question 84:

What is the ratio of the number of Underground passengers on Monday compared to that on Saturday?

A. 1:0.13

B. 1:0.25

C. 1:0.40

D. 1:1.50

E. 1:4.08

Question 85:

The tollbooths charge £4 per car and an additional £1 per passenger (including the driver). 80% of this payment is tax. How much tax is paid at the tollbooths next week from Monday-Friday if there are 4,219 commuters everyday split in the ratio of 2:1.7:1 - underground passenger : car passenger (including driver) : car ratio?

A. £1,938.45

B. £4,219.00

C. £4,560.50

D. £5,198.40

E. £6,498.96

SET 19

Music practice rooms are available seven days a week, with each day being split into three sessions: morning (8am-2pm), day (2pm-8pm) and night (8pm-2am). The table below gives the prices for the hourly rental of the music practice rooms. Some information is missing. The "two sessions" column indicates the hourly charge if two sessions are booked on the same day.

| Type of room | Deposit | Cost per Hour | | | |
		1-2 hours (night session)	3-6 hours (night session)	Two sessions	All day
Basic (no piano)	£10.00	-	-	£11.00	£8.00
Standard (upright piano)	£25.00	£20.00	£18.00	£16.00	£12.00
Superior (baby grand piano)	£50.00	£30.00	£26.00	£22.00	£16.50
Deluxe (grand piano)	-	£45.00	£38.00	£30.00	£20.00

NB: All prices above include VAT (25%)

Question 86:
The hourly rate for a day session is 10% more expensive than a night session. What is the total cost, excluding the deposit, for 3 hours in the Superior room during a day session?
A. £59.40
B. £70.20
C. £78.00
D. £84.18
E. £85.80

Question 87:
The total cost for two 6 hour sessions in the Deluxe room is £460. How much is the deposit?
A. £64
B. £75
C. £82
D. £100
E. £136

Question 88:
Mike books a Basic room and a Standard room for a full night session. The total cost is £221 including deposit. What is the hourly rate for a full night session in a Basic room?
A. £12.50
B. £13.00
C. £15.00
D. £16.83
E. £18.83

Question 89:
The hourly rate for a morning session up to 6hrs is 5% cheaper than a night session. The deposit remains the same. A Superior room is booked for 90 minutes one morning, all costs paid up front. How much is paid at the start of the session? (Assume half hours can be booked at half the hourly rate.)
A. £97.25
B. £92.75
C. £95.00
D. £90.50
E. £90.25

Question 90:
A Basic room is booked for 18 hours each day for three full weeks. What is the total cost of this booking excluding VAT and deposit?
A. £1,935.36
B. £2,419.20
C. £2,459.52
D. £3,024.00
E. £3,074.40

SET 20

A group of 180 people took part in a perception study and were asked to count how many differences they could spot between two similar pieces of short video footage. The results are given below

		Age (years)					
		10 to 16	16 to 22	22 to 34	34 to 48	48 to 65	65+
Differences correctly spotted	<5	9	10	10	16	15	19
	5 to 10	7	12	9	8	8	5
	11 to 15	11	8	6	2	8	9
	15+	3	2	0	1	2	0

Question 91:

What percentage of people under the age of 22 spotted more than 10 differences?

A. 31.3%   B. 33.3%   C. 38.7%   D. 46.7%   E. 63.2%

Question 92:

75% of the results for the people who spotted 5 to 10 differences correctly were removed from the study. What percentage of the remaining people aged 16-22 spotted more than 15 differences?

A. 6.3%   B. 6.9%   C. 8.5%   D. 8.7%   E. 9.4%

Question 93:

25% of people who correctly spotted over 10 differences, also *incorrectly* spotted over 10 differences. How many people was this?

A. 11
B. 12
C. 13
D. 14
E. 15

Question 94:

10,000 people aged 48 or older take this test. Using the data, estimate how many spotted fewer than five differences to the nearest 50.

A. 2,300
B. 2,900
C. 4,500
D. 5,100
E. 5,150
F. 5,200

Question 95:

The test is repeated with the same population. The number of 16-34 year olds who spot 11-15 differences increases by 50%. All other age groups experience no change. What is the new ratio between 16-34 year olds and the total number of people in the other age groups who spot 11-15 differences?

A. 1:3
B. 4:17
C. 14:44
D. 14:51
E. 21:51

SET 21

The pie chart below shows the favourite sports of some high school students. Every student plays only their favourite sport in games lessons. The school has 1300 students, with an exact 50:50 split between boys and girls.

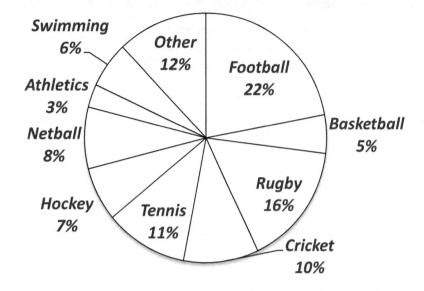

Question 96:
What is the difference between the number of boys that play football and the number that play netball in games lessons?

A. 90   C. 104   E. 182
B. 91   D. 180   F. 286

Question 97:
The senior football teams are picked from the two most senior years – a total of 350 students. Only those whose favourite sport is football play. At least 11 people are needed per team. What is the maximum number of teams that could be made? Assume that the values given in the chart are representative of these years.

A. 4   B. 5   C. 6   D. 7   E. 8

Question 98:
All those whose favourite sport is basketball are boys and all those whose favourite sport is netball are girls. 80% of the basketball boys are invited to play netball. What proportion of the netball-playing population do they then make?

A. 17%   B. 25%   C. 33%   D. 42%   E. 50%

Question 99:
One quarter of students in the *Other* category have a favourite sport which is a ball sport. In the whole school, how many students have a favourite sport which is a ball sport?

A. 39   B. 117   C. 572   D. 1,066   E. 1,183

Question 100:
Only boys play cricket. Only girls play hockey. The gender split for tennis follows that of the school as a whole. How many more boys play cricket or tennis than girls play hockey or tennis?

A. 39   B. 58   C. 59   D. 111   E. 112

SET 22

The number of apples picked by a company per year is given below, along with the quality of the apples. 30% of edible apples are sold as they come. Passable apples and the remaining edible apples are processed into cider. Apples which are No Good are not used for human consumption, and are instead discarded for animal food.

	1998	1999	2000	2001	2002	2003
Edible	1,100,547	1,398,663	1,563,327	1,443,599	1,763,870	1,931,784
Passable	2,983,411	2,691,553	3,008,941	2,790,456	2,651,399	2,439,012
No Good	400,001	391,747	398,014	568,440	494,309	571,221

Question 101:

What is the percentage increase in the number of apples used for human consumption from 1998 to 2003?

- A. 7%
- B. 10%
- C. 22%
- D. 76%
- E. 93%

Question 102:

What percentage of all No Good apples was produced in the year most apples could not be used for humans?

- A. 11.6%
- B. 11.8%
- C. 13.9%
- D. 19.9%
- E. 20.2%

Question 103:

2004 saw a three-fold increase on 2003 in the number of No Good apples. The total number of apples fit for consumption remained the same. What was the difference in number between processed and No Good apples in 2004 to the nearest apple?

- A. 2,077,598
- B. 2,224,675
- C. 2,478,954
- D. 2,675,133
- E. 2,765,131

Question 104:

The next six-year period saw an overall 20% increase on the period 1998-2003 in the total number of edible apples picked. How many were sold as they came between 2004 and 2009?

- A. 3,588,698
- B. 3,321,646
- C. 3,312,644
- D. 2,392,465
- E. 2,208,430

Question 105:

Generally, 20 apples give 1 litre of cider. Given that 2004 saw the same number of apples fit for human consumption as 2003, roughly how many litres of cider were produced in 2004?

- A. 122,000 l
- B. 189,600 l
- C. 215,400 l
- D. 247,100 l
- E. 988,400 l

SET 23

Jen tracks her daily jogs using an app which gives her data on her performance. Her app tells her that her average speed is 5 mph.

Conversion factor: 1 mile = 1.6 km

Question 106:

On wet days, Jen's average speed decreases by 8%. How many kilometres does she cover in 40 minutes?

A.   3.1 km
B.   3.3 km
C.   4.9 km
D.   5.3 km
E.   7.4 km

Question 107:

Jen begins training for a marathon (26 miles). She starts off by trying to complete a marathon over the space of four equally long jogs. Estimate how long each jog is. Assume dry conditions.

A.   42 minutes
B.   46 minutes
C.   1 hour 18 minutes
D.   1 hour 25 minutes
E.   1 hour 30 minutes

Question 108:

After starting marathon training, her average speed decreases to her old wet speed; her average wet speed remaining 8% slower than this. Estimate, therefore, how long it would take her to cover 12km in the rain.

A.   1 hour 38 minutes
B.   1 hour 46 minutes
C.   2 hours 17 minutes
D.   2 hours 37 minutes
E.   2 hours 50 minutes

Question 109:

After bringing her average speeds back to their original values, Jen starts a new regime. She goes on four jogs, each being 50% further than the last. Her first jog is 4km long. How long does the final jog take in dry conditions?

A.   1 hour 8 minutes
B.   1 hour 41 minutes
C.   1 hour 50 minutes
D.   2 hours 9 minutes
E.   2 hours 42 minutes

Question 110:

Lots of training later, Jen completes the marathon in a time of 3hrs 42mins on a dry day. What is the percentage increase in Jen's dry average speed compared to her original one?

A.   7%
B.   12%
C.   41%
D.   52%
E.   53%

SET 24

The table below gives the prices per person per week for different luxury holiday accommodations with different swimming facilities. Some types of accommodation offer a choice between swimming facilities. Some information is missing. Additional days are charged at 1/7 of the weekly cost.

	Studio	Apartment	Villa	Palazzo
No pool	£50.00	£70.00	£95.00	£155.00
Shared pool	£60.00	£80.00	-	-
Private pool	-	£100.00	-	£325.00
Beachfront	-	-	£220.00	£480.00

Question 111:

Villas are available with a private pool, and currently they are on sale: 20% off the standard price, where the standard price sits halfway between that of an apartment with a private pool and a palazzo with a private pool. How much would this cost for two people for one week?

A. £323   B. £332   C. £340   D. £415   E. £664

Question 112:

A group of twelve rents out a beachfront palazzo for four weeks. A booking fee is required from each member of the group, in this case charged at 10% of the weekly cost per person. What is the total cost of the booking?

A. £23,040

B. £23,161

C. £23,616

D. £25,344

E. £25,614

Question 113:

A couple rents an apartment with a shared pool for 20 days. The total cost is £492.89. How much is the booking fee?

A. £35.55

B. £35.57

C. £35.75

D. £37.55

E. £37.75

Question 114:

A family of four stays at a beachfront villa for two weeks, with no booking fee. Due to a complaint, they are refunded 20% of the standard charge. How much does the family pay?

A. £1,408

B. £1,760

C. £1,920

D. £2,340

E. £2,620

Question 115:

A company hires three palazzi with private pools for a week for the grand total of £19,500. The booking fee is 10% of the total cost. Assuming each palazzo has the same number of people staying in it, how many people are there in each palazzo?

A. 18   B. 20   C. 22   D. 54   E. 60

SET 25

FastFoodCo is a fast food take-away that delivers directly to customers' homes. Delivery rates are £3.00 for orders less than £10, £1.50 for orders from £10 - £15 and free for orders over £15. Below is a selection from their menu (delivery and food prices exclude 20% VAT, which is payable on all orders). VAT is added after delivery and any discounts have been taken into account.

Item	Cost
Green Curry	£3.95
Chicken Curry	£2.95
Noodles	£2.95
Chicken Tikka	£4.95
Vegetarian Curry	£3.95

Question 116:
John orders a green curry, noodles and a vegetarian curry. What is the total price?

A. £16.62
B. £14.82
C. £14.52
D. £12.35

Question 117:
Katy orders 3 noodles, 2 chicken tikkas and a green curry. Her total is:

A. £22.44
B. £25.67
C. £27.24
D. £29.04

Question 118:
John orders 2 noodles and a vegetarian curry. What is his total price?

A. £15.42
B. £14.24
C. £13.62
D. £12.14

Question 119:
Katy orders a green curry, 3 noodles and a vegetarian curry. What is her total?

A. £21.89
B. £20.10
C. £18.52
D. £18.09

Question 120:
A final 'two for the price of one' offer is applied for noodles. John orders 4 noodles, 2 chicken tikkas and a green curry. What is his total?

A. £18.20   B. £21.33   C. £22.51   D. £23.70   E. £24.31

SET 26

The graph below shows the first quarter profits (in GBP) of four suppliers of prescription medicine.

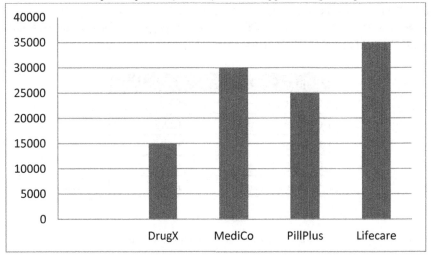

Question 121:

What percentage of total first quarter profits were earned by MediCo?

A. 26.6%

B. 28.6%

C. 30.4%

D. 33.3%

Question 122:

What percentage of the total first quarter profit is from MediCo and Lifecare combined?

A. 56.8%

B. 59.5%

C. 61.9%

D. 62.3%

Question 123:

PillPlus offers a 10% discount on all products in the second quarter. As a result, their sales increase and profit increases by 15%.

Assuming that the profits of all other suppliers remain constant into the second quarter, what percentage of the total second quarter profits did PillPlus make?

A. 16.4%

B. 23.8%

C. 26.4%

D. 27.3%

Question 124:

During the third quarter, all profits fall by 10% from second quarter values. Lifecare then buys DrugX. What percentage of the third quarter profits was made by Lifecare?

A. 46.0%

B. 46.6%

C. 47.9%

D. 48.2%

Question 125:

Production costs are increased in the fourth quarter, resulting in all profits falling by a further 5%, despite an increase in sales. The information given in question 124 still applies. How much money does Lifecare make in this quarter?

A. £41,800

B. £42,750

C. £43,490

D. £47,002

SET 27

The chart below shows the cost of a variety of cars and optional extras. All prices are excluding 20% VAT, which must be paid by all customers.

Model	Price	Leather Seats	Sound System	Easy-Park Technology
Racer	£15,000	£395	£195	£395
Stuntman	£12,500	£345	£145	£295
Saloon	£21,500	£495	£245	£445
Pod	£18,000	£445	£395	£495

Question 126:
What is the total cost of the Stuntman, with all optional extras?
A. £15,942
B. £15,904
C. £15,894
D. £15,616

Question 127:
What is the price difference between the Saloon and the Pod (with all optional extras)?
A. £3,900
B. £4,020
C. £4,040
D. £4,100

Question 128:
What is the difference in price between the Racer (with no optional extras) and the Stuntman with all optional extras?
A. £2,040
B. £2,048
C. £2,058
D. £2,142

Question 129:
There is a 10% discount on the Racer and all its optional extras. What is the difference in price between the Pod with no optional extras and the Racer with all optional extras?
A. £4,236.20
B. £4,285.50
C. £4,336.20
D. £4,438.40

Question 130:
A final offer on the Saloon is 20% off, including all options. What is the difference in final price between the Saloon with Leather seats and Easy-Park technology and the Pod with only basic features?
A. £18.60
B. £37.20
C. £48.30
D. £57.60

SET 28

The graph below shows the total amount of CO_2 (in Tonnes) emitted by the country Aissur in each year from 2000 onwards.

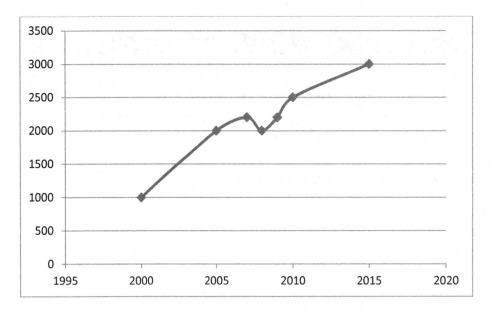

Question 131:

What was the rate of increase of CO_2 emissions between 2000 and 2005?

A. 250 Tonnes/year   B. 225 Tonnes/year   C. 200 Tonnes/year   D. 100 Tonnes/year

Question 132:

The economic crash of 2008 caused global CO_2 emissions to decrease due to a decrease in industrial output. How much less CO_2 was emitted in the year 2010 compared to if emissions had continued to rise at the same rate seen from 2000 to 2005.

A. 500 Tonnes   B. 750 Tonnes   C. 1,000 Tonnes   D. 2,500 Tonnes

Question 133:

What is the percentage increase in CO_2 emissions from 2005 to 2015?

A. 25%   B. 33%   C. 50%   D. 150%

Questions 134 – 135 require the following information:

In 2015, the government of Aissur voted on a new energy bill. The bill seeks to reduce the rate of CO_2 increase over the past 5 years by 50% over the next 5 years, and keep the increase at this level thereafter.

Question 134:

If the new energy bill is successful in meeting its aims, how much CO_2 will be saved by the end of 2020 relative to the 2010 – 2015 trend continuing?

A. 200 Tonnes   B. 250 Tonnes   C. 500 Tonnes   D. 750 Tonnes

Question 135:

What will the total CO_2 be in 2020 according to this new act?

A. 2,750 Tonnes   B. 3,000 Tonnes   C. 3,250 Tonnes   D. 3,500 Tonne

SET 29

The chart below shows the price per item for different styles of printing. The price is lower when larger orders are made, as shown in the table.

Type	1	10+	100+
Single sided black & white	£0.10	£0.07	£0.05
Single sided colour	£0.25	£0.20	£0.15
Double sided black & white	£0.15	£0.12	£0.10
Double sided colour	£0.45	£0.30	£0.25

Question 136:

What is the price per job of 74 single sided black & white sheets?

A. £3.70

B. £5.18

C. £5.24

D. £7.40

Question 137:

How many double-sided colour sheets can you buy for £100?

A. 222

B. 333

C. 400

D. 425

A 10% discount is offered for orders above 50 units, applying to the whole order. All other offers still apply.

Question 138:

What is the price of 150 units of double sided black & white?

A. £13.50

B. £15.50

C. £16.20

D. £20.25

Question 139:

Compared to buying 150 double sided black & white sheets individually, how many sheets worth (at the standard price for 1 sheet) is saved by buying in one transaction at the discounted price?

A. 65 sheets

B. 60 sheets

C. 53 sheets

D. 50 Sheets

Question 140:

What is the total cost of an order of double sided pages, with 227 requiring black and white printing and 34 requiring colour printing?

A. £22.38

B. £29.61

C. £32.90

D. £34.32

SET 30

4 sets of 300 volunteers take part in a clinical trial for a new drug, which is aimed at reducing the effects of asthma. The responses received are recorded below.

Group	Positive	Negative	No Effect
1	75%	20%	5%
2	65%	30%	5%
3	70%	15%	15%
4	55%	25%	20%

Question 141:
How many people reacted positively overall?

A. 135
B. 265
C. 523
D. 795

Question 142:
How many more people reacted negatively from set 2 compared to set 3?

A. 15
B. 33
C. 45
D. 56

Question 143:
What proportion of those tested overall reacted negatively?

A. 21%
B. 23%
C. 26%
D. 28%

After modifications to the drug, a new survey of 300 volunteers was taken. The results of this are shown below:

Group	Positive	Negative	No Effect
5	82%	15%	3%

Question 144:
What was the percentage increase in the success rate (i.e. the percentage of people reacting positively) in the 5th group compared to the first 4 groups?

A. 7.81%
B. 15.75%
C. 17.93%
D. 23.77%

Question 145:
Across all groups, including group 5, how many people reacted negatively to the drug?

A. 275   B. 315   C. 355   D. 380

SET 31

The graph below shows the total number of views for two rival local television dramas, The Last Chase and The Final Frontier, across the 4 yearly quarters in 2014.

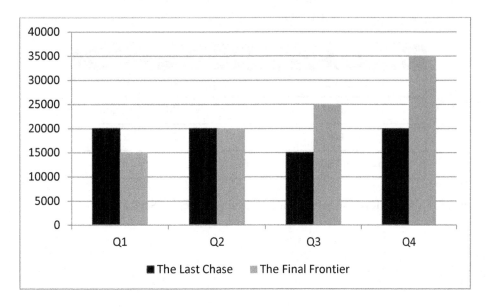

Question 146:
What is the difference between the total number of views of the Final Frontier and The Last Chase during 2014?
A. 10,000   B. 15,000   C. 20,000   D. 25,000

Question 147:
Broadcasters earn £2,500 from advertisements per 1,000 views. What is the difference in money earned through advertising between the two shows in 2014?
A. £45,000   B. £50,000   C. £55,000   D. £60,000

Question 148:
If the number of views of The Final Frontier continues to increase at same rate it did from Q1 – Q3 of 2014, how many views will it have during the final quarter of year 2015?
A. 50,000   B. 55,000   C. 60,000   D. 65,000

Question 149:
If the number of views of The Final Frontier continues to increase at same rate it did from Q1 – Q3 of 2014, how many views will it have in 2015 in total?
A. 180,000   B. 190,000   C. 200,000   D. 250,000

Question 150:
Under different circumstances, at the end of the third quarter of 2014, the broadcasters decide to terminate The Last Chase. As a result, half of The Last Chase's views instead transfer to The Final Frontier. How many views will The Final Frontier have at the end of the final quarter of 2014 under these circumstances?
A. 25,000   B. 35,000   C. 37,500   D. 45,000

SET 32

The table below shows the average time, in minutes, spent waiting for GP appointments by patients, according to a series of surveys from 2014. On average, 20% of patients who wait between 11 and 30 minutes and 40% of those who wait for more than 30 minutes register a complaint during a customer satisfaction survey. No patients who waited for 10 minutes or less registered complaints.

	0-10	11-30	30+	Survey size
England	60%	30%	10%	100,000
Scotland	55%	25%	20%	50,000
Wales	50%	25%	25%	25,000
Northern Ireland	60%	25%	15%	25,000

Question 151:
How many patients waited for less than half an hour for an appointment in Scotland?
A. 12,500
B. 27,500
C. 40,000
D. 45,000

Question 152:
What percentage of patients across the UK waited for more than half an hour for an appointment?
A. 10%
B. 15%
C. 20%
D. 25%

Question 153:
How many complaints are received from this survey at the end of the year?
A. 20,250
B. 21,500
C. 23,000
D. 24,250

Question 154:
What proportion of patients complained about waiting times by the end of the 2014 survey?
A. 12.1%
B. 11.5%
C. 11.0%
D. 10.7%

Question 155:
In January 2015, the government announced a target to reduce the number of patients waiting for longer than 30 minutes for an appointment by 50%, and by 25% for those waiting between 11-30mins. Proportionally, what will be the decrease in the number of complaints recorded by an identical survey at the end of 2015, if all targets are met?
A. 40%
B. 38%
C. 36%
D. 34%

SET 33

The graph below shows the price of crude oil in US Dollars during 2014:

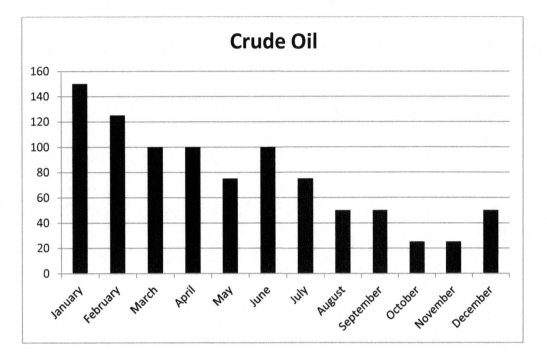

The total oil production, in millions of barrels per day, is shown on the graph below:

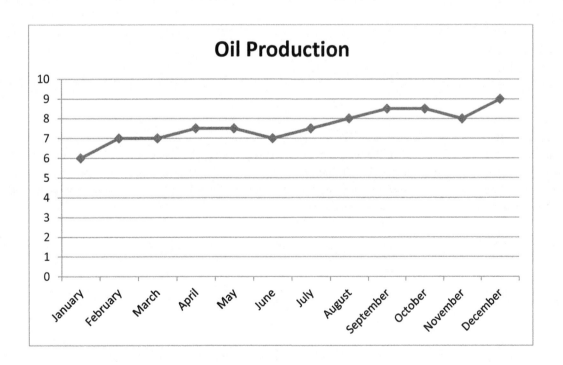

Question 156:
At what rate did the price of oil fall between January and March of 2014?

A. $16.70 per month
B. $20.00 per month
C. $22.70 per month
D. $25.00 per month

Question 157:
What was approximate total oil production in 2014?

A. 1,750 million barrels
B. 2,146 million barrels
C. 2,300 million barrels
D. 2,700 million barrels

Question 158:
How much did oil sales total in July 2014?

A. $0.56 Billion
B. $16.9 Billion
C. $17.4 Billion
D. $21.1 Billion

Question 159:
Oil prices have been falling due to a high supply. On average, the price of extraction & production of oil makes up 40% of the total price. The rest of the price is profit. How much profit was made from oil sales during June 2014?

A. $8.4 Billion
B. $12.6 Billion
C. $13.0 Billion
D. $21.0 Billion

Question 160:
Profit from oil extraction is 60% of the total sale price. This profit is split between the oil companies and the nation producing the oil in a ratio of 5:2. Of the oil company profits, 30% are used for corporation tax in the companies' home countries. Given that the overall sales value was $204 billion over the year, how much corporation tax was paid in 2014 (to 2 decimal places).

A. $26.23 Billion
B. $36.74 Billion
C. $43.71 Billion
D. $67.57 Billion

SET 34

The chart below shows the severity of asthma amongst a sample of 5 groups of 50 people of different ages. The average cost of asthma inhalers per patient is £50 per year. The population of the United Kingdom averaged 50 million during the period of interest. Children aged 0-5 years made up 7% of the population and children aged 5-10 years made up 10% of the population.

Children below the age of 10 who suffer from mild asthma have a half chance of developing respiratory problems in adult life. This figure is 90% for children below the age of 10 who suffer severe asthma. Children without asthma will not develop respiratory problems.

A review into doctors' practices concluded that between 1990 and 1995, 35% of mild asthma diagnoses of children between 0-10 were incorrect.

Age	No Asthma	Mild	Severe
0-5	80%	15%	5%
5-10	75%	20%	5%
10-21	85%	12%	3%
21-30	95%	3%	2%
30+	95%	4%	1%

Question 161:
How many people surveyed suffer from asthma?

A. 25　　　　　　　B. 35　　　　　　　C. 45　　　　　　　D. 55

Question 162:
What is the proportion of children surveyed who are likely to develop respiratory problems?

A. 13.00%　　　　　B. 13.25%　　　　　C. 13.50%　　　　　D. 14.25%

Question 163:
How many 0-10 year olds from the survey have been incorrectly diagnosed with asthma?

A. 6.1%　　　　　　B. 6.9%　　　　　　C. 7.4%　　　　　　D. 8.0%

Question 164:
What proportion of children below the age of 10 who were correctly diagnosed with asthma will develop respiratory problems?

A. 9%　　　　　　　B. 10%　　　　　　C. 11%　　　　　　D. 12%

Question 165:
How much money was wasted on mistakenly prescribing medication to children who were wrongly diagnosed with asthma from 1990 to 1995?

A. £133 million　　B. £157 million　　C. £187 million　　D. £255 million

SET 35

The following table shows data related to equity shares issued by five public sector companies on 1 March 2015.

Company	Number of equity shares (million)	Current market price Per share (£)	Percentage of equity share held by UK government
A	10	60	75%
B	20	50	50%
C	30	40	33.33%
D	40	30	25%
E	50	20	12.5%

Question 166:
If the government disinvested 50% of its stake in A at current market price, what (in £) is the amount of revenue generated by the government through the disinvestment?

A. 375 Million   B. 325 Million   C. 275 Million   D. 225 Million

Question 167:
If the government disinvested 25% of its stake in B at current market price, the amount of revenue generated by the government through the disinvestment would be (in £):

A. 125 Million   B. 150 Million   C. 175 Million   D. 200 Million

Question 168:
The government disinvested its entire stake in C at a price of £35 per share. What would have been the additional revenue generated by the government had it done the given disinvestment at the given market price?

A. £25 Million   B. £50 Million   C. £75 Million   D. £100 Million

Question 169:
If the share price of D fell to £25 on 2 March 2015, then what was the decline in the total value of D's shares held by the government from that of the previous day?

A. £25 Million
B. £50 Million
C. £75 Million
D. £100 Million

Question 170:
If the share price of E rose to £25 on 2 March 2015, then what was the increase in the total value of E's shares held by the government over that of the previous day (in £)?

A. £30.25 Million
B. £30.75 Million
C. £31.25 Million
D. £31.75 Million

Question 171:
Which of the following will fetch higher revenue for government?

A. Redeeming all its stock from company A.
B. Redeeming all its stock from company B.
C. Both of the above will fetch the same value.
D. None of the above.

SET 36

The table below shows the production of some agricultural crops in Harvestland in the years 2011-12 and the targets that were earlier set for that growing season.

Crop	Targeted production For 2011-12 (tonnes)	Actual production for 2011-12 (tonnes)	% Increase in production from 2010-11
Food grains	120	100	25
Oil seeds	60	50	25
Sugarcane	50	40	10
Cotton	40	30	20
Jute	25	20	25

Question 172:
The production of food grain (in tonnes) in 2010-11 was:
A. 40
B. 60
C. 80
D. 100

Question 173:
What was the difference in targeted production in 2011-12 and actual production in 2010-11 for oil seeds (in tonnes)?
A. 10
B. 20
C. 30
D. 40

Question 174:
How much more sugarcane should have been produced in order to meet the target in 2011-12 (in tonnes)?
A. 5
B. 10
C. 15
D. 20

Question 175:
What was the combined production of Cotton and Jute in year 2010-11 (in tonnes)?
A. 11
B. 21
C. 31
D. 41

Question 176:
How much more food grain was produced than oil seeds in 2010-11 (in TONNES)?
A. 10   B. 20   C. 30   D. 40

Question 177:
Cotton constituted what percentage of total crops in year 2011-12?
A. 10   B. 12.5   C. 15   D. 17.5   E. 30

SET 37

The table given below shows the sales volume of four products A, B, C and D manufactured by a company from January to April in the year 2014.

	January	February	March	April
Product A	9,500	10,250	10,500	11,000
Product B	6,500	7,000	7,250	7,500
Product C	3,500	3,750	4,000	4,250
Product D	2,500	3,100	3,500	4,000

Question 178:

In February, sale of product B constituted what percentage of total sales of all 4 products put together?

A. 26%

B. 27%

C. 28%

D. 29%

Question 179:

Which of the following products recorded maximum percentage increase from March to April?

A. Product A

B. Product B

C. Product C

D. Product D

Question 180:

In May 2014, the sales of product C witnessed an increase of 20% over the previous month. The sales of D were the same as those of C. What was the percentage increase in the sales of D in May relative to April?

A. 22.5 %

B. 25.0 %

C. 27.5 %

D. 30.0 %

Question 181:

By what percentage did the combined sales of product A and product C increase from January to April?

A. 17.0 %   B. 17.1 %   C. 17.2 %   D. 17.3 %

Question 182:

Assume a different scenario, that May 2015 witnessed a 20% growth in sales for products A and B, and a 30% growth in sales for products C and D over April values. What was the total sales value in May for all the products combined?

A. 32,925   B. 33,925   C. 34,925   D. 35,925

Question 183:

Assume a different scenario, that May 2015 witnessed 20% growth in sales of product A and 10% growth in sales for the other 3 products (B, C and D). Sales of A constituted what percentage of total sales in May 2015?

A. 40.25 %   B. 41.25 %   C. 42.25 %   D. 43.24 %

SET 38

A courier company uses three modes of transportation for delivering consignments – Road, Rail and Air. The following table shows the percentage distribution of the total number of consignments delivered, the revenue generated and the cost incurred, across the three modes of transportation in 2014.

Mode of transportation	Number of consignments (%)	Revenue (%)	Cost (%)
Rail	30	35	25
Road	45	20	25
Air	25	45	50

Question: 184

In 2012, the profit made by Courier Company was 30% of the total revenue. The company made a profit of £2.5 million. What was the total revenue?

A. £3.6 Million
B. £7.2 Million
C. £8.3 Million
D. £25 Million

Question 185:

In 2014, the cost per consignment was the lowest through which method?

A. Rail
B. Road
C. Air
D. Equal between road and rail

Question 186:

In 2014, the cost per consignment through rail was £5 and the revenue per consignment through rail was £20. What was the ratio of the total revenue through rail to the total cost through rail? Assume the number of consignments is equal to that given in the table.

A. 4:1   B. 5:1   C. 6:1   D. 7:1   E. 8:1

Question 187:

In 2013, the total costs of the company are £54,000. What is the total cost of air transportation in the year 2013?

A. £13,500
B. £17,000
C. £27,000
D. £32,000
E. More information needed

Question 188:

In 2014, if the total number of consignments delivered was 17,145, then what was total number of consignments delivered using rail and road?

A. 11,670   B. 11,974   C. 12,463   D. 12,859

SET 39

The following table provides partial information about the composition of three different alloys, A, B and C. Each of these alloys contains five different elements: Zinc, Tin, Lead, Copper and Nickel, and no other substances. An alloy, Alloy G, the composition of which is not given in the table, contains alloys A, B, C in the ratio 2:1:3. It is also known that in Alloy G, Tin, Lead and Copper are present in equal quantities.

Alloy	Zinc	Tin	Lead	Copper	Nickel
A	10%	40%			10%
B	25%	15%	50%	5%	5%
C	15%		20%		35%

Question 189:
Find the percentage of Lead in alloy A.

A. 8.33 %

B. 4.16 %

C. 2.70 %

D. 2.08 %

Question 190:
Find the percentage of Tin in alloy C.

A. 31.3 %

B. 15.8 %

C. 10.6 %

D. 7.9 %

Question 191:
An alloy X contains A, B and C in equal proportion. What is the percentage of Zinc in this alloy?

A. 12.50 %

B. 16.67 %

C. 25.00 %

D. 33.33 %

Question 192:
Find the percentage of Tin and Copper combined in alloy C.

A. 15 %

B. 20 %

C. 25 %

D. 30 %

Question 193:
Find the percentage of Tin in alloy G.

A. 11.11 %

B. 21.11 %

C. 31.11 %

D. 41.11 %

Question 194:
How many elements have exactly the same concentration in Alloy G?

A. One   B. Two   C. Three   D. Four

SET 40

The following table chart represents the number of people in the USA surveyed by CNN-Time in an opinion poll for "*The most influential person of the year 2001*". The number of people surveyed is 11,500.

Response	Percentage
Voted in favour of George Bush	39
Voted in favour of Donald Rumsfield	5
Voted in favour of Robert Guiliani	4
Voted in favour of Bill Clinton	2
Voted in favour of Lady Politicians	17
Non-respondents	33
Total	**100**

Question 195:
How many people voted in favour of Hillary Clinton, who received 60% of total votes polled for lady politicians?
A. 1,173   B. 1,223   C. 1,253   D. 1,273

Question 196:
If everyone who voted in favour of Robert Guiliani is a citizen of New York, then out of all the people surveyed, the number of citizens from New York is:
A. 460
B. 960
C. 1,040
D. Cannot be determined.

Question 197:
Out of the respondents, 20% are not US citizens. Given that only US citizens voted for George Bush, determine the percentage of US citizens who voted in favour of Bush.
A. 42.8%   B. 45.3%   C. 46.6%   D. 48.8%

Question 198:
Out of the total people surveyed, 40% are employees of the Federal Government and out of these 10% are in favour of Rumsfield. Find the number of people who are in favour of Rumsfield but are NOT employees of the Federal Government.
A. 105   B. 110   C. 115   D. 120

Question 199:
A mid-year survey has also been done on the same group of people. In that survey 16% of the people were in favour of Bill Clinton. Find the decrease in the number of people who voted in favour of Bill Clinton from mid-year survey to the actual survey.
A. 1,210   B. 1,410   C. 1,610   D. 1,810

Question 200:
A mid-year survey has also been done on the same group of people. In that survey 40% of the people were in favour of Bush. Find the decrease in the number of people who voted in favour of Bush from mid-year survey to the actual survey.
A. 115   B. 230   C. 460   D. 920

Abstract Reasoning

The Basics

The abstract reasoning section of the UKCAT will test your ability to think beyond the information that is readily available to you in form of the information provided by the question. The idea behind this section of the paper is to test how well the candidate is able to respond to questions that may go beyond the scope of their knowledge or require them to apply their existing knowledge in an unusual way. This is thought to be helpful in determining how well a student will be able to interpret information such as scans, X-rays or other test results as a clinician.

This section of the test examines pattern recognition and the logical approach to a series of symbols in order to match symbols to one group or another. The questions are grouped into 11 image sources, with 5 questions on each. Each image source contains two sets of six images, Set A and Set B. All of the images within each set are linked to each other by a common rule, but the rule must be different for Set A and Set B. The task is to identify the rules for each set, then for the 5 options you need to decide where they belong. If an option follows the same rule as the shapes in Set A, then it belongs in Set A, and likewise for Set B. If the image obeys neither the rule for Set A nor the rule for Set B, then it is correct to say it belongs in neither set and you choose the "neither" option.

> **Top tip!** If a shape fits the rules for **both sets**, then the correct response is always **"neither"**

In this section of the UKCAT, you have to answer 55 questions in only 14 minutes, so it is mathematically the most time pressured section of the UKCAT. But in terms of timing, think of it in terms of the image sets. There are 11 separate image sets, so you have 78 seconds per image set to work out the two rules and decide which set each option belongs in. Now by far the hardest task is deducing the rules – once you have them, matching the options to the correct set is straightforward. Therefore as a rule of thumb, you have about 60 seconds to work out the patterns, then quickly match the options to the set they each belong in.

Techniques

Timings

As with the rest of the test, you have to keep an eye on the time to keep track of how you're doing. Make sure that you stay within your time limit of 78 seconds for each block of 5 questions. When divided up to 15 seconds per question it might not seem like a lot, but actually given the format of the questions you will begin to realise that it is enough. As mentioned above, keep ticking on at a steady rate of about 55–60 seconds to find the rule then about 18–23 seconds to decide which set the 5 different options fit into. Your **practice will increase both your speed and overall likelihood of finding the rule**, but despite thorough preparation you still may fail to spot the pattern. If you can't see it, don't despair – simply make reasonable guesses (you have a 33% success rate by chance alone), flag for review (in case you have spare time at the end to check back and have another go) and move swiftly on.

Pattern Recognition

By far the most important ability in this section is to correctly identify patterns, as the matching process is straightforward once you have identified the rules. Some people are naturally better at this than others. You might be the sort of person who sees these patterns easily and can quickly put a name to the rule, or you might be the sort of person who finds it takes them more time and effort to work out what's going on. In reality, everyone lies on a sliding scale, but one thing is certain. You can improve your speed and accuracy on this section by having a methodical system that can be repeated and applied to all shape-sets. One such system is the **NSPCC** system. This provides a logical structure for working through each set of images, looking for different components of a possible pattern.

In this system, the letters stand for:

<u>N</u>umber ➜ <u>S</u>ize ➜ <u>P</u>osition ➜ <u>C</u>olour ➜ <u>C</u>onformation

Using this system, you consider each of the following aspects of the images in sequence, looking each time for commonly used patterns. We recommend this because it begins by looking for the simplest and most common potential patterns – if they are present, you are sure to get the pattern quickly and easily. If the first few patterns you look for are not present, then you look further on in the sequence to check for harder and less commonly tested patterns until you arrive at the answer.

Practice

It's very important to practice for this section as the style of questions are unlikely to be familiar. Practicing well gives you three key advantages. Firstly, you get used to the types of patterns which are likely to be asked in the real exam. This makes it more likely you will spot the patterns quickly as you will have seen them before, and it also trains up your implicit recognition system, meaning that if you take an "educated guess" you are more likely to be right. Secondly, it gives you practice implementing a pattern recognition system, like **NSPCC**. With practice you will become better at using the system, and therefore quicker and more accurate overall. Thirdly, you will gain a feeling for the time it takes to answer different types of question. This will allow you to better plan your time on the day, making the most out of every second you have.

Guessing

If you practice well you shouldn't have to guess very many questions, but it might be necessary if you just can't figure out a pattern. Guessing in this section of the test has a reasonable probability of success. Since there are only three options per question there is a 33% chance of guessing any one question correctly, and if all 5 questions in a data set are guessed then there is and 87% chance of gaining at least one mark from the section. However there is more to it than that.

Whilst the best way to answer these questions correctly is to formally deduce the rule and apply it (using a pattern recognition system like **NSPCC** helps here), humans do have an innate instinct for pattern recognition. This innate instinct is not necessarily right and can lead you astray, but in a quick guessing situation, it can be applied cleverly to boost your chances of guessing correctly. That is to say, in some questions the overall look of the image will feel as though it should be placed in a particular set – you wouldn't be able to say exactly why, but to you it would look much more like one group than the other. Learning to harness this power can help give you a much better guessing accuracy. Below is a simple example to demonstrate:

Set A	Set B	?
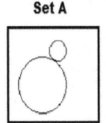	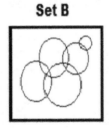	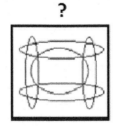

By quickly looking at the images provided for Set A and B, you get a general feel for what the contents are like. If asked which set the question image belongs to, you might be tempted to say Set B – it kind of look more complicated and cluttered then Set A. It just looks more like the image. Now whilst this reasoning is not the full rule, in instances like this it can lead you to the correct answer quickly, even if you don't properly identify the underlying pattern.

How to use the NSPCC system

The **NSPCC** system is a good way of working through possible patterns in a structured way. Whilst no structured response can be perfect, this system should solve about 90% of patterns quicker and more reliably than by trusting intuition alone.

Using the system, it is important that you are thorough. Sometimes the pattern can be subtle and you could easily miss out on it if not taking care. You have to examine the details closely: count corners, sides of shapes, check where they are etc. **You shouldn't be looking AT the shapes; you should be looking FOR patterns.** You should be working quickly, checking one thing, and if it's not that checking the next item in your list until you find the rule. Now to look at the system step by step.....

Number

Looking at "number" is about counting as many things as possible. How many dots? How many squares? How many sides? How many corners? How many right angles? Also have a look at how many different types of shapes you can find in the frames. Sometimes you might find one type of shape only in Set A and not in Set B for example. A good rule of thumb: block arrows have 7 sides, so don't count all the sides individually every time you see one!

Size

It is quite common to find patterns in the size of the shapes. Is one shape always bigger than the others? Is there always a big shape in the centre, or in the corner? Are there smaller shapes inside larger ones?

Position

Look for patterns in where shapes are positioned. You might, for instance, always find a square in the top right corner in one set and a circle in the top right corner of the other set. Look for Look also for touching and overlap of shapes – when you see this, make careful note of the type of contact. Is it tangential? Does it cut the shape in equal pieces, or is it off centre? Is there a certain shape that always makes this contact?

Colour

The shading of different shapes can constitute a pattern. Whilst this is often the easiest pattern to spot, it takes its place lower down in the system as it can often be a distracter. Most diagrams contain some amount of shading, but only occasionally is the primary pattern centred upon this. Look for shapes that are always shaded. Are all triangles black in one set and all circles black in the other, for example? On the other hand, are some shapes never shaded?

Conformation

These are the hardest patterns to spot, as they are the more complex patterns that can't be found by looking at the more geometric aspects. Conformation describes the pattern by which the shapes are arranged within the box – so you have to take a step back and look at the box as a whole in order to spot them. Look for patterns to the arrangement, like shapes arranged in a horizontal, vertical or diagonal line. Look also for the influence of one shape on another. For example, the presence of a white circle might signal a 90 degrees clockwise rotation of one shape and the presence of a black circle might signal a 90 degrees anticlockwise rotation, for example. When there are arrows, look at where they are pointing: are they all pointing in the same direction or at the same thing? You're looking for second order patterns, how things change based upon other aspects of the image.

Top tip! Give yourself plenty of time to systematically work out the rules. Once you have found them, answering the questions will be quick.

Example 1

Start by applying the NSPCC system

Set A   Set B

Test Shape 1   Test Shape 2

Start by applying the NSPCC system. Number: count the number of shapes, sides, angles and so on looking for a pattern (I can't see one). Size: are all shapes the same size (yes they are). Position: is there a pattern to where certain shapes are (not obviously). Colour: Is there a pattern to the shading (yes, the shading is dependent upon the shape of the cross). If you didn't get that, look back now to identify what the pattern is before reading on.

We can use our observations to devise the following rules:
Set A: (+)-shaped crosses have four white shapes and (X)-shaped crosses have two white and two black shapes.
Set B: (+)-shaped crosses have two white and two black shapes and (X)-shaped crosses have four black shapes.

Applying these rules tells us Test Shape 1 belongs to Set B and Test Shape 2 belongs to Set A.

Example 2

Set A   Set B

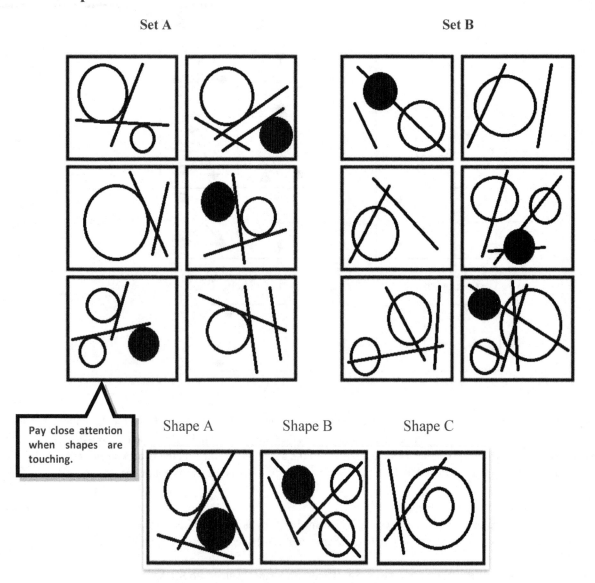

Pay close attention when shapes are touching.

Shape A   Shape B   Shape C

Start by applying the NSPCC system. Once again there is no pattern for number or size, but when reaching position you should note that shapes are touching and intersecting. Look more closely at this to work out what the pattern is.

It turns out that the rules for the set are as follows:

Set A: Every circle is touched tangentially by at least one line

Set B: Every circle is intersected by at least one line

Applying these rules tells us Shape 1 belongs to Set A, Shape 2 belongs to Set B and Shape 3 belongs to neither set, as the middle circle is neither touched tangentially nor intersected by any line.

A Final Word

This section is all about pattern recognition. The more you see the better you will become. Once you're familiar with the main types of patterns which come up, you'll be able to solve the majority of questions without difficulty. Remember that **you're looking to identify a rule** for each set of boxes, something which links them all together. Then, you can decide which set each question item fits into (or indeed neither). Start using the **NSPCC** system, then practice makes perfect!

Abstract Reasoning Questions

SET 1

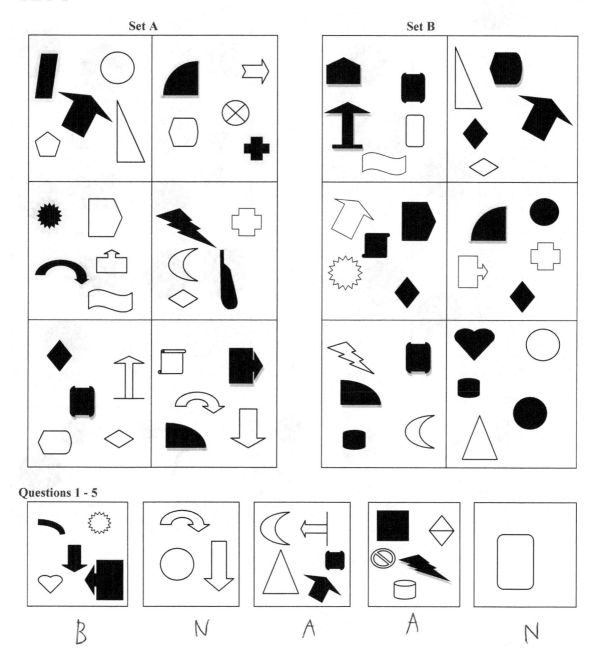

Set A

Set B

Questions 1 - 5

B   N   A   A   N

SET 2   2 shade   2 shade

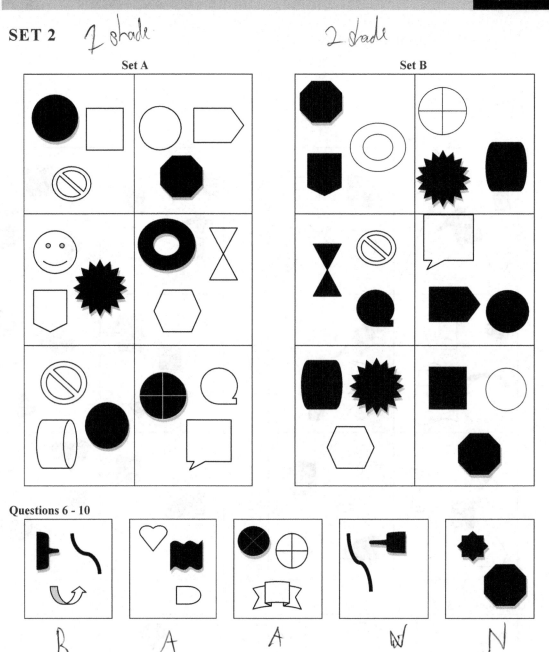

Set A   Set B

Questions 6 - 10

B   A   A   N   N

SET 3

triangle top left

4 sides in bottom right

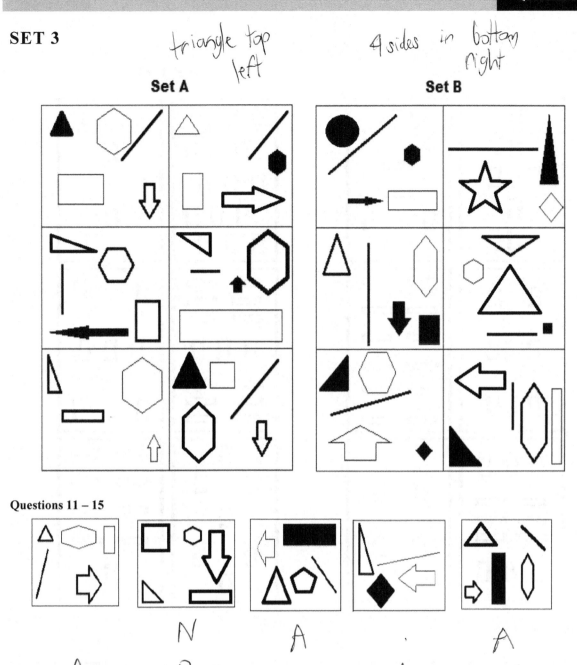

Set A

Set B

Questions 11 – 15

A   N   A   .   A
      B   N   A   ✓

SET 4 Even Odd

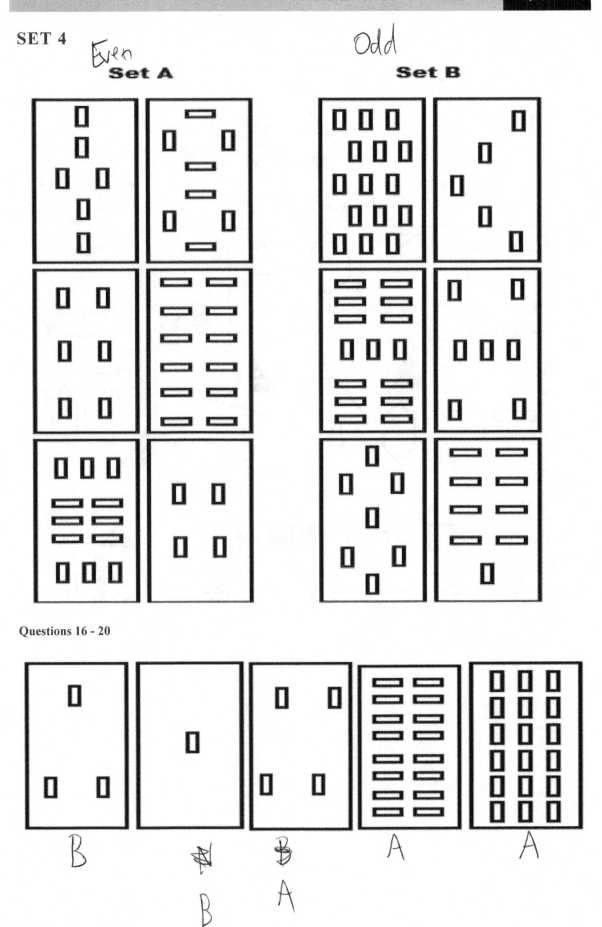

Set A **Set B**

Questions 16 - 20

B ~~N~~ ~~B~~ A A

B A

SET 5

No intersect

intersect

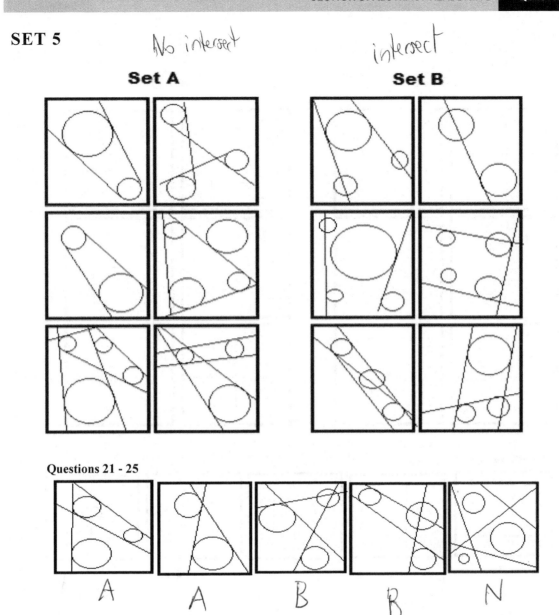

Set A

Set B

Questions 21 - 25

A   A   B   B   N

SET 6

Set A   Set B

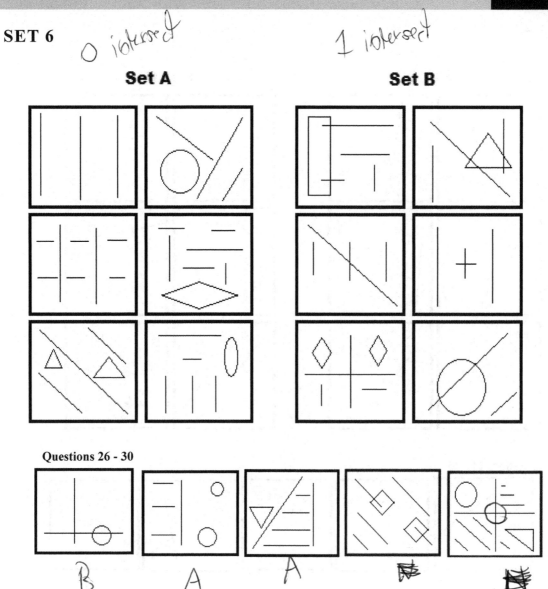

Questions 26 - 30

SET 7   *10 dots*   *9 dots*

Set A   ## Set B

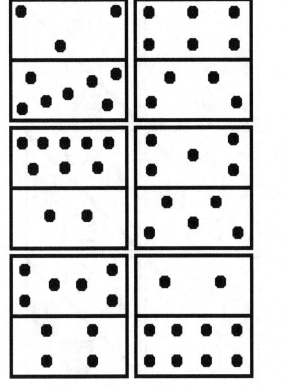

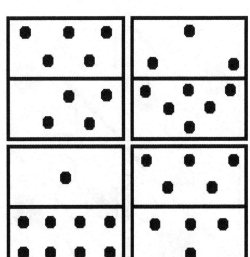

Questions 31 - 35

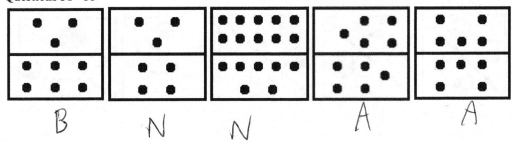

B   N   N   A   A

SET 8

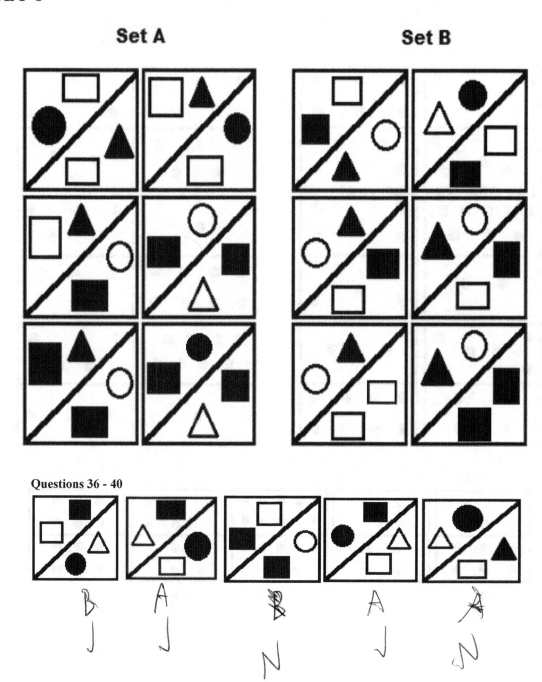

Set A

Set B

Questions 36 - 40

SET 9

5 point star center

triangle bottom left

Set A

Set B

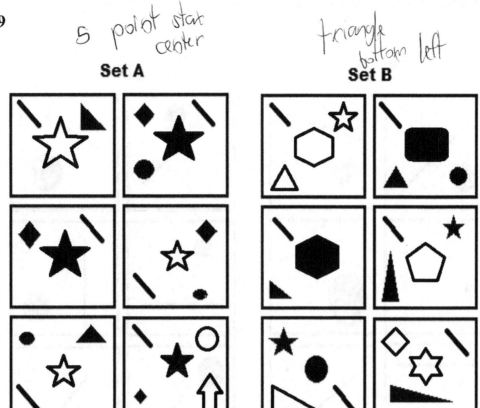

Questions 41 - 45

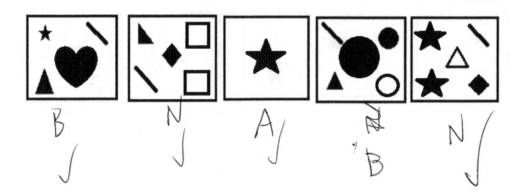

B ✓

N ✓

A ✓

B ✓

N ✓

SET 10

circle bottom left

dots top right

Set A   **Set B**

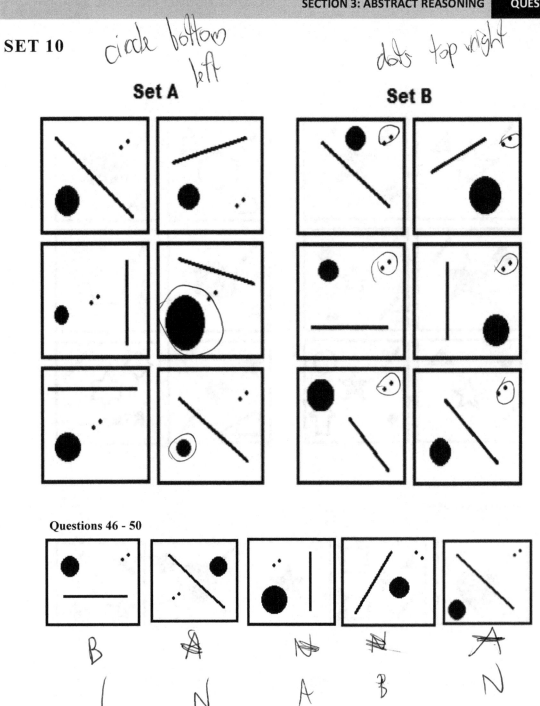

Questions 46 - 50

B   A   N   N   A

√   N   A   B   N

SET 11

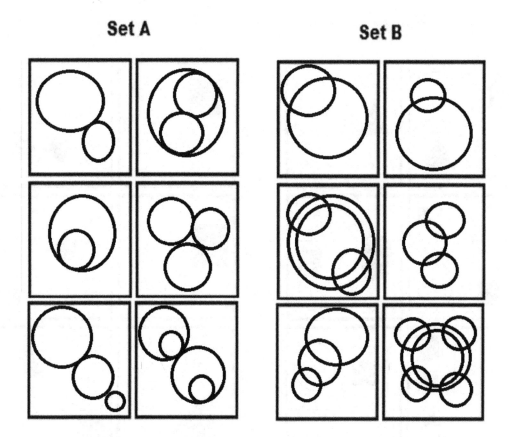

Questions 51 - 55

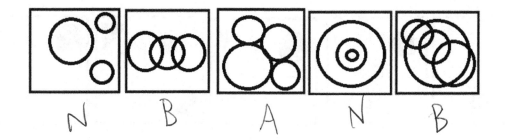

SET 12

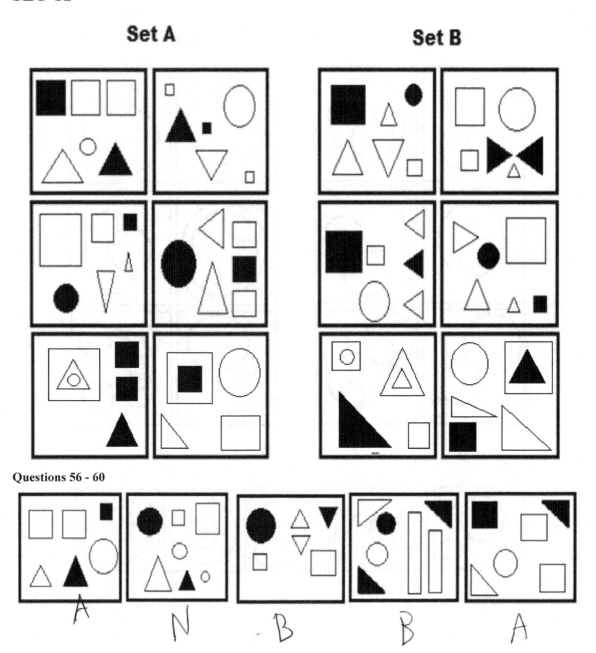

Set A

Set B

Questions 56 - 60

SET 13

sum edges = odd *sum edges = even*

Set A

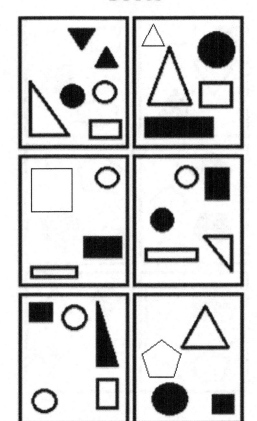 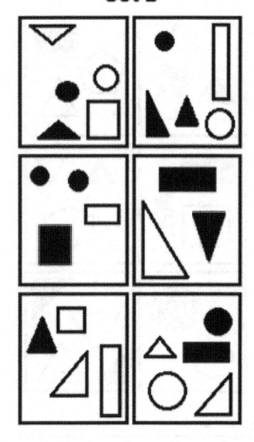

Set B

Questions 61 - 65

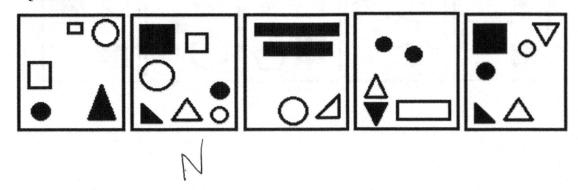

N

SET 14

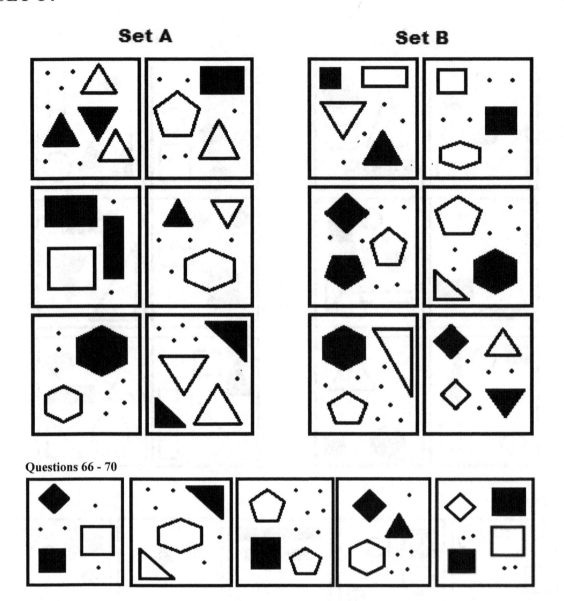

Set A   **Set B**

Questions 66 - 70

SET 15

4 right angles

6 right angles

Set A

Set B

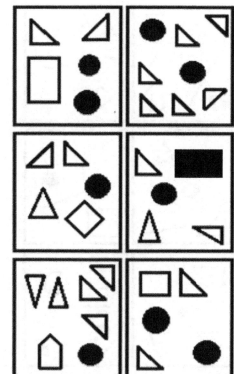

Questions 71 - 75

 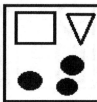   

SET 16

white shape smaller black

black shape smaller white

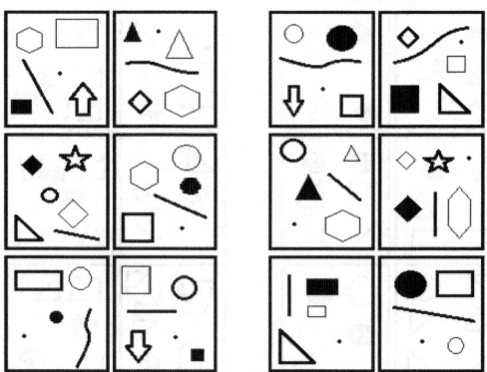

Set A   Set B

Questions 76 - 80

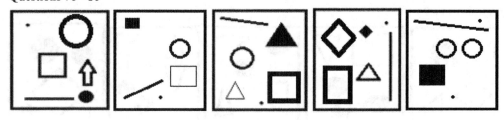

SET 17

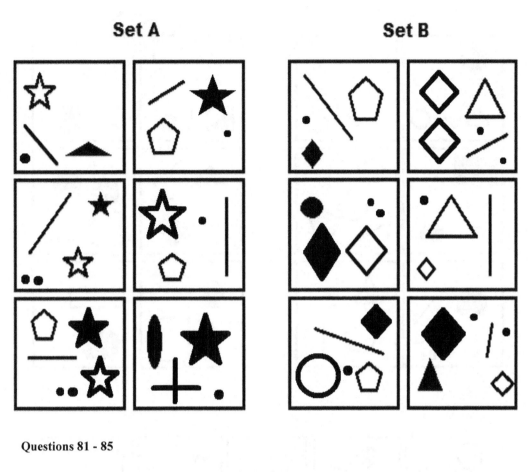

Set A   Set B

Questions 81 - 85

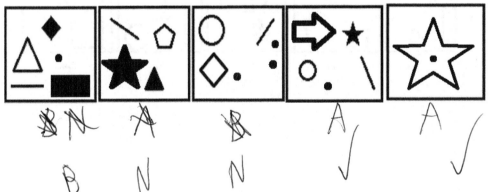

SET 18

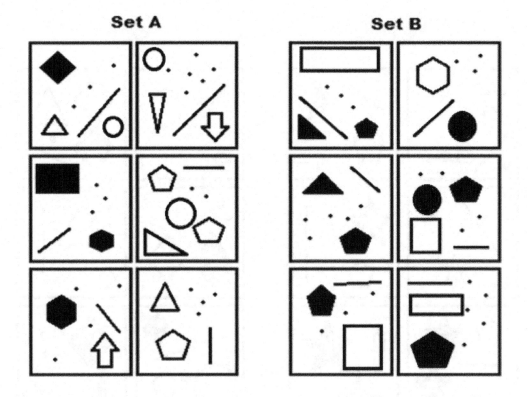

Set A   Set B

Questions 86 - 90

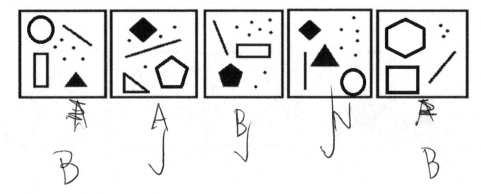

B   A   B   N   B

SET 19

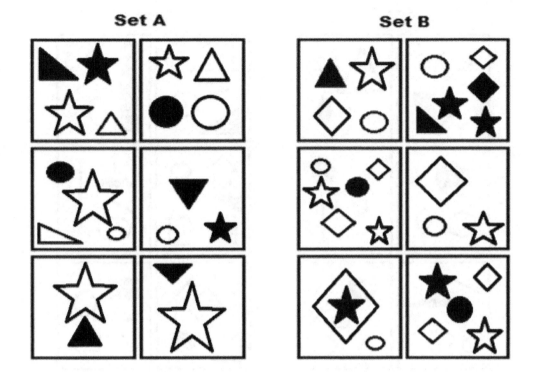

Questions 91 - 95

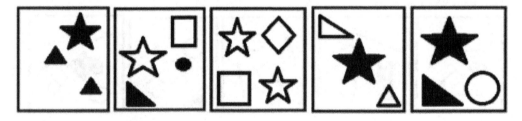

SET 20

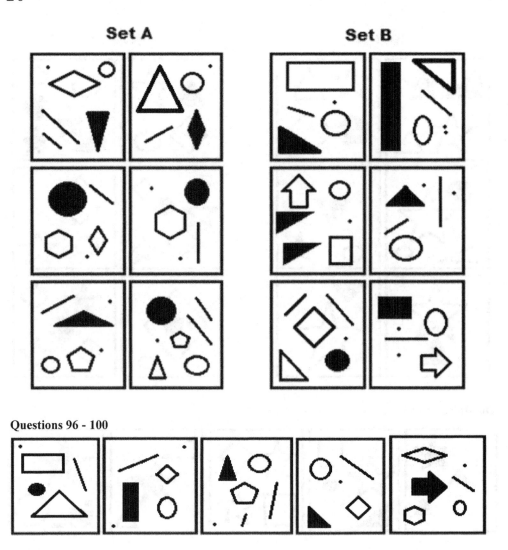

Questions 96 - 100

SET 21

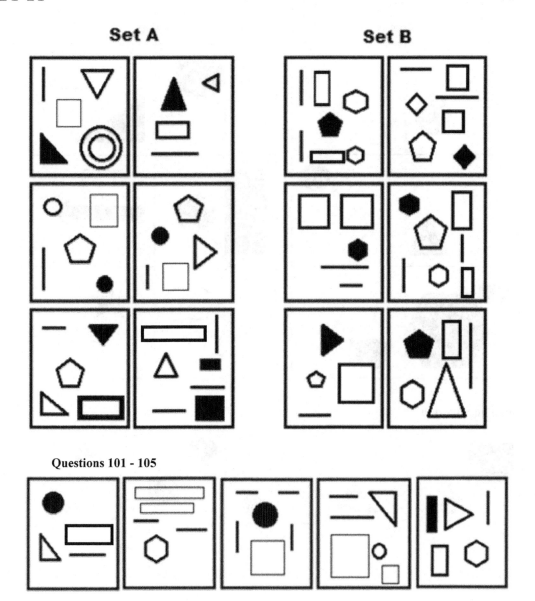

Set A   **Set B**

Questions 101 - 105

SET 22

Set A   Set B

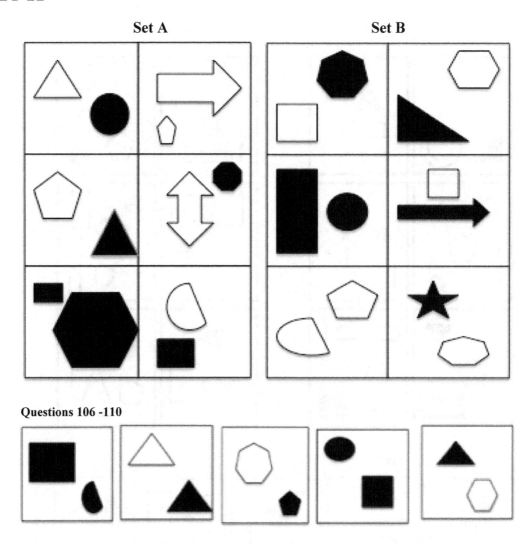

Questions 106 -110

SET 23

Set A   Set B

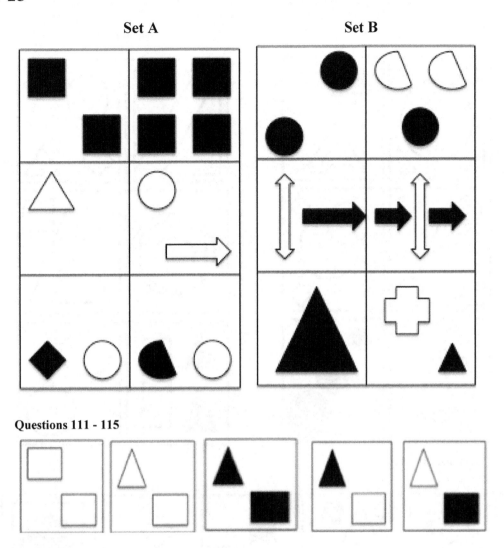

Questions 111 - 115

SET 24

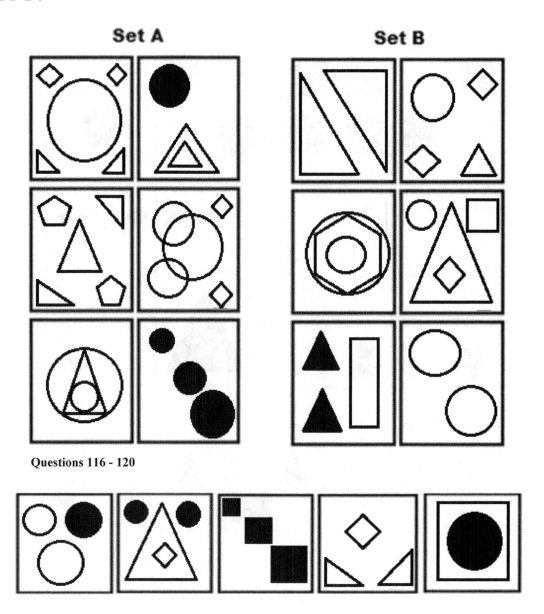

Set A

Set B

Questions 116 - 120

SET 25

Set A   Set B

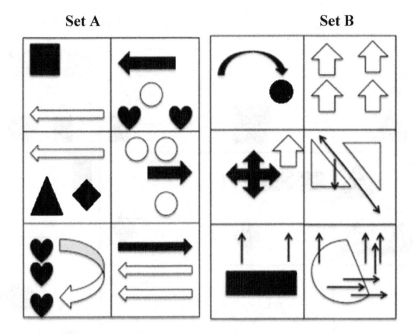

Questions 121 - 125

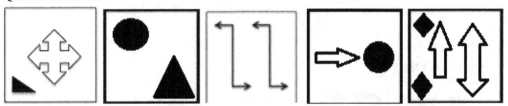

SET 26

Set A   Set B

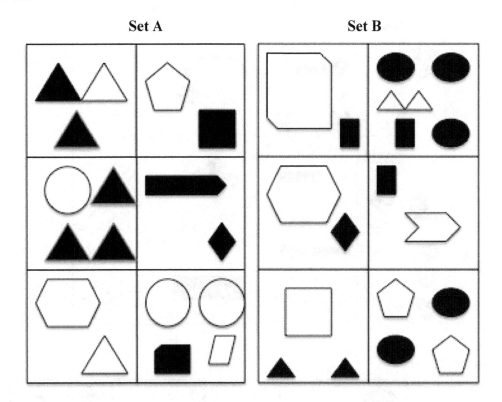

Questions 126 - 130

SET 27

Set A   Set B

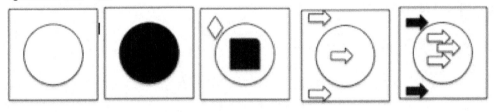

Questions 131 - 135

SET 28

Set A   Set B

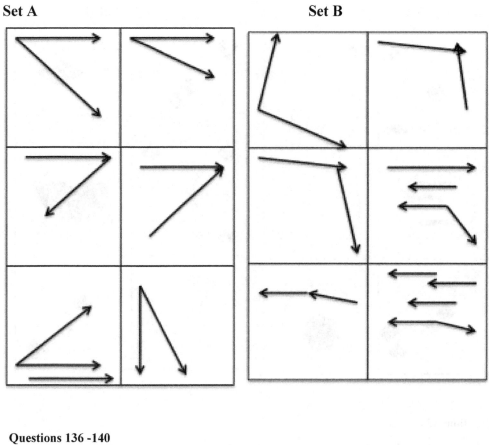

Questions 136 -140

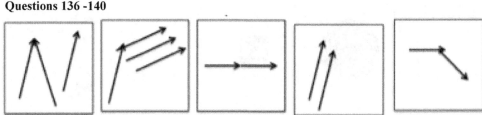

SET 29

Set A   Set B

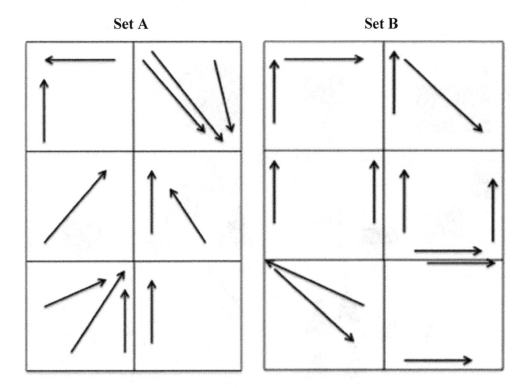

Questions 141 -145

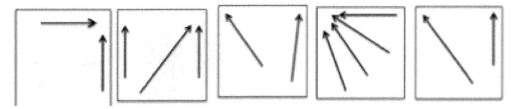

SET 30

Set A   Set B

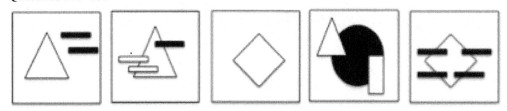

Questions 146 -150

SET 31

Set A   Set B

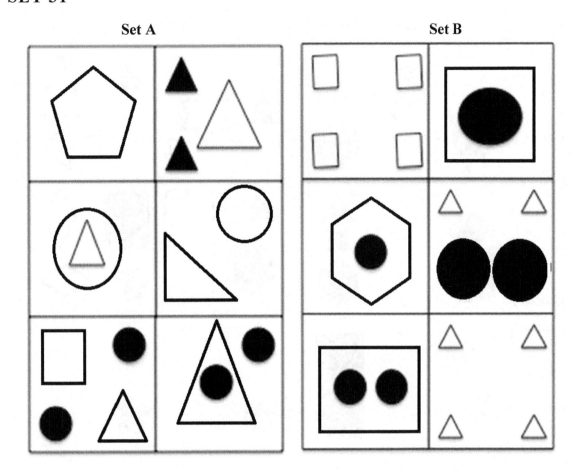

Questions 151 -155

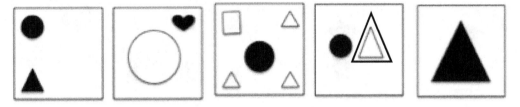

SET 32

Set A   Set B

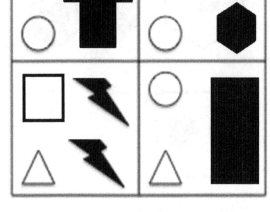
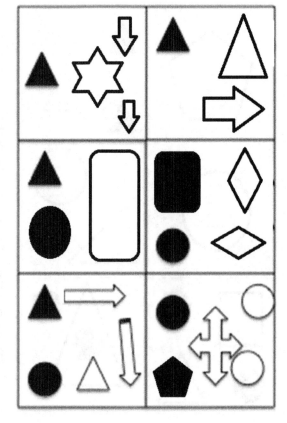

Questions 156 - 160

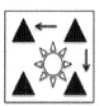

SET 33

Set A   Set B

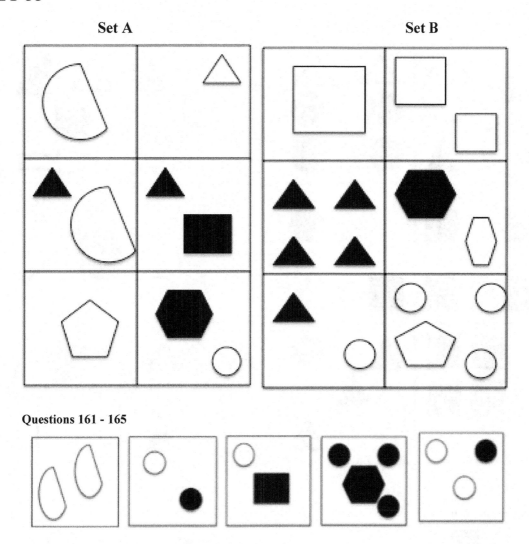

Questions 161 - 165

SET 34

Set A   Set B

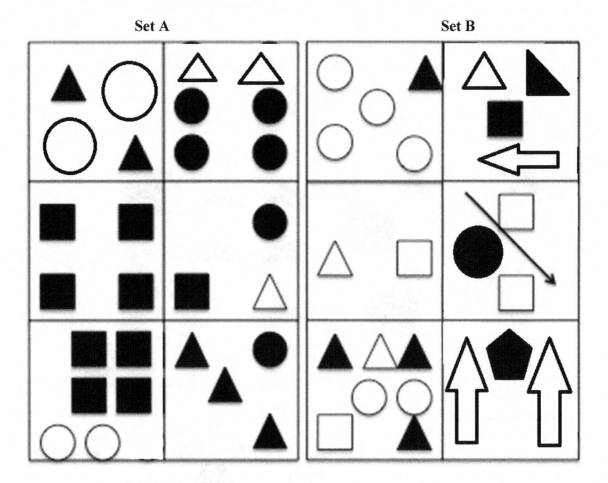

Questions 166 - 170

SET 35

Set A   **Set B**

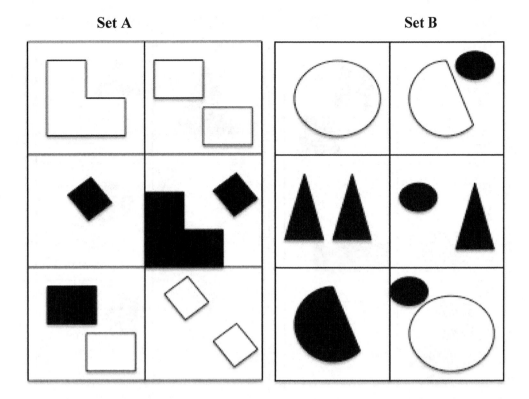

Questions 171 - 175

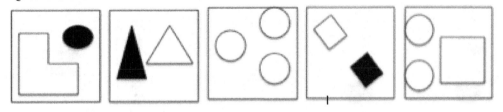

SET 36

Set A

Set B

Questions 176 - 180

SET 37

Set A   Set B

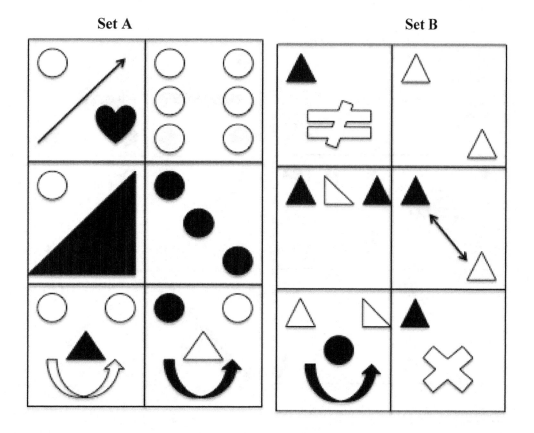

Questions 181 - 185

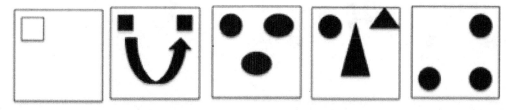

SET 38

Set A   Set B

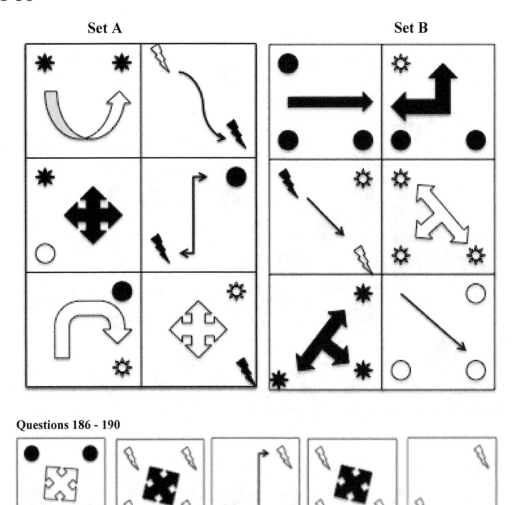

Questions 186 - 190

SET 39

Set A   Set B

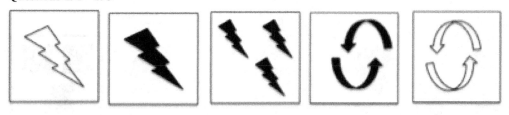

Questions 191 - 195

SET 40

Set A   Set B

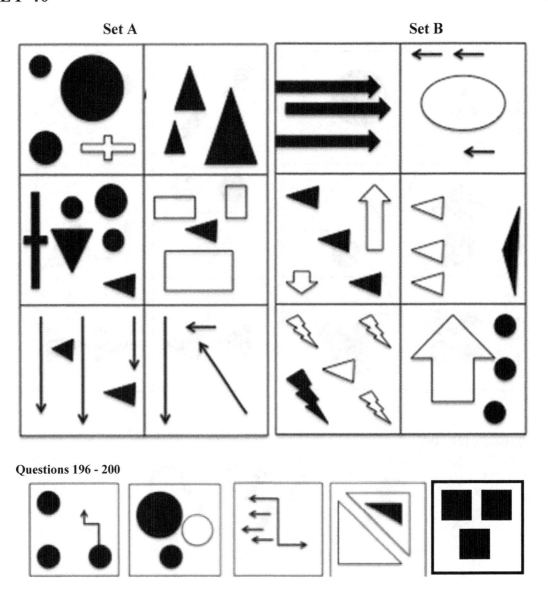

Questions 196 - 200

Decision Analysis

The Basics

Section 4 is the "decision analysis" section – this tests your ability to translate and work in a coded language. The idea is that this measures your ability to make decisions on the basis of limited information. Section 4 is the most time generous section of the UKCAT – you are given 31 minutes to answer 28 questions, equating to 66 seconds per question. This is the only section of the UKCAT where you have more than a minute per question. Unlike the other sections of the UKCAT, you must answer every question in order; you cannot move on until you have provided an answer to both parts of each question (the answer and your confidence rating), and will be prompted to complete the question by an on-screen error message if you try to move on before answering the question.

In each question, you are given a situation and some code. You are given a translation for the code, so the task is not to work out what the code means, but to translate between coded information and English. The majority of the questions require you to translate the coded language into English, but there are also questions that ask you to work the other way.

This is possibly the most unusual section of the UKCAT, and the style of question is least likely to be familiar to you. However don't be alarmed – with the clear approach you will learn in this book, you'll be armed with the right skills to tackle even the hardest decision analysis questions. With the right skills and enough practice, you'll be amazed at how good you can become.

Format of codes

This will become clear after you have looked at a few questions, but it is useful to understand what is meant by a code when reading this guide. At the beginning of the section, you will be given a scenario and a table showing you the code translations. The table contains words corresponding to letters, numbers or symbols – these are the codes. The questions will then use the code supplied until any new code is provided. As the table will only supply codes for a limited number of words, different or unusual phrasing and grouping of words may be required to increase the complexity. Read on to see how this works.

There are only three possible types of question:

➢ **Type 1:** You have to work from code to English. In this type, the question gives a sentence in the code and you have to choose the best interpretation of the code from a choice of English sentences.
➢ **Type 2:** You have to work from English to code. In this type, the question gives an English sentence and you have to choose the best translation into code from a choice of different responses in code.
➢ **Type 3:** You have to create new code. You are provided with a sentence to translate into code, but the current code is insufficient to give an accurate translation. In this type, you have to pick one additional word to be added to the code in order to improve the code to give a better translation of the text. You will choose from words in English.

Ensure you have practised all three types sufficiently; you may find a difference in your ability to answer the different question styles, and by realising this you can focus on the questions you find most difficult. Whilst it can be tempting to continue practicing the questions you enjoy and find easier, keep your eyes on the goal. Your aim is to do well in the UKCAT and get into medical school, so think about your aim and work on those tough questions to boost your score!

Question Answering Strategy

To do well in this section you need to get into the thought process of the person who wrote the code. Code in the UKCAT is written according to certain conventions and rules. If you want to make things much easier for yourself, learn about these **three** simple principles: omissions and introductions; commas; brackets.

Omissions & Introductions

This is the most simple code principle to understand, and also the most useful. It will help you answer the majority of questions in this section by a straightforward process of elimination.

It is a simple extension of what you already know. You know you are supposed to choose the best response, but how do you determine that? Now imagine you're presented with a code and are asked to choose the best translation for the code. From a logical standpoint, this task can be simplified into two questions which allow you to determine the best answer.

1) Which is the answer that uses **the most** information **in** the code?
2) Which is the answer that introduces **the least** new information **not in** the code?

If you approach every question with these two questions in mind, your task will be made very much simpler. You can use each question to eliminate less-than-perfect responses to leave you with the right one.

Commas

Commas are used to separate different items in the code. Two words in the same "phrase" between commas might relate to the same thing or action, or might be happening at the same period of time – but their actual meanings are not joined together (as in the case with **brackets**). For example: "**me, morning sun, food eat**" might mean "I eat breakfast at dawn" but probably wouldn't mean "my sunlight shines on the food I eat", because the concept of "me" is not grouped with a reference to the sun. There is no new meaning that is greater than the sum of the components of the code; the commas simply help to make the arrangement of the ideas clearer.

Brackets

Brackets are stronger than commas and are used to introduce new meanings to the code. Two words which are together in a bracket have a single, and often more complex, meaning which is a compound of the two words within it. For example: "**(water death)**" might mean "drowning" rather than, for instance, "someone was killed near the lake"; likewise "**(light capture)**" might mean "photograph" and "**(pen name)**" might mean "signature". Notice how the linking effect is stronger than for commas. Whereas "**run circle**" might mean a person running in a circle, "**(run circle)**" might take on a new meaning to mean a place where people run in a circle, such as a "running track". Apply these principles for yourself in the practice questions to see how they work!

Write out the Code

Writing out the "translation" of each phrase word-by-word on your whiteboard can be really helpful. Doing this makes it easy for you to mentally re-arrange the code until it makes sense. This is especially helpful as you get further through the section and the codes become increasingly complex.

You can ask for a replacement whiteboard, this can take time – plan ahead so the test centre staff have time to help you before it's too late! The marker is permanent, so you can't erase your working.
Make full use of your whiteboard and use shorthand.

To speed up your working, **consider using symbols to replace words** to condense your text. Writing out each code into English longhand is both tedious and time consuming. Try to come up with shorthand symbols for common words (such as female and male, opposite and negative, increase and decrease, hot and cold, water, street, walk etc.); if you devise these when you are practising, you can use them in the test to save time. Be comfortable with using the shorthand and make the symbols easily recognisable to make sure you don't get confused under pressure.

Top tip! Focus on eliminating answers. First, eliminate any answers that introduce information that is not in the code. Then eliminate answers that fail to translate items in the code. By keeping to a clear and logical method you make this section much simpler.

Answering questions

Which is closest?

In this section, you can never work out the right answer empirically. Instead, you need to compare the answers and choose the best. The right answer will contain all elements of the code, with as little addition as possible. Follow a structured question answering strategy to eliminate answers and find the best one.
Base your best judgement on the codes only.

Try to avoid making decision on what you would expect to be correct, or what seems the most logical statement. The section is looking at your ability to make the judgement from the codes given, and not any prior knowledge. The translation can sometime be peculiar, so don't let that throw you off. The task is to translate the code – if you've gone through the steps and arrived at an unusual answer, then it may well be the best translation of the code and the right answer.

> ***Top tip!*** When working from English to code (**type 2**), don't attempt to translate any but the very simplest sentences into code. Most codes will allow for multiple different ways of coding the message, so this is unlikely to produce and exact match and will waste time. **Instead, focus on working through each code in the options** and eliminate any which are poor translations, leaving you with the correct answer.

Confidence Ratings

In each question in this section, after you have chosen your answer you are asked to provide a confidence rating – to say how confident you are that your response is correct. This is rated on a scale from 1 to 5, with 1 being the least confident you are right and 5 being the most confident. The idea behind this is that it measures your awareness of your own decision making, as it is important to be aware of the risk of making mistakes when decisions are made on the basis of limited information.

For 2015 entry, confidence ratings were not used as a part of the scoring process, and **for 2016 entry they will not be used** either. Therefore you are advised to select an answer without wasting any time on it and move immediately on. Many candidates choose to tick the same confidence box for every question in order to avoid having to waste any energy at all thinking about it.

Remember to practice

By practicing plenty of examples you build your familiarity, reinforce your question answering strategy and gain confidence. If you're confident going into the UKCAT, you will better apply your skills and perform as well as you can!

Worked Examples

Operators	Basic Codes
A Old	1. I
B Future	2. They
C Good	3. Small
D Opposite	4. Study
E Increase	5. Anticipation
F Combine	6. Talk
	7. Hot
	8. Travel
	9. Book
	10. Land

Choose the best meaning for the following code: B, 1 (E4), 5, CE

A. I think I will do better in the future.
B. I used to study more and do better.
C. Next year I will study more and hope to do better.
D. Next time we will study more and perform better.
E. My teachers want me to study harder so I do better.

> There is no mention of teachers in the code, so forget this option immediately!

Worked Answer:

Firstly, find and write out the literal translation – *Future, I (increase study), anticipation, good increase.*
The best option should include all the meanings of the literal words, be in the correct tense, use correct singular/plural and not add any additional words. When selecting your answer make sure all of these criteria are satisfied.

A. I think I will do better in the future (**fault!** no use of study).
B. I used to study more and do better (**fault!** past tense rather than future).
C. Next year I will study more and hope to do better (this seems a good fit).
D. Next time we will study more and perform better (**fault!** uses we rather than I).
E. My teachers want me to study harder so I do better (**fault!** addition of my teachers).

Choose the code which most accurately reflects the following sentence: We are going to Antarctica next year.

A. B, (1, 8), 10 (D7)
B. BD, E1, 8, 10 (D7)
C. B, E1, 8 (10, 7)
D. E1, 8, (D7, 10), B
E. E1, BD (6), (B, 8), 10 (D7)

> Antarctica is not mentioned in the simple code, so we must look for a different way of expressing it.

Worked Answer:

When translating from English to code, it is often best to work backwards from the code and eliminate any incorrect responses. If you try to produce a code it is likely it will not fit any of the options, as there are many different ways to code a similar meaning. For example, Antarctica is not in the code, so we must translate it using a compound word in brackets. The phrase (cold land) might be appropriate, but as there is no word for cold in the code either, we might be looking for the translation of (hot opposite land). Alternatively, we might be looking for something describing the location of Antarctica – so work backwards from the code to stay on track.

A. B, (1, 8), 10 (D7) – Uses **I travel** rather than **we.**
B. BD, E1, 8, 10 (D7) – **Incorrect tense**, uses past rather than future.
C. B, E1, 8 (10, 7) – No opposite term for hot, suggests **Antarctica is hot.**
D. E1, 8, (D7, 10), B – Good fit.
E. E1, BD (6), (B, 8), 10 (D7) – **Added code** for "talked" which is not mentioned in question.

Decision Analysis Questions

Use the following to answer questions 1 – 22:

You are a soldier stationed at a base near an enemy camp. A river and forest separate your base and the enemy's base. The soldiers at your base have developed a code to communicate by radio what they observe when scouting the enemy camp. The code is limited, so it cannot be used to communicate everything, but you and your fellow soldiers have to use it as best you can. The code is as follows:

Code:	Meaning:	Code:	Meaning
1	Fast	U	Weapon
2	Over	V	River
3	High	W	Trees
4	Between	X	Water
5	Large	Y	Infantry
6	Toward	Z	Vehicle
7	Many	*	Opposite
8	Good	$	Increase

For questions 1-10, what is the best translation of the following code:

Question 1

5Z (1*), 2V, Y, 2V

A. A truck carrying several soldiers has crossed the bridge.
B. A tank and some soldiers have crossed the bridge.
C. A plane carrying several soldiers has crossed the bridge.
D. A vehicle and soldiers have charged across the bridge.

Question 2

135Z, 2W

A. A truck is moving through the forest.
B. A tank is crushing down trees.
C. A group of infantry is charging through the forest.
D. A plane is flying over the forest.

Question 3

7Y, 5U, Z(5*), 2V

A. A few heavily-armed soldiers and a truck have crossed the bridge.
B. A large group of heavily-armed soldiers and a tank have crossed the bridge.
C. A large group of lightly-armed soldiers and a truck have crossed the bridge.
D. A large group of heavily-armed soldiers and a car have crossed the bridge.

Question 4

75Z, 6W; (7*)Y, 2V

A. A large group of tanks and soldiers have crossed the bridge.
B. A formation of tanks is moving away from the forest while a small group of soldiers are crossing the bridge.
C. A large group of tanks is moving to the forest while a large group of soldiers are crossing the bridge.
D. A formation of tanks is moving to the forest while a small group of soldiers are crossing the bridge.

~ 143 ~

Code:	Meaning:	Code:	Meaning
1	Fast	U	Weapon
2	Over	V	River
3	High	W	Trees
4	Between	X	Water
5	Large	Y	Infantry
6	Toward	Z	Vehicle
7	Many	*	Opposite
8	Good	$	Increase

Question 5

You are manning the radio at your base and receive the code 7U, 4XW. What does this code most likely mean?

A. A large group of infantry are based along the river and forest.
B. The path between the forest and river has been fortified with machine guns.
C. A large group of trucks are moving between the forest and the river.
D. Several armed boats are guarding the river.

Question 6

4VW, 7Z(5*)

A. A large group of motorcycles is moving from the river to the forest.
B. A small group of motorcycles is moving between the forest and the river.
C. A large group of motorcycles is meeting at the river.
D. A small group of tanks is moving through the forest to the river.

Question 7

5(XZ)(1*), 2X

A. A tank is crossing the bridge.
B. A large boat is crossing the river.
C. A large plane is flying over the river.
D. A large group of boats is crossing the river.

Question 8

(13Z) 2V, 7YW

A. A boat has crossed the river while a large group of soldiers have fortified the forest.
B. A plane has crossed the river while soldiers move through the forest.
C. A boat carrying a large group of soldiers is heading for the forest.
D. Planes carrying soldiers are flying over the river and forest.

Question 9

7Y, 6*V, 7Z, 6*V, 7U, 6*V

A. The enemy is attacking with heavily-armed soldiers and heavily-armed tanks.
B. A large group of soldiers, trucks and machine guns have moved toward the river.
C. The enemy is retreating away from their position.
D. A large group of soldiers, tanks, planes and machine guns have moved along the riverbank.

Code:	Meaning:	Code:	Meaning
1	Fast	U	Weapon
2	Over	V	River
3	High	W	Trees
4	Between	X	Water
5	Large	Y	Infantry
6	Toward	Z	Vehicle
7	Many	*	Opposite
8	Good	$	Increase

Question 10

7Z, 7Y, 7U, 3Z, 6V

A. The enemy forces are advancing toward the river.
B. A large group of trucks, soldiers, weapons and planes is crossing over the river.
C. The enemy have soldiers and support vehicles in the river.
D. A large group of tanks and heavily-armed infantry have boarded planes to cross the forest.

For questions 11 – 20, what is the best code for you to transmit back to your base?

Question 11

You observe four tanks crossing the bridge while several squads of soldiers creep through the forest.
A. 45Z, 2V, 4Y, W
B. 5Z, 5Z, 5Z, 5Z, 2V, 1Y, W
C. 5Z 5Z 5Z 5Z, 2V; Y, (1*) W
D. 5Z*, 2V, Y*, W

Question 12
You observe two boats carrying soldiers across the river while a tank crosses the bridge.

A. (XZ)Y, (XZ)Y, 2V; (5Z) 2V
B. XZ, 2V, 5Z(Y), 5Z(Y), 2V
C. VZ, VZ, 2V, 5Z, 2V
D. 7XZ, Y, 2V, 5Z, 2V13.

Question 13
You observe a plane flying overhead while soldiers board trucks.

A. 3Z, Z(5*)
B. 3Z, 7U5Z
C. 5U, 7(5*)
D. Z(Y$), 3Z2

Question 14
You observe several defensive machine-gun locations along the riverbank and two squads of soldiers in the forest.

A. Y, Y, W; 7U, V
B. 7Y, W, 7U, V
C. YW, UV
D. YU, VW

Code:	Meaning:	Code:	Meaning
1	Fast	U	Weapon
2	Over	V	River
3	High	W	Trees
4	Between	X	Water
5	Large	Y	Infantry
6	Toward	Z	Vehicle
7	Many	*	Opposite
8	Good	$	Increase

Question 15

You observe three boats crossing the river while two tanks cross the bridge.

A. 7XZ, 2V, 5*Z 5*Z, 2V

B. (XZ) (XZ) (XZ), 2V; 5Z, 5Z, 2V

C. (XZ) (XZ) (XZ), V; 5Z, 5Z, V

D. 75XZ, 6V, 75Z, 2V

Question 16

You observe soldiers boarding a well-armed helicopter while two boats cross the river.

A. 3YZU; (XZ) (XZ) 2V

B. (3Z5U) Y$; (XZ) (XZ) 2V

C. XZ XZ, 2V; 7Y, 3Z (5U)

D. 3Z(5U, Y), 7XZ, 2V

Question 17

You observe every available land vehicle and soldier crossing the bridge while every available boat crosses the river.

A. Y Y, 2V, 5Z 5Z, 2V, 5*Z, 5*Z, 2V, 7XZ, 7XZ, 2V

B. 7Y, 2V, 13Z, 2V, 75Z, 2V, 7(XZ), 2V

C. 7Y, 75Z, 75*Z, 7(XZ), 2V

D. 7Y, 2V, 7Z, 2V, 7(XZ), 2V

Question 18

You observe infantry boarding a boat and a few trucks stationed in the forest.

A. (XZ)Y$, V, Z, W

B. 7XZ, Y, V, 75Z, W

C. (XZ)Y$, Z(7*), W

D. XZY(V$), 75Z(W)

Question 19

You observe a large group of planes quickly flying toward your base.

A. 713, Z2V, Z2W

B. 73Z, 2V(1), 2W(1)

C. 2V, 2W, 3Z(1), 3Z(1)

D. 2V, 2W, 73*Z(1)

Code:	Meaning:	Code:	Meaning
1	Fast	U	Weapon
2	Over	V	River
3	High	W	Trees
4	Between	X	Water
5	Large	Y	Infantry
6	Toward	Z	Vehicle
7	Many	*	Opposite
8	Good	$	Increase

Question 20

You observe two tanks in the forest while a large group of trucks full of soldiers cross the bridge.

A. 5Z, 5Z, W, 7(ZY), 2V
B. 75Z, 2W, 75*(ZY), 2V
C. 5*Z, 5*Z, W, 75Z(Y), 2V
D. 5Z, 5Z, W, 5*Z 5*Z, 2V(Y)

Question 21

You need to convey "rockets are targeted to fire towards base".
Which one of the following words would be the most helpful to have included in the code in order to convey the new message?

A. Target
B. Rocket
C. Fire
D. To

Question 22

You need to convey: "enemy soldiers are preparing to destroy the bridge."
Which one of the following words would be the most helpful to have included in the code in order to convey the new message?

A. Enemy
B. Bridge
C. Destroy
D. Soldier

Use the following to answer questions 23 – 43:

You are translating an ancient manuscript written in a language that is not well understood. Some of the symbols are understood, but not perfectly. You are working to make get a general sense of what the manuscript says, not to translate it perfectly or precisely. Your best understanding of the symbols used in the manuscript is as follows:

Symbol	Meaning	Symbol	Meaning
1	Water	A	Move
2	Fire	B	Breathe
3	Trees	C	Cold
4	Air	D	Food
5	Hill	E	Human
6	Earth	F	Fight
7	Home	G	Up
8	Spear	H	Large
9	Opposite	I	Good

For questions 23-32, what is the best translation of the following code:

Question 23

EE, (1A)

A. The people walked on the water.
B. The people went to the lake.
C. The man went to the river.
D. The people swam through the river.

Question 24

B, E, 4, C

A. He drank the cold water.
B. She breathed in the cold air.
C. The cold air gave him a cold.
D. The cold woman breathed.

Question 25

(32) EE, A

A. The people moved away from the forest fire.
B. The people used water to put out the fire.
C. The people burned the trees for warmth.
D. The soldiers lit their arrows on fire.

Question 26

1, A, 5

A. The hill was carved by the flood.
B. The river flows from the hills.
C. The hill moves along the river.
D. The fire crept up the hill.

Symbol	Meaning	Symbol	Meaning
1	Water	A	Move
2	Fire	B	Breathe
3	Trees	C	Cold
4	Air	D	Food
5	Hill	E	Human
6	Earth	F	Fight
7	Home	G	Up
8	Spear	H	Large
9	Opposite	I	Good

Question 27

(IE) 7,3, (D9)

A. He made his home in the woods, where there was only water to drink.
B. The starving hero painstakingly made his way home.
C. The hero lived in the forest, where she suffered from starvation.
D. He went to the woods to cut down trees to build a home.

Question 28

(6A), H, 3, (G9)

A. The forest was destroyed by the big earthquake.
B. The earthquake pushed soil down through the forest.
C. The trees grew up out of the ground.
D. The trees slid down the mountain.

Question 29

E(I9), A, 8, (F9), EE

A. The hero and the villain fought to the death.
B. The hero crafted a spear ready for the fight.
C. The village was peaceful after the villain was killed.
D. The villain put down his spear and made peace with the others.

Question 30

E(I), A3, 3G9, G2

A. The strong man cut down a tree to show his might.
B. The hero went to the forest and cut down a tree to light a fire.
C. She saw the tree falling, so she moved out of its way.
D. The hero cut down trees to save the people from the forest fire.

Question 31

HE, H7, G5

A. The queen's castle is at the top of the hill.
B. The hero's home is in the forest.
C. The king had the castle built on the highest mountain.
D. The queen was kept prisoner in the castle.

Symbol	Meaning	Symbol	Meaning
1	Water	A	Move
2	Fire	B	Breathe
3	Trees	C	Cold
4	Air	D	Food
5	Hill	E	Human
6	Earth	F	Fight
7	Home	G	Up
8	Spear	H	Large
9	Opposite	I	Good

Question 32

(E,I9), 2, (4,I9), B9

A. The villain set the forest ablaze.
B. The villain was so strong that he could even breathe smoke.
C. The villain suffocated in the smoke.
D. The villain drowned in the lake.

For questions 33 – 35, what is the best translation of the following code:

Question 33

"The battle was fought in the woods."

A. EE, F, (H3)
B. EE, F3(6)
C. FH3, E, 59, E
D. EE, (FH), 3

Question 34

"The forest burned to the ground

A. (H3)2, G9, 6
B. (H3)4, G9, 3
C. 34, G, 6
D. 32, B9, 6

Question 35

"The villain brought terror upon the land, drying up the river and poisoning the air."

A. E(I9), 6H, (1A)(I9), 4(I)
B. E, 6(I9), 1(G), 4(I9)
C. E(I9), A6, G9, 19
D. E(I9), 6(I9), (1A)(19), 4(I9)

Question 36

You are aware of a section of this manuscript that tells the story of a war fought over farmland. If you were trying to locate the section with this story, which symbols should you look for?

A. 4, E, 5
B. D, 3, A
C. E, F, D
D. A, D, 4

Symbol	Meaning	Symbol	Meaning
1	Water	A	Move
2	Fire	B	Breathe
3	Trees	C	Cold
4	Air	D	Food
5	Hill	E	Human
6	Earth	F	Fight
7	Home	G	Up
8	Spear	H	Large
9	Opposite	I	Good

Question 37

You are aware of a section of this manuscript that tells the story of an army capturing a village. If you were trying to locate the section with this story, which symbols should you look for?

A. E, F, 4
B. F, 7, E
C. F, 9, E
D. 8, F, 2

Question 38

You want to encode: "The hero fell in love with the lady." Which of the following words would be the most helpful addition to the above code?

A. Hero
B. Fall
C. Love
D. Lady

Question 39

You want to encode: "The villain's army burned down the hero's home." Which of the following words would be the most helpful addition to the above code?

A. Villain
B. Army
C. Burn
D. Hero

Some teenagers are going to the local theme park. Discover more about their trip by cracking the codes below:

Operator codes	Specialist codes	
A Increase	1 Theme	13 Up
B Decrease	2 Park	14 Fall
C Plural	3 Ride	15 Loop
D Plus	4 King	16 Fun
E Opposite	5 Short	17 You
F Negative	6 Cart	18 Go
G Positive	7 Scary	19 Enough
H Combine	8 Friend	20 This
I Past	9 Dry	21 Tidal
J Future	10 Wave	
K Question	11 Height	
L Every	12 Sick	

For questions 40-44, what is the best translation of the following code:

Question 40

E17, 18, B(E4), H(1,2), D, C8

A. I am going to the Princess theme park with a friend.

B. I am going to the Princess theme park with friends.

C. We are going to the Princess theme park with friends.

D. You are going to the Princess theme park with friends.

E. I am going to the Queen theme park with friends .

Question 41

C3, D, A(C15), D, (C14,D,C(E13)), A7

A. The rides with lots of loops and ups-and-downs are very scary.

B. The ride with lots of loops and ups-and-downs are very scary.

C. The rides with lots of loops and ups-and-downs are scary.

D. The rides with the loop and ups-and-downs are scary.

E. The rides with lots of loops and ups-and-downs are lots of fun.

Question 42

18, F(H(E5, 19)), 20, 3

A. I am not tall enough for this ride.

B. I am too tall for this ride.

C. You are not tall enough for that ride.

D. You are not tall enough for this ride.

E. You are too tall for this ride.

Question 43

H(21,10), 3, I, C(E17), A(E9)

A. The tidal wave ride made us wet.

B. The tidal wave ride will make us very wet.

C. The tidal wave ride made us very wet.

D. The tidal wave ride was very wet.

E. The tidal wave ride made me very wet.

Question 44

E17, J12, 20, 3; 20, F16!

A. I will be sick on this ride; this is not fun!

B. You will be sick on this ride; this is not fun!

C. I will be sick on this ride; this is fun!

D. I feel sick on this ride; this is not fun!

E. I was sick on this ride; it was not fun!

Use the following to answer questions 45 – 55:

You are asked to build a workbench. The following table applies to a kit of materials that you are using to construct the workbench. Use the code to answer the following questions:

Code	Meaning	Code	Meaning
0	Black	a	Nail
1	Red	b	Block
2	White	c	Beam
3	Blue	d	Screw
4	Green	e	Wood
5	Yellow	f	Metal
6	Grey	g	Glue

For questions 45-49, what is the best translation of the following code:

Question 45.

2fc, 3fc, 3d, 4eb

A. Attach a white metal beam and a blue metal beam to a green wooden block and a blue metal block.
B. Use blue screws to attach a white metal beam and a blue metal beam to a green wooden block.
C. Screw two blue metal beams to a green wooden block.
D. Use blue screws to attach two white metal beams to a green wooden block.

Question 46

5eb, 5eb, 5fb, a, 4fb

A. Nail three wooden yellow blocks to one green metal block.
B. Nail two wooden yellow blocks and one metal yellow block to one green metal block.
C. Screw two wooden yellow blocks to a metal yellow block and a green metal block.
D. Attach two wooden yellow blocks and one metal yellow block to a green metal block with a black nail.

Question 47

The next step of your instructions reads as follows: a0, 1c, 3ec 3ec. Which of the following is the most accurate interpretation of this step?

A. Nail the red beam to two wooden blue beams.
B. Attach the red metal beam to two wooden blue beams.
C. Using black nails, attach the red beam to two wooden blue beams.
D. Using black nails, attach the red metal beam to two wooden blue beams.

Question 48

6eb, gd, 1eb.

A. Glue a grey wooden block to a red wooden block.
B. Attach a grey wooden block to a red wooden block with screws.
C. Use glue and a screw to attach a grey metal block to a red wooden block.
D. Use glue and a screw to attach a grey wooden block to a red wooden block.

Code	Meaning	Code	Meaning
0	Black	a	Nail
1	Red	b	Block
2	White	c	Beam
3	Blue	d	Screw
4	Green	e	Wood
5	Yellow	f	Metal
6	Grey	g	Glue

Question 49

23fc, 23fc, d, 45eb.

A. Screw two light blue wooden beams to a teal wooden block.

B. Attach two light blue wooden beams to a green and yellow block with screws.

C. Screw two blue and white metal beams to a green and yellow wooden block.

D. Using white screws, attach two blue and white wooden beams to a green and yellow wooden block.

For questions 50 – 53, what is the best code to translate:

Question 50

"Screw the white wooden beam to the black metal beam."

A. 2ec, d, 0fc

B. 2c, ed, 0fc

C. 2de, d0, cf

D. 2ec, d, 2fc

Question 51

"Nail the two red wooden blocks to the white wooden block."

A. eb1, 1eb, d, eb

B. 1b(2), a, 2eb

C. 1eb, 1eb, a, 2eb

D. 1eb, 1eb, 2d, 2eb

Question 52

"Screw three blue and yellow wooden beams into the green metal block."

A. 35ec, 35ec, 35ec, d, 4fb

B. 35ec, 35ec, 36ec, d, 4fb

C. 35ec(3), 4d, fb

D. d, 4fb, 35ce, 35ce, 25ce

Question 53

"Glue the red metal beam to the two black wooden blocks."

A. 1fc, 0g, eb eb

B. 1fc, g, 0eb(2)

C. 0eb, 0eb, g, fc

D. D.1fc, g, 0eb 0eb

Question 54

If you were encoding, "Glue the white wooden block to the exact centre of the grey wooden beam," which of the following words would be most helpful to have included in the code?

A. To   B. Centre   C. Of   D. Exact

Question 55

If you were encoding, "Screw the pink block to the end of the white beam and secure it with glue," which of the following words would be most helpful to have included in the code?

A. Pink   B. End   C. And   D. Secure

You are working as a land surveyor and your partner has made notes in code:

Notation	Meaning	Notation	Meaning
A	Soil	1	Overgrown
B	Gravel	2	Dry
C	Rock	3	Stable
D	Wet	4	Unstable
E	Slippery	5	Even
F	Bare	6	Uneven
G	Packed	7	Suitable for buildings
H	Loose	8	Suitable for roads
I	Ground	9	Opposite

For questions 56-66, what is the best translation of the following code:

Question 56

C, 248

A. This is stable, dry rock but a road could be built here.

B. This is unstable, dry rock on which a road could be built.

C. This is unstable, overgrown rock on which a road could be built.

D. This is unstable, dry rock on which a building could be built.

Question: 57

A, 3G, 7

A. This is stable, packed rock on which a building could be built.

B. This is unstable, packed soil on which a building could be built.

C. This is stable, packed soil on which a building could be built.

D. This is stable, wet soil on which a road could be built.

Question 58

(DA) 1, 4

A. This is an unstable, overgrown marsh on which nothing can be built.

B. This is an unstable, rocky lake on which nothing can be built.

C. This is a stable lake, over which could be built a bridge.

D. This is a dried lake bed on which nothing could be built.

Question 59

B, DH, 4

A. This is loose, unstable gravel on which a road could be built.

B. This is loose, wet, unstable gravel on which nothing can be built.

C. This is loose, unstable gravel on which nothing can be built.

D. This is loose, wet, unstable soil on which nothing can be built.

Question 60

5C, E, 3, 7

A. This is slippery, unstable rock that is not suitable for any construction

B. This is a rocky hill that is unstable, but could still support a road.

C. This is stable, but shifty gravel that could support construction.

D. This is stable, slippery rock on which a building could be built.

Question 61

A, 6G, 3, 8

A. This is stable, packed, even soil on which a road can be built.

B. This is unstable, loose, even soil on which a road can be built.

C. This is stable, packed, uneven soil on which a road could be built.

D. This is stable, packed, uneven soil that can support a building.

Notation	Meaning	Notation	Meaning
A	Soil	1	Overgrown
B	Gravel	2	Dry
C	Rock	3	Stable
D	Wet	4	Unstable
E	Slippery	5	Even
F	Bare	6	Uneven
G	Packed	7	Suitable for buildings
H	Loose	8	Suitable for roads
I	Ground	9	Opposite

Question 62

A, DHF, 3, 8

A. This is loose, wet, soil with no growth. It is stable enough for a road to be built.
B. This is very loose and muddy soil that cannot support any type of construction.
C. This is an overgrown bog, but it could support a road.
D. This is a marshy wetland with shifty soil that cannot support any construction.

Question 63

B, 1H, 53, 7

A. This is loose, stable gravel that is even overgrown enough for the construction of buildings.
B. This is overgrown, loose gravel that is flat and stable enough for a building to be built.
C. This is a paved lot that is ready for the construction of a building.
D. This is a grassy area that is stable and flat enough for road construction.

Question 64

C, E6, (89)

A. This is a hilly, rocky area, on which a building could not be built.
B. This is a loose, flat slab of rock on which a building could be built.
C. This is a flat, rocky plain. It would not be a good site for a road.
D. This is loose, slippery rock, so a road could not be built here.

Question 65

A(23), (61I), 7

A. This is a flat, cleared forest on which a building can be built.
B. This is an undulating meadow on which a building can be built.
C. This is a hilly plain on which a road could be built.
D. This is a grassy, forested area, which could be cleared and used for the construction of buildings.

Question 66

(AD), F5H, 8

A. This is an overgrown, flat area on which a road can be built.
B. This is a barren, wet, flat area which is not suitable for any construction.
C. This is a barren, muddy, flat field on which a road can be built.
D. This is a hilly, unstable, wetland that is not suitable for any construction.

Notation	Meaning	Notation	Meaning
A	Soil	1	Overgrown
B	Gravel	2	Dry
C	Rock	3	Stable
D	Wet	4	Unstable
E	Slippery	5	Even
F	Bare	6	Uneven
G	Packed	7	Suitable for buildings
H	Loose	8	Suitable for roads
I	Ground	9	Opposite

For questions 67 – 73, what is the best code to translate:

Question 67
Land that is extremely sandy.

A. (4C), 2, 3
B. 3, D, (HB)
C. AB, G, 1
D. 4, (HCA)

Question 68
Land that is extremely muddy.

A. 4, H, C
B. (AD), H
C. H, 4, 1
D. (AD9), H

Question 69
Rainforests get a lot of rain but deserts don't.

A. (1DI), D, (2I), (9D)
B. (1I), D, (2I), (9D)
C. (1I), D, (2I), 2
D. (2I), D, (1I), (9D)

Question 70
Land that mostly consists of a bog.

A. D, H, 4
B. D, F, 1
C. 4, 5, A
D. H, D, 7

Question 71
Land that is grassy and full of large rocks.

A. A, C, D
B. 1, (GB)
C. (1A) C
D. G, C, H

Notation	Meaning	Notation	Meaning
A	Soil	1	Overgrown
B	Gravel	2	Dry
C	Rock	3	Stable
D	Wet	4	Unstable
E	Slippery	5	Even
F	Bare	6	Uneven
G	Packed	7	Suitable for buildings
H	Loose	8	Suitable for roads
I	Ground	9	Opposite

Question 72

Land that is very hilly and barren.

A. 6, E, F

B. F, G, 4

C. A, C, 6

D. 6 (19)

Question 73

Land that is very flat and lush.

 GA, 15

A. 5I, 1

B. C, 5, 6

C. 19, A, F

Question 74

Land that is full of dry, rocky craters.

A. 6, C, 4

B. C, 6, H

C. E, C, 6

D. 2, A, C

Question 75

You are sent out to survey a plot that turns out to be a lake. Which of the following would be most helpful to have included in the code?

A. Wet

B. Water

C. Land

D. Crater

Question 76

You are sent out to survey a plot of land that already has a building on it. Which of the following would be most helpful to have included in the code?

A. Already

B. Build

C. Structure

D. Here

Question 77

You are sent out to survey a plot of land that is frozen over. Which of the following would be most helpful to have included in the code?

A. Cold

B. Snow

C. Ice

D. Hard

Use the following information to answer questions 78 – 100:

You are the communications officer for a merchant ship in the Caribbean. Your job is to communicate with other ships and to cooperate with them as best you can.

There are three main languages used in the Caribbean: Spanish, English and French. Spanish is spoken in Cuba, Puerto Rico and the Dominican Republic. English is spoken in Jamaica, the Bahamas and the Virgin Islands. French is spoken in Haiti, St. Barthélemy and Guadeloupe.

Before contacting each other by radio, ships fly flags that display symbols to communicate. These symbols are not perfectly suited to every situation, but you and the other ships must use them as best you can. The ships all use the same symbols, but the meaning of the symbols depends on the language spoken by the crew. Ships in the Caribbean normally sail with the flag of their nation displayed.

	French	English	Spanish
1	You	We	State purpose
2	Port	Merchant	Continue on
3	Military	You	Stop
4	Distress	Distress	Merchant
5	Merchant	Continue on	Distress
6	Stop	Toward	Military
7	Return	Return	Return
8	State purpose	Stop	You
9	Destination	State purpose	We
10	Continue on	Destination	Port
11	We	Port	Destination
12	Toward	Military	Toward

Question 78
You come to a ship sailing under a Cuban flag. The ship displays the following symbols to you: 3, 1. What should you do to cooperate with this ship?
A. Stop and tell the ship why you are in the area.
B. Continue on your way and signal the ship with your purpose for being in these waters.
C. Attempt to help the distressed crew members on the other ship.
D. Stop to acknowledge the ship and then continue on your way.

Question 79
You come to a ship flying the Jamaican flag. The ship displays the following symbol to you: 10, 3, 5. What should you do to cooperate with this ship?
A. Attempt to help the distressed crew members on the other ship.
B. Explain to the other ship that you are a merchant vessel and go on your way.
C. Tell the other ship your destination and go on your way.
D. Follow the other ship to its destination.

Question 80
You come to a ship flying the Puerto Rican flag. The ship displays the following symbols to you: 3, (4,9), 81. What should you do to cooperate with this ship?
A. Tell the ship what you are doing in the area and go on your way.
B. Continue on to your destination.
C. Attempt to help the distressed crew members on the other ship.
D. Stop and explain your reason for being in the area.

	French	English	Spanish
1	You	We	State purpose
2	Port	Merchant	Continue on
3	Military	You	Stop
4	Distress	Distress	Merchant
5	Merchant	Continue on	Distress
6	Stop	Toward	Military
7	Return	Return	Return
8	State purpose	Stop	You
9	Destination	State purpose	We
10	Continue on	Destination	Port
11	We	Port	Destination
12	Toward	Military	Toward

Question 81

You come to a ship flying the flag of St. Barthélemy. The ship displays the following symbols to you: 16, (3,11), 92,19. What should you do to cooperate with this ship?

A. Stop and tell the ship your destination.
B. Identify yourself as a merchant vessel.
C. Stop to acknowledge the other ship and then go about your business.
D. Follow the other ship to its destination.

Question 82

You come to a ship flying the flag of the Bahamas. The ship displays the following symbols to you: 83, (12,1), (1,3, 6, 11). What should you do to cooperate with this ship?

A. Identify yourself as a merchant vessel and tell the ship your reason for being in the area.
B. Continue going about your business.
C. Stop and tell the ship your destination.
D. Stop to acknowledge the ship and follow it to port.

Question 83

You come to a ship flying a flag of the Virgin Islands. The ship displays the following symbols to you: 8, (12,1), 3,5,6,10. What should you do to cooperate with this ship?

A. Tell the ship your reason for being in the area.
B. Attempt to help the distressed crew members on the other ship.
C. Stop to acknowledge the ship and continue on to your destination.
D. Stop and explain your reason for being in the area.

Question 84

You come to a ship flying the Dominican flag. The ship displays the following symbols to you: 9,6; 8, 12, 11; 1. What should you do to cooperate with this ship?

A. Stop to acknowledge the ship and then go about your business.
B. Tell the ship where you are going and why.
C. Attempt to help the distressed crew members on the other ship.
D. Follow the ship to its destination.

	French	English	Spanish
1	You	We	State purpose
2	Port	Merchant	Continue on
3	Military	You	Stop
4	Distress	Distress	Merchant
5	Merchant	Continue on	Distress
6	Stop	Toward	Military
7	Return	Return	Return
8	State purpose	Stop	You
9	Destination	State purpose	We
10	Continue on	Destination	Port
11	We	Port	Destination
12	Toward	Military	Toward

Question 85

You come to a ship flying the Haitian flag. The ship displays the following symbols to you: 8,1; 10. What should you do to cooperate with this ship?

A. Stop to acknowledge the ship and then go on your way.
B. Tell the ship where you are going.
C. Tell the ship why you are in the area and go on your way.
D. Follow the ship to its destination.

Question 86

You come to a ship flying the flag of Guadeloupe. The ship displays the following symbols to you: (4,11), 6,8. What should you do to cooperate with this ship?

A. Explain to the ship that you are a merchant vessel.
B. Stop to acknowledge the ship and go on your way.
C. Tell the ship where you are going and go on your way.
D. Attempt to help the distressed crew members on the other ship.

Question 87

A ship approaches you with no indication of its country of origin. It displays the symbols 6, 8. Which code is the ship most likely using?

A. French
B. Spanish
C. English
D. They are all equally likely.

Question 88

A ship approaches you with no indication of its country of origin. It displays the symbols 4,9; 2, 8. Which code is the ship most likely using?

A. French
B. Spanish
C. English
D. They are all equally likely.

	French	English	Spanish
1	You	We	State purpose
2	Port	Merchant	Continue on
3	Military	You	Stop
4	Distress	Distress	Merchant
5	Merchant	Continue on	Distress
6	Stop	Toward	Military
7	Return	Return	Return
8	State purpose	Stop	You
9	Destination	State purpose	We
10	Continue on	Destination	Port
11	We	Port	Destination
12	Toward	Military	Toward

Question 89

A ship approaches you with no indication of its country of origin. It displays the symbols (12,1), 8, 9. Which code is the ship most likely using?

A. French
B. Spanish
C. English
D. They are all equally likely.

Question 90

A ship approaches you with no indication of its country of origin. It displays the symbols 3, 1, 8. Which code is the ship most likely using?

A. French.
B. Spanish.
C. English.
D. They are all equally likely.

Question 91

You approach a ship from Guadeloupe and want to address it using its own code. You want to express that you are a merchant ship and would like to go about your business without being stopped. Which of the following would be the best message for you to send?

A. (4, 9), 2, 12, 11
B. 5, 10, 9, 11
C. 5, 11; 10, 11; 12, 9
D. 10, 12, 12, 9, 3

Question 92

You approach a Puerto Rican ship and want to address it using its own code. You want to explain to the ship that you are a merchant vessel and are on your way to port. Which of the following would be the best message for you to send?

A. 6, 9; 11, 12
B. 4, 9; 11, 10
C. 9, 11; 4, 10, 11
D. 9, 10; (11,12)

	French	English	Spanish
1	You	We	State purpose
2	Port	Merchant	Continue on
3	Military	You	Stop
4	Distress	Distress	Merchant
5	Merchant	Continue on	Distress
6	Stop	Toward	Military
7	Return	Return	Return
8	State purpose	Stop	You
9	Destination	State purpose	We
10	Continue on	Destination	Port
11	We	Port	Destination
12	Toward	Military	Toward

Question 93

You approach a Haitian ship and want to address it using its own code. You want to explain to the ship that you do not want it to stop, you just want each of you to go about your business. Which of the following would be the best message for you to send?

A. 9, 10, 11(12), 8
B. 10,1; 10,11, 12, 9
C. 6, 8, 10,11
D. 4(11), 1, 10, 12, 9

Question 94

You approach a Jamaican ship and want to address it using its own code. You want the ship to stop and explain to you what they are doing. Which of the following would be the best message for you to send?

A. 8, (2,1) 9,3
B. 1, 2, 5, 3
C. 8, (2,1) 10,3
D. 6, 5(11), (8,1)

Question 95

A Bahamian ship that orders you to follow them to port approaches you. Before complying, you want to use the ship's own code to find out if it is a merchant or a military vessel. Which of the following would be the best message for you to send?

A. 12, 93, 1, 12
B. 2,1, 9,3, 2,12
C. 4, 9, 1,8, 4, 6
D. (5,11), 8, 5, 3

Question 96

Your ship is in need of help and is approached by a Cuban ship. You want to ask for help using the Cuban ship's own code. Which of the following is the best message for you to send?

A. 4,9, 8
B. 4(9), 5, 6
C. 7(8), 9(5)
D. 3, 5,9

	French	English	Spanish
1	You	We	State purpose
2	Port	Merchant	Continue on
3	Military	You	Stop
4	Distress	Distress	Merchant
5	Merchant	Continue on	Distress
6	Stop	Toward	Military
7	Return	Return	Return
8	State purpose	Stop	You
9	Destination	State purpose	We
10	Continue on	Destination	Port
11	We	Port	Destination
12	Toward	Military	Toward

Question 97

You approach a Dominican ship and want to address it using its own code. You want to know where the ship is going. Which of the following is the best message for you to send?

A. (7,8), 11,8
B. 11, 12, (9,8)
C. 8, 1, (11,8)
D. 1, 11, 2, 8

Question 98

Which of the following would be most useful to have in the code if you were trying to communicate: "this ship is on a peaceful mission."

A. Ship
B. Peaceful
C. Mission
D. Opposite

Question 99

Which of the following would be most useful to have in the code if you were trying to communicate: "Give up control of your vessel and follow my ship into port."

A. Give up
B. Control
C. Follow
D. Vessel

Question 100

Which of the following would be most useful to have in the code if you were trying to communicate: "where did you start your journey?"

A. Your
B. Journey
C. Where
D. Opposite

Use the code below to discover what went on when this family went on holiday to the seaside

Operating codes		Specialist codes		
A Increase	1 Holiday	11 Day	21 Boat
B Decrease	2 Good	12 I	22 Catch
C Plural	3 Water	13 Play	23 Make
D Plus	4 Hot	14 Castle	
E Opposite	5 Sand	15 Swim	
F Negative	6 Child	16 Eat	
G Positive	7 Parent	17 Next to	
H Combine	8 Toy	18 Weather	
I Past	9 Fish	19 Inside	
J Future	10 Go	20 Food	

For questions 100 -106, what is the best translation of the following code:

Question 101

C12, I10, H(A(6,7)), 1.

A. We went on holiday to visit family.
B. We went on a family holiday.
C. We are going on a family holiday.
D. I went on holiday with my family.
E. We went on holiday with the children.

Question 102

H (J11), (A4)18, H((A3)5)

A. Tomorrow it will be warm weather at the beach.
B. Today the weather is very hot at the beach.
C. Tomorrow the sand and water will be very hot.
D. Tomorrow it will be very hot weather at the beach.
E. The weather will be very hot tomorrow.

Question 103

C6, I13, H(C (5,8))

A. The children played with their buckets and spades.
B. The children played in the sand.
C. The children are playing on the beach.
D. The children played with their toys on the beach.
E. The children will play with their buckets and spades.

Question 104

H (A (6,7)), I16, 4(9D20), 17, A3

A. The family ate fish and chips by the sea.
B. We all ate hot fish and chips on the beach.
C. The family ate in a restaurant beside the sea.
D. The family ate hot fish and chips beside the sea.
E. The family will eat hot fish and chips next to the sea.

	Operating codes		Specialist codes	
	A Increase	1 Holiday	11 Day	21 Boat
	B Decrease	2 Good	12 I	22 Catch
	C Plural	3 Water	13 Play	23 Make
	D Plus	4 Hot	14 Castle	
	E Opposite	5 Sand	15 Swim	
	F Negative	6 Child	16 Eat	
	G Positive	7 Parent	17 Next to	
	H Combine	8 Toy	18 Weather	
	I Past	9 Fish	19 Inside	
	J Future	10 Go	20 Food	

Question 105

H (J11), F (J15), A3, A(E2(18))

A. Tomorrow we will not swim because of very bad weather.
B. Tomorrow we will swim in the sea because of the weather.
C. Today we did not swam in the sea because of bad weather.
D. Tomorrow we will not swim in the sea because of very good weather.
E. Tomorrow we will not swim in the sea because of very bad weather.

Question 106

C7, C6, (H (22,9) D21), A3

A. The parents took the children fishing out at sea.
B. The parents took the children on a fishing boat.
C. The parents took the children on a fishing boat on the sea.
D. The parents took a child fishing on a boat.
E. The parents took the children to catch fish.

Question 107

What is the best way to code this sentence? 'The children build sand castles all day'

A. C6, 23, H (5,14), C11.
B. C6, 23, H (5,14), A11.
C. C6, 23, C (H (5,14)), A11.
D. 6, 23, C (H (5,14)), A11.
E. 6, 23, H (5,14), A11.

Archaeologists doing a dig in Eastern Africa discover secret messages written in code. Help them to crack the code and translate the sentences below to learn what happened in this far-away land long ago.

Operating Codes	Specialist Codes	
A Increase	1 Old	11 Find
B Decrease	2 Language	12 Write
C Plural	3 Queen	13 Recent
D Plus	4 Cave	14 Prince
E Opposite	5 Tribe	15 Weapon
F Negative	6 War	16 Relationship
G Positive	7 Man	17 Hidden
H Combine	8 Live	18 Take
I Past	9 Wall	19 Story
J Future	10 Love	20 Rare

For questions 108-114, what is the best translation of the following code:

Question 108

A1, 2, I11, 12, H (4,9)

A. A modern language was found written on a cave wall.
B. A very old language was hidden in a cave.
C. An ancient language was found written on a cave wall.
D. An ancient language was found inside a cave.
E. A very old language will be found written on a cave wall.

Question 109

3, 17, I, H (10,16), H (6,7)

A. The queen was in a secret relationship whilst at war.
B. The queen had a secret romance with a warrior.
C. The queen secretly hated the warrior.
D. The queen will fall in love with a warrior.
E. The queen hid from the warrior.

Question 110

E3, I (E8), 6, A (E13)

A. The old queen died at war long ago.
B. The king died at war not too long ago.
C. The king died a long time ago.
D. The king died at war recently.
E. The king died at war long ago.

Question 111

H (5(E3)), I (E10), H (3,E3, 14)

C. The tribe chief loved the royal family.
D. The tribe chief hated the royal family.
E. The local tribe hated the royal family.
F. The tribe chief hated the King and Queen.
G. The royal family hated the tribe chief.

Operating Codes	Specialist Codes	
A Increase	1 Old	11 Find
B Decrease	2 Language	12 Write
C Plural	3 Queen	13 Recent
D Plus	4 Cave	14 Prince
E Opposite	5 Tribe	15 Weapon
F Negative	6 War	16 Relationship
G Positive	7 Man	17 Hidden
H Combine	8 Live	18 Take
I Past	9 Wall	19 Story
J Future	10 Love	20 Rare

Question 112

H (6,7) 15, I(E18), 3.

A. The warrior took the weapon from the Queen.
B. The man's sword was given to him by the Queen whilst at war.
C. The warrior will take a weapon from the Queen.
D. The warrior's sword was given to him by the Queen.
E. The warrior's sword was given to him by the King.

Question 113

H (12,2), E17, 17(C19).

A. The written language revealed many secrets.
B. The writing hid many secrets.
C. The written language revealed many stories.
D. The written language revealed a secret.
E. The writing will reveal a story.

Question 114

What is the best way to code this sentence? 'The tribe go to war with the royal family often.'

A. 5, 6, H (3,E3, 14), E20.
B. 5, F, 6, H (3,E3,14), E20.
C. 5,6, H (3,E3,14), 20.
D. 5, 6, E3,E20.
E. H(6,7), 6, H(3,E3,14), E20.

Local traffic reports and transport updates involve the use of code so that workers can communicate freely.

Operating Codes	Specialist codes	
A Increase	1 Woman	11 Fast
B Decrease	2 Van	12 Day
C Plural	3 Black	13 Lock
D Plus	4 Old	14 Find
E Opposite	5 Bad	15 Want
F Negative	6 Driver	16 Work
G Positive	7 Travel	17 School
H Combine	8 Distance	18 Short
I Past	9 Crash	19 Find
J Future	10 Road	

For questions 115-120, what is the best translation of the following code:

Question 115

B (E1), I15, E4, E3, B2.

A. The boy wanted a new white van.
B. The boy wanted a new white car.
C. The boy wants a new white car.
D. The boy wanted a new black car.
E. The girl wanted a new white car.

Question 116

C (E1), F, A (E5),C6, C1.

A. Men are better drivers than women.
B. The man is not a better driver than the woman.
C. Men are not better drivers than women.
D. Men are not worse drivers than women.
E. Men are worse drivers than women.

Question 117

H ((A2)(C6)), 7, A(E18), C8.

A. The lorry driver travels very long distances.
B. Lorry drivers travel for a very long time.
C. Van drivers travel very long distances.
D. Lorry drivers travel short differences.
E. Lorry drivers travel very long distances.

Question 118

I, A5, 9, H (11,10), A (I12)

A. There was a serious accident on the motorway last week.
B. There was a serious accident on the motorway today.
C. There was a bad crash on the road a few days ago.
D. There was a bad crash on the road last week.
E. There might be a crash on the motorway soon.

Operating Codes	Specialist codes	
A Increase	1 Woman	11 Fast
B Decrease	2 Van	12 Day
C Plural	3 Black	13 Lock
D Plus	4 Old	14 Find
E Opposite	5 Bad	15 Want
F Negative	6 Driver	16 Work
G Positive	7 Travel	17 School
H Combine	8 Distance	18 Short
I Past	9 Crash	19 Find
J Future	10 Road	

Question 119

B (E1), I (E19), B2, E13

A. The boy found his car key.
B. The boy went to unlock his car.
C. The girl lost his car key.
D. The boy lost his car key.
E. The boy lost the key to his van.

Question 120

1, J7, 16, J (E12), H(11,10)

A. The woman will travel to work tomorrow via the motorway.
B. The woman will travel to work tomorrow night via the motorway.
C. The woman will travel to work tonight via the motorway.
D. The women will drive to work on the motorway.
E. The women will travel to work tomorrow night on the motorway.

Question 121

What is the best way to code this sentence? 'The van driver was lost as he travelled to work'

A. H (2,6), 19, 7, 16.
B. H (2,6), E19, 7, 16.
C. H (2,6), I (E19), 7, 16.
D. H (2,6), I (E19), 7, 17.
E. H (2,6), I (E19), 10, 17.

It is during medieval times and the royal family has complete control over the land. The King has been informed that local people have been spying on them and communicating information with one another using code.

Operating codes		Specialist codes	
A Plural	1 Me	11 Party	
B Opposite	2 You	12 Loss	
C Negative	3 Woman	13 Marry	
D Common	4 Ice		
E Combine	5 Castle		
F Increase	6 Hunted		
G Decrease	7 Young		
H Positive	8 Noble		
I Plus	9 Weapon		
	10 Animal		

For questions 122-126, what is the best translation of the following code:

Question 122

E (1,2), 6, E(8,7,3), 5, B4

A. We searched the young queen when the castle was frozen.

B. Many hunted for the princess when the castle was on fire.

C. We searched for the princess when the castle was icy.

D. We searched for the princess when the castle was on fire.

E. Many searched for the princess when the castle was on fire.

Question 123

E(8(B3)), 6, (BD)10, 8(7(B3))

A. The King hunted for a rare beast with his Queen.

B. The King hunted for a rare beast with his son.

C. The King hunted for a common animal with his son.

D. The Queen hunted for a rare beast with her son.

E. The princess hunted for a rare beast with the prince.

Question 124

8(B3), I (8,3), 11, (B12)

A. The prince and princess celebrated the victory.

B. The King and Queen did not celebrate the victory.

C. The King and Queen celebrated the victory.

D. The King and Queen had a party even though they lost.

E. The man and woman had a party for their victory.

Question 125

F (A (B3)), 13, E(8,7,3)

A. The man wanted to marry the princess.

B. The princess married many men.

C. Many women wanted to marry the prince.

D. Not many men wanted to marry the princess.

E. Many men wanted to marry the princess.

Question 126

8(7(B3)), 13, (C8), 3

A. The prince married a poor woman.

B. The prince did not marry a poor woman.

C. The prince married a noble woman.

D. The prince met a poor woman.

E. The princess married a poor man.

Staff in the UK Space Agency communicate with their astronauts in outer space using code. Help them to translate the codes so that information can be relayed quickly and efficiently between them.

Operator codes		Specialist codes		
A Increase	1 Space	11 Heavy	21 Science
B Decrease	2 Mars	12 Slow	22 Nearby
C Plural	3 Planet	13 Earth	
D Plus	4 Star	14 Cold	
E Opposite	5 Moon	15 Dark	
F Negative	6 Ship	16 Off	
G Positive	7 Man	17 Return	
H Combine	8 Alien	18 Day	
I Past	9 Walk	19 Small	
J Future	10 Life	20 Understood	
K Question			

For questions 127-132, what is the best translation of the following code:

Question 127

C(H(1,7)), E11, 12, 5

A. The astronaut is light and slow on the moon.
B. The astronauts are light and slow on the moon.
C. Men are light and slow when in space.
D. The astronaut is heavy and fast on the moon.
E. The astronauts are heavy and slow on the moon.

Question 128

(1D6), J(F17), 13, 5, E18

A. The spaceship returned to earth today.
B. The spaceship will not return home from the moon tonight.
C. The spaceship will not return home from the moon today.
D. The spaceship returned to the moon from earth tonight.
E. The spaceship set off for Earth from the moon.

Question 129

H (13,4) A(E14), D, E15

A. The star is very hot and bright.
B. Stars are very hot and bright.
C. The sun is cold and dark.
D. The sun is very hot and bright.
E. Space is cold and dark.

Question 130

1, A (E19), F20

A. Space is vast and poorly understood.
B. Space is vast but well understood.
C. Space is small and poorly understood.
D. Space is small but we have a lot of knowledge.
E. Space is very large and misunderstanding.

Operator codes	Specialist codes		
A Increase	1 Space	11 Heavy	21 Science
B Decrease	2 Mars	12 Slow	22 Nearby
C Plural	3 Planet	13 Earth	
D Plus	4 Star	14 Cold	
E Opposite	5 Moon	15 Dark	
F Negative	6 Ship	16 Off	
G Positive	7 Man	17 Return	
H Combine	8 Alien	18 Day	
I Past	9 Walk	19 Small	
J Future	10 Life	20 Understood	
K Question			

Question 131

C (H(21,7)), K, (8,I,10), E22 13

A. The scientist wonders whether there is life other than that on Earth.
B. Science has questioned the existence of aliens.
C. Scientists have found alien life away from Earth.
D. There is a question of alien life away from Earth.
E. Scientists question whether there is alien life away from Earth.

Question 132

2, (A(E11), 13), (A11, 5)

A. Mars is heavier than the Earth and the moon.
B. The Earth is heavier than Mars and the moon.
C. Mars is heavier than the Earth but lighter than the moon.
D. Mars is lighter than the Earth and the moon.
E. Mars is lighter than the Earth but heavier than the moon.

All emergency services must communicate with one another in a common code shown below:

Operator codes	Specialist codes	
A Increase	1 Fire	12 Fast
B Decrease	2 Danger	13 Drive
C Plural	3 Crime	14 Inside
D Plus	4 Smoke	15 Phone
E Opposite	5 Trap	16 Sad
F Negative	6 Building	17 Local
G Positive	7 Emergency	
H Combine	8 Vehicle	
I Past	9 Man	
J Future	10 Safe	
K Question	11 Service	

For questions 133-137, what is the best translation of the following code:

Question 133

A(E9), 2, (5,D,14,D,6)

A. There is a woman in danger trapped inside the building.
B. There are women trapped inside the building.
C. There are women in danger trapped inside.
D. There are women in danger trapped inside the building.
E. There are women in danger inside the building.

Question 134

C(H(7,11)), K, 1, 3

A. The police wonder if the fire was a crime.
B. The emergency fire was a crime.
C. There is the question that the fire was a crime.
D. The police know the fire was a crime.
E. The police have a question about the fire.

Question 135

C(1,D,9), I(E16), E5, 1, 10

A. The men were happy to escape the fire and be safe.
B. The firemen were happy to escape the fire and be safe.
C. The firemen did not escape the fire and be safe.
D. The firemen were sad to escape the fire and were not safe.
E. The fireman was happy to escape the fire and be safe.

Question 136

C(H(17,9)), I15, H(7,1,11)

A. The firemen called the emergency services.
B. The local men called the police.
C. The local women called the fire brigade.
D. The local men called the fire brigade.
E. The local men did not call the fire brigade.

Question 137

H(7,1,8), I13, 12, (1,D,6)

A. The fire engine will drive quickly to the burning house.
B. The firemen drive quickly to the burning house.
C. The fire engine drove quickly to the burning house.
D. The fire engine drove slowly to the burning house.
E. The fire engine drove quickly to the house.

You are a teacher in a primary school and you notice that children have been passing notes in code:

Operator codes	Specialist codes	
A Increase	1 School	12 Adult
B Decrease	2 Book	13 Music
C Plural	3 Dress	14 Pretty
D Plus	4 Long	15 Old
E Opposite	5 Boy	16 Nice
F Negative	6 Write	17 Day
G Positive	7 Learn	18 Parent
H Combine	8 Home	19 Trip
I Past	9 Play	
J Future	10 Love	
K Question	11 Teach	

For questions 138-140 and 142, what is the best translation of the following code:

Question 138

14(E5), B3, A(E4), 1

A. The girl's dress was too short for school.
B. The girl's dress was too short today.
C. The girl's skirt was too long for school.
D. The boy wore a dress to school.
E. The pretty girl's skirt was too short for school.

Question 139

C(5,D,E5), 10, H(13(12,11))

A. The children love their music teacher.
B. The boys and girls love to learn music.
C. The children love their teacher.
D. The children don't like their music teacher.
E. The children love to teach music to the adults.

Question 140

C(E5), E10, E15, H((7(E6))2)

A. The girls hate their new writing book.
B. The girls hate their new reading book.
C. The girls love their new reading book.
D. The girls hate to read books.
E. The boys hate their new reading book.

Question 141

What is the best way to translate this sentence? 'The older girls were mean to the younger girls'

A. A15(C(E5)), I16, A(E15)(C(E5)).
B. A(E15)(C(E5)), I(E16), A15(C(E5)).
C. A15(C5), I(E16), A15(C5).
D. A15(C(E5)), I(E16), A(E15)(C(E5)).
E. A15(E5), I(E16), A(E15)(E5).

Question 142

1, J, H(17,19), D, C18

A. The school went on a day trip with the parents.
B. The school will be going on an overnight trip with the parents.
C. The school will be going on a day trip with the parents.
D. The school will be going on an overnight trip with the parents.
E. The school will be going on a day trip without the parents.

Over the past few years, NHS hospitals have experienced an increase in the number of patients seeking their services. This has had knock-on effects throughout the entire healthcare system. Translate these sentences below to understand some of the difficulties facing hospitals today

Operator codes	Specialist codes	
A Increase	1 Summer	13 Money
B Decrease	2 Patient	14 Drug
C Plural	3 Hospital	15 Doctor
D Plus	4 Cold	16 Student
E Opposite	5 Expect	17 Nurse
F Negative	6 Weather	18 Asks for
G Positive	7 Eat	19 Safe
H Combine	8 Water	20 Excess
I Past	9 Hospital	21 Protest
J Future	10 Remember	
K Plenty	11 People	
L Because of	12 Bed	

For questions 143-150, what is the best translation of the following code:

Question 143

A (C2), 5, 9, J(E1)

A. No more patients are expected in hospital next winter.
B. Many more patients were expected in hospital last winter.
C. Many more patients are not expected in hospital next winter.
D. Many more patients were not expected in hospital last winter.
E. Many more patients are expected in hospital next winter.

Question 144

C2, F10, E7, K8, 9

A. Patients remember to drink plenty of water whilst in hospital.
B. Patients forget to drink plenty of water whilst in hospital.
C. Patients forget to eat enough in hospital.
D. Patients forget to drink plenty whilst in hospital.
E. Patients used to forget to drink plenty of water in hospital.

Question 145

A11, I(F5), A(E4)(1,D,6)

A. Many people did not anticipate the very hot summer.
B. Many people did not expect the very cold summer.
C. I did not anticipate the very hot summer.
D. Many people anticipate a very hot summer.
E. Many people will not anticipate a very hot summer.

Question 146

What is the best way to code this sentence? 'The hospital has no beds as there is less money'

A. 3 K(C12), L, A13.
B. 3, (EK)(C12), L, 13.
C. 3, (EK)(C12), L, B13.
D. C3, (EK)(C12), L, B13.
E. C2, (EK)(C12), L, B13.

Operator codes	Specialist codes	
A Increase	1 Summer	13 Money
B Decrease	2 Patient	14 Drug
C Plural	3 Hospital	15 Doctor
D Plus	4 Cold	16 Student
E Opposite	5 Expect	17 Nurse
F Negative	6 Weather	18 Asks for
G Positive	7 Eat	19 Safe
H Combine	8 Water	20 Excess
I Past	9 Hospital	21 Protest
J Future	10 Remember	
K Plenty	11 People	
L Because of	12 Bed	

Question 147

2, A18, A(C, 14), H(16,17)

A. The patient asks for a drug from the student nurse.
B. The patient requests more drugs from the nurse.
C. The patient demands more drugs from the student and the nurse.
D. The patient demands more drugs from the student nurse.
E. The patient demands more drugs from the student.

Question 148

C2, A (E19), L, 15,

A. The doctor was in danger from his patients.
B. The doctor and patients were in danger.
C. The patients were safe with their doctor.
D. The patients were in grave danger from their doctor.
E. The patients were very angry with their doctor.

Question 149

(E20) 14, L, A (C2), L, H (4,6)

A. There are excess drugs because of increased patients from the cold weather.
B. There is a drug shortage because of increased patients from the cold weather.
C. There are excess drugs because of fewer patients due to warm weather.
D. There is a drug shortage because of increased patients from the warm weather.
E. There is a drug shortage because of fewer patients due to the cold weather.

Question 150

H3(C(15,D,17)) J, 21

A. The hospital staff went on strike.
B. The nurses staged a protest.
C. The hospital doctors staged a protest.
D. The hospital doctors will stage a protest.
E. The hospital staff will go on strike.

The city of London has many train stations – both underground and over-ground. The network of train lines is very complex, and so drivers must communicate in code to understand each other. Help them ensure trains are on time and passengers are kept safe by translating this code into the sentences below.

Operator codes	Specialist Codes	
A Increase	1 Train	13 This
B Decrease	2 Station	14 Towards
C Plural	3 Above	15 Conductor
D Plus	4 Compartment	16 Driver
E Opposite	5 Ground	17 Car
F Negative	6 Sit	18 City
G Positive	7 Early	19 Personal
H Combine	8 Start	20 Emergency
I Past	9 Busy	
J Future	10 Evening	
K Plenty	11 Day	
L Because of	12 Empty	

For questions 151-155, what is the best translation of the following code:

Question 151
H((E3,5)1), A9, 13 E10

A. The underground train is very busy this evening.
B. The underground train is very busy this morning.
C. The underground train is busy this morning.
D. The over-ground train is very busy this morning.
E. The underground train is not very busy this morning.

Question 152
E13, H(1,4), 12; 13, H(1,4), E12

A. The other train is full; this carriage is empty.
B. The other carriage is full; this carriage is empty.
C. The other train is empty; this train is full.
D. The other carriage is empty; this carriage is full.
E. This carriage is empty; the other carriage is full.

Question 153
H(3,5)D1, 14, 18, J(E7)

A. The over-ground train from London is delayed.
B. The over-ground train to London will be delayed.
C. The over-ground train from London will be delayed.
D. The over-ground train to London was delayed.
E. The underground train to London will be delayed.

Operator codes	Specialist Codes	
A Increase	1 Train	13 This
B Decrease	2 Station	14 Towards
C Plural	3 Above	15 Conductor
D Plus	4 Compartment	16 Driver
E Opposite	5 Ground	17 Car
F Negative	6 Sit	18 City
G Positive	7 Early	19 Personal
H Combine	8 Start	20 Emergency
I Past	9 Busy	
J Future	10 Evening	
K Plenty	11 Day	
L Because of	12 Empty	

Question 154

J(H(13,11)), 19, JF, 17, E10

A. Tomorrow I will drive in the morning.
B. Tomorrow I will drive in the evening.
C. Tomorrow I will not drive in the morning.
D. Yesterday I did not drive in the morning.
E. Tomorrow I will not drive in the evening.

Question 155

H(1,16), I, H(20(E8)), J13, 2

A. The train driver stopped at the next station.
B. The train driver made an emergency stop at the station.
C. The train made an emergency stop at the next station.
D. The train driver will make an emergency stop at the next station.
E. The train driver made an emergency stop at the next station.

Question 156

What is the best way to code this sentence? 'The London underground has many stations'

A. 18, H((E3,5)1), A(C2).
B. 18, H((E3,5)1), C2.
C. 18, F, H((E3,5)1), A(C2).
D. 18, H(3,5)D1, A(C2).
E. 18, H((E3,5)1), 2.

A group of university students are throwing a party for people in their year. Find out what went on at the party by translating the codes below.

Operator codes	Specialist code	
A Increase	1 Boy	13 Blue
B Decrease	2 Party	14 Yellow
C Plural	3 Friend	15 Pink
D Plus	4 Music	17 Light
E Opposite	5 Conversation	18 Word
F Negative	6 Angry	19 Song
G Positive	7 Happy	20 That
H Combine	8 Like	21 Day
I Past	9 I	22 Dull
J Future	10 Exercise	
K Plenty	11 Wear	
L Question	12 Dress	

For questions 157-162, what is the best translation of the following code:

Question 157
H(1,3), D, H((E1)3), I(H(6,5)), 2

A. The boyfriend and the girlfriend spoke at the party.
B. The boyfriend and the girlfriend went to the party.
C. The boyfriend and the girlfriend were angry at the party.
D. The boyfriend and the girlfriend argued at the party.
E. The boy and girl argued at the party.

Question 158
L, E9, 8, H(2,10)?

A. Would you like to dance?
B. Do you like to party?
C. Would you like to exercise?
D. Can I dance with you?
E. Will you dance with me at the party?

Question 159
9, J11, H(13,14), 12, J(E21)

A. I wore a green dress at the party last night.
B. I will wear a green dress at the party tomorrow night.
C. I will wear a green dress at the party today.
D. I will wear a blue and yellow dress at the party tomorrow night.
E. I will wear a purple dress at the party tomorrow night.

Operator codes	Specialist code	
A Increase	1 Boy	13 Blue
B Decrease	2 Party	14 Yellow
C Plural	3 Friend	15 Pink
D Plus	4 Music	17 Light
E Opposite	5 Conversation	18 Word
F Negative	6 Angry	19 Song
G Positive	7 Happy	20 That
H Combine	8 Like	21 Day
I Past	9 I	22 Dull
J Future	10 Exercise	
K Plenty	11 Wear	
L Question	12 Dress	

Question 160

A(9,C3), J, 2

A. Lots of friends will be at the party.
B. Lots of my friends were at the party.
C. Lots of my friends will be at the party.
D. None of my friends will be at the party.
E. None of my friends were at the party.

Question 161

9, 8, C(H(18,19)), E20, 19

A. I like the lyrics to that song.
B. I don't like the lyrics to this song.
C. We don't like the lyrics to this song.
D. We like the lyrics to this song.
E. I like the lyrics to this song.

Question 162

C17, I, A(E22), I(E21)

A. The lights were too dark last night.
B. The lights are too bright tonight.
C. The lights are too dark tonight.
D. The lights were too bright last night.
E. The lights were bright last night.

Discover what happened when a family went on their usual camping trip to the nearby woods at the foot of the mountain by translating the codes below:

Operator codes	Specialist codes		
A Increase	1 Tent	13 Day	25 See
B Decrease	2 House	14 Year	26 Pretty
C Plural	3 Walk	15 Parent	
D Plus	4 Hill	16 Children	
E Opposite	5 Tree	17 Light	
F Negative	6 Camp	18 Far away	
G Positive	7 Cook	19 Down	
H Combine	8 Fire	20 Help	
I Past	9 Scared	21 Descend	
J Future	10 Go	22 Sleep	
K Question	11 I	23 Outside	
L Every	12 Like	24 Sky	

For questions 163-170, what is the best translation of the following code:

Question 163

11, 9, A(C5), E13

A. I am scared of the woods in the daytime.
B. I am scared of the woods in the dark.
C. I used to be scared of the woods at night.
D. I am scared of the woods at night.
E. I was scared of the woods in the daytime.

Question 164

H(C15,16), 12, 10, 6, L14

A. The family like to go camping every year.
B. The family like to go camping sometimes.
C. The parents like to go camping every year.
D. The children like to go camping every year.
E. The family don't like to go camping every year.

Question 165

C11, J7, E18, H(7,8)

A. We cooked by the campfire.
B. I will cook by the campfire.
C. We will cook by the campfire.
D. I cooked by the campfire.
E. We will cook away from the campfire.

Question 166

J13, J(A3), E19, C(A4)

A. Today we will jog up some mountains.
B. Tomorrow we will walk up a mountain.
C. Tomorrow we will jog up a mountain.
D. Tomorrow we will jog up some mountains.
E. Tomorrow we will jog down a mountain.

Operator codes	Specialist codes		
A Increase	1 Tent	13 Day	25 See
B Decrease	2 House	14 Year	26 Pretty
C Plural	3 Walk	15 Parent	
D Plus	4 Hill	16 Children	
E Opposite	5 Tree	17 Light	
F Negative	6 Camp	18 Far away	
G Positive	7 Cook	19 Down	
H Combine	8 Fire	20 Help	
I Past	9 Scared	21 Descend	
J Future	10 Go	22 Sleep	
K Question	11 I	23 Outside	
L Every	12 Like	24 Sky	

Question 167
16, I(F20), C15, 1, E19

A. The children did not help the parents put the tent down.
B. The children did not help the parents put the tent up.
C. The children do not help the parents put the tent up.
D. The children do not help the parents put the tent down.
E. The children helped the parents put the tent up.

Question 168
15, H((E21),(E19)), C5

A. The children will climb trees.
B. The children are climbing the tree.
C. The children are climbing down trees.
D. The children are climbing trees.
E. The children climbed down the tree.

Question 169
K, E(C11), 22, E23, 1, J(E13)?

A. Can I sleep inside the tent tomorrow night?
B. Can we sleep inside the tent tonight?
C. Can you sleep outside the tent tomorrow night?
D. Can you sleep outside the tent tonight?
E. Can you sleep inside the tent tomorrow night?

Question 170
11, 25, C(H(24,17)), E17, E13, 24

A. I can't see the stars in the dark night sky.
B. I can see the stars in the dark night sky.
C. I can see lights in the dark night sky.
D. I can see a star in the dark night sky.
E. I can see the stars in the dark sky.

Air traffic control at Heathrow Airport uses codes to communicate with each other and pilots in the air. Sometimes these messages are interrupted by passengers communicating with each other. Help them to distinguish between them by translating these codes.

Operator codes	Specialist codes		
A Increase	1 Plane	13 Bag	25 In
B Decrease	2 Wing	14 Holiday	26 Smooth
C Plural	3 Road	15 Clothes	27 Old
D Plus	4 Fly	16 Travel	28 Small
E Opposite	5 Land	17 Document	29 Light
F Negative	6 Window	18 Security	30 Trust
G Positive	7 Driver	19 Give	31 Picture
H Combine	8 Worker	20 On	
I Past	9 Seat	21 Remember	
J Future	10 Brave	22 You	
K Question	11 Height	23 Belong	
L Every	12 Sand	24 Look	

For questions 171-177, what is the best translation of the following code:

Question 171
2, I(H(E19, E20)), H(1,3)

A. The plane will land on the runway.
B. The plane will take off from the runway.
C. The plane took off from the runway.
D. The plane took off from the road.
E. The plane is taking off from the runway.

Question 172
K, 22, E21, E22, H(16,17)?

A. Did I forget my passport?
B. You forgot my passport.
C. Did you forget your passport?
D. Did you forget my passport?
E. I forgot your passport.

Question 173
F24, E25, 6, 22, E10, C11

A. Don't look out of the window if you are afraid of heights.
B. Look out of the window if you are afraid of flying.
C. Look out of the window if you are not afraid of heights.
D. Don't look out of the window if you are not afraid of heights.
E. Don't look into the window if you are afraid of heights.

Operator codes	Specialist codes		
A Increase	1 Plane	13 Bag	25 In
B Decrease	2 Wing	14 Holiday	26 Smooth
C Plural	3 Road	15 Clothes	27 Old
D Plus	4 Fly	16 Travel	28 Small
E Opposite	5 Land	17 Document	29 Light
F Negative	6 Window	18 Security	30 Trust
G Positive	7 Driver	19 Give	31 Picture
H Combine	8 Worker	20 On	
I Past	9 Seat	21 Remember	
J Future	10 Brave	22 You	
K Question	11 Height	23 Belong	
L Every	12 Sand	24 Look	

Question 174

H (1,7), 5, 1, H (1,5), 26

A. The pilot lands the plane on the runway bumpily.
B. The pilot lands the plane on the runway smoothly.
C. The driver lands the plane on the runway smoothly.
D. The pilot takes off from the runway smoothly.
E. The pilot will land the plane on the runway smoothly.

Question 175

H(1,8), I19, E22, A(E28), 9

A. The air hostess will give me a bigger seat.
B. The plane had bigger seats.
C. The air hostess gave me a bigger seat.
D. The air hostess gave me a big seat.
E. The pilot gave me a bigger seat.

Question 176

H(23,E22), H(E28,14,13), I, A(E29)

A. My big suitcase will be too heavy.
B. My big suitcase was too light.
C. Your big suitcase was too heavy.
D. My bag was too heavy.
E. My big suitcase was too heavy.

Question 177

18, I(E30), 22, H(16,17), 31

A. Security liked your passport photo.
B. Security will doubt your passport photo.
C. Security trusted your passport photo.
D. Security doubted my passport photo.
E. Security doubted your passport photo.

A large multinational company has just opened a London office. The head office wants to know how the new branch is getting on. Help them to crack the code below to find out.

Operator codes	Specialist codes	
A Increase	1 Building	13 Tall
B Decrease	2 Work	14 Inside
C Plural	3 Meeting	15 Personal
D Plus	4 Room	16 Belonging
E Opposite	5 Desk	17 Large
F Negative	6 We	18 Leader
G Positive	7 Staff	19 Before
H Combine	8 Day	20 Social
I Past	9 Smart	21 Fun
J Future	10 Wear	
K Question	11 Clothes	
L Every	12 Cold	

For questions 178-182, what is the best translation of the following code:

Question 178
6, J, (7,D, 3), H(3,4)

A. We will have our meeting in the staff room.
B. Our staff meeting was in the meeting room.
C. We had our staff meeting in the meeting room.
D. We will have our staff meeting in the meeting room.
E. We will have all staff in the meeting room.

Question 179
A (J8), 6, J10, A (E9), 11, 2

A. Next week we will wear casual clothes to work.
B. Next week we will wear very smart clothes to work.
C. Yesterday we wore very casual clothes to work.
D. Today we are wearing very casual clothes to work.
E. Next week we will wear very casual clothes to work.

Question 180
H(2,4), A(E12), I8

A. The office was very hot yesterday.
B. The office was hot yesterday.
C. The office is very hot today.
D. The office was very cold yesterday.
E. The office will be very hot tomorrow.

Operator codes	Specialist codes	
A Increase	1 Building	13 Tall
B Decrease	2 Work	14 Inside
C Plural	3 Meeting	15 Personal
D Plus	4 Room	16 Belonging
E Opposite	5 Desk	17 Large
F Negative	6 We	18 Leader
G Positive	7 Staff	19 Before
H Combine	8 Day	20 Social
I Past	9 Smart	21 Fun
J Future	10 Wear	
K Question	11 Clothes	
L Every	12 Cold	

Question 181

H (2,4), 14, H ((A13), 1)

A. I work in a tower block.
B. The office is a very tall building.
C. We work in a very tall building.
D. The office is in a tower block.
E. The office is in a small building.

Question 182

H (15,16), 5, A(E17)

A. My desk is too big.
B. Your desk is too small.
C. The belongings on my desk are too small.
D. My desk is too small.
E. My desk is small.

Question 183

What is the best way of coding this sentence? 'The bosses had an office party after work'

A. 7, I, H(2,5), H(21,20), E19, 2.
B. C18, I, H(2,5), H(21,20), E19, 2.
C. C18, I, H(2,5), H(21,20), 19, 2.
D. C18, I, 7, H(21,20), E19, 2.
E. C18, J, H(2,5), H(21,20), E19, 2.

A family are on safari in South Africa. Discover more about their adventure by translating the codes below:

Operator codes		Specialist codes	
A Increase	1 Cat	13 Father	25 See
B Decrease	2 Dog	14 Drive	26 Sky
C Plural	3 Dry	15 Day	27 This
D Plus	4 Land	16 After	28 Season
E Opposite	5 Spotty	17 Meet	29 Lost
F Negative	6 Stripy	18 Water	30 Throughout
G Positive	7 Horse	19 Far from	31 Shrink
H Combine	8 Tree	20 Protect	32 Small
I Past	9 Eat	21 Sun	
J Future	10 Fast	22 Cold	
K Question	11 Food	23 Female	
L Every	12 Child	24 Run	

For questions 178-182, what is the best translation of the following code:

Question 184

C(A1), I9, H(6,7)
A. The lions ate the zebras.
B. The lion ate the zebra.
C. The lions ate the zebra.
D. The lion ate the zebras.
E. The lions are eating the zebra.

Question 185

I, F11, C (A2), 9
A. There was no food for the dogs to eat.
B. There is no food for the wolves to eat.
C. There was no food for the wolves to eat.
D. There will be no food for the wolves to eat.
E. There was food for the wolves to eat.

Question 186

H(B,12), H(6,7), E29, E13
A. The baby horse has found its mother.
B. The baby zebra has found its mother.
C. The baby zebra has lost its mother.
D. The baby zebra has found its father.
E. The baby zebra will find its mother.

Question 187

H(5(A1)), 24, A10, A(C1)
A. The tiger runs the fastest of the big cats.
B. The cheetah is the fastest big cat.
C. The cheetah is the biggest of the big cats.
D. The cheetah is the fastest of the big cats.
E. The cheetah runs the fastest of the big cats.

Question 188

H(C12,13,E13), I14, H(30,15), 25, A1
A. The family will drive all day to see a lion.
B. The family drove yesterday to see a lion.
C. The family drove all day to see a lion.
D. The family drove all day but didn't see a lion.
E. The mother and father drove all day to see a lion.

Operator codes		Specialist codes	
A Increase	1 Cat	13 Father	25 See
B Decrease	2 Dog	14 Drive	26 Sky
C Plural	3 Dry	15 Day	27 This
D Plus	4 Land	16 After	28 Season
E Opposite	5 Spotty	17 Meet	29 Lost
F Negative	6 Stripy	18 Water	30 Throughout
G Positive	7 Horse	19 Far from	31 Shrink
H Combine	8 Tree	20 Protect	32 Small
I Past	9 Eat	21 Sun	
J Future	10 Fast	22 Cold	
K Question	11 Food	23 Female	
L Every	12 Child	24 Run	

Question 189

H(C1,C2,C7), 17, E19, A18

A. The animals assemble around the watering hole.
B. The animals meet far from the watering hole.
C. The animals will assemble around the watering hole.
D. The animal assembles around the watering hole.
E. The cats meet around the watering hole.

Question 190

C8, 20, H(C1,C2,C7), A(E22), 21

A. Trees provide shelter for the animals from the hot sun.
B. The tree provides shelter for the animals from the very hot sun.
C. Trees provide shelter for the animals from the extreme heat.
D. Trees provide shelter for the animals from the very hot sun.
E. Trees provide shelter for the animal from the very hot sun.

Question 191

E23, C(A1), H(24,16), 23, C(A1)

A. The male lion chases the female lion.
B. The female lions chase the male lions.
C. The male lions chase the female lions.
D. The male lion chases the female lions.
E. The male lions chase the female lion.

Question 192

I, F, H (26,18), 4, A3

A. There will be no rain so the land will be very dry.
B. There is no rain so the land is very dry.
C. There was no rain so the land was very dry.
D. There was lots of rain so the land is not very dry.
E. There was no rain but the land is not very dry.

Question 193

C8, I(E31), A(E32), 27, 28

A. The trees grew very tall this year.
B. The trees grew tall this summer.
C. The trees did not grow very tall this summer.
D. The tree grew very tall this summer.
E. The trees grew very tall this summer.

A corporate bank communicates in code to discuss the financial difficulties in your area. Crack the code to find out more about what they are saying.

Operator codes	Specialist codes	
A Increase	1 Bank	13 Old
B Decrease	2 Money	14 Bad
C Plural	3 Boss	15 Paper
D Plus	4 Worker	16 Into
E Opposite	5 Worry	17 Loan
F Negative	6 Parent	18 Gain
G Positive	7 Child	19 Place
H Combine	8 Give	20 Coin
I Past	9 University	
J Future	10 Charity	
K Question	11 Country	
L Every	12 Take out	

For questions 194-200, what is the best translation of the following code:

Question 194
H(C7,C6), I5, 2

A. The family was worried about money.
B. The parents were worried about money.
C. The family will be worried about money.
D. The family worry about money.
E. The family was not worried about money.

Question 195
H(9,4), I(H(1,17)), 2

A. The professor stole some money.
B. The professor will borrow some money.
C. The University borrowed some money.
D. The professor borrowed some money.
E. The professor did not borrow any money.

Question 196
1, J8, A2, 10

A. The bank is giving lots of money to charity.
B. The bank did not give much money to charity.
C. The bank gave lots of money to charity.
D. The bank will give money to charity.
E. The bank will give lots of money to charity.

Question 197
C(H(1,4)), A(C11), E18, A2

A. The banks made many countries lose lots of money.
B. The bankers made many countries lose lots of money.
C. The banker made many countries lose lots of money.
D. The bankers made many countries lose money.
E. The bankers did not make many countries lose lots of money.

Operator codes	Specialist codes	
A Increase	1 Bank	13 Old
B Decrease	2 Money	14 Bad
C Plural	3 Boss	15 Paper
D Plus	4 Worker	16 Into
E Opposite	5 Worry	17 Loan
F Negative	6 Parent	18 Gain
G Positive	7 Child	19 Place
H Combine	8 Give	20 Coin
I Past	9 University	
J Future	10 Charity	
K Question	11 Country	
L Every	12 Take out	

Question 198

E13, H(1,3), A(E14)

A. The old bank manager was very good.
B. The new bank manager is good.
C. The new bank manager is very good.
D. The new bank is very good.
E. The new bank manager is not very good.

Question 199

7, J(E12), H(2,15), 16, 1

A. The child will take out a check from the bank.
B. The child deposited a check in the bank.
C. The parent will deposit a check in the bank.
D. The child will deposit a check in the bank.
E. The child will take out notes from the bank.

Question 200

C6, I(F5), 7, H(18,19), 9

A. The family were pleased about their child getting into university.
B. The parents were not worried as the child had not got into university.
C. The parents were worried as their child had got into university.
D. The parents were not worried as their child had got into university.
E. The parents were pleased as their child had not got into university.

Situational Judgement

The Basics

Situational judgment is a psychological aptitude test; it is an assessment method used to evaluate your ability in solving problems in work-related situations. Situational Judgement Tests (or SJTs) are widely used in medicine as one of the criteria when deciding on applicants; it is used for the Foundation Programme and GP applications.

The aim of the situational judgment section is to assess your ability to understand situations that you could encounter as a medical student or doctor and how you would deal with them. It is a method to **test some of the qualities required in a healthcare professional** (e.g. integrity and ability to work in a team).

In the UKCAT, the situational judgment section consists of 20 scenarios with 67 items. Each scenario will have 3-6 items. You will have 27 Minutes to complete this section, which translates to approximately 24 seconds per item. Ensure you're careful to mark your intended answers when working at this pace.

This is the last section of your exam, you are almost near the end- only twenty seven more minutes to go. You still need to stay focused; it might seem obvious, but make sure you read the whole scenario and understand it prior to answering. When answering, imagine you are the person in the scenario. The majority of the scenarios will be about medical students, imagine you are in their shoes.

The series of scenarios include possible actions and considerations. Each scenario is comprised of two sets of questions. In set one you will be asked to assess the "appropriateness" of options in relation to the scenario.

The four possible <u>appropriateness</u> choices are:

➢ *A very appropriate thing to do* – This is an ideal action.
➢ *Appropriate, but not ideal* – This option can be done but not necessarily the best thing to be done.
➢ *Inappropriate, but not awful* – This should not be done, but if it does occur the consequences are not terrible.
➢ *A very inappropriate thing to do* – This should not be done in any circumstances, as it will make the situation worse.

In set two, you will be asked to assess the "importance" of options in relation to the scenario,

The four possible <u>importance</u> options are:

➢ *Very important* – something that is essential to take into account.
➢ *Important* – something you should take into account but is not vital.
➢ *Of minor importance* – something that may be considered, but will not affect the outcome if it is not taken into account.
➢ *Not important at all* – something that is not relevant at all.

Section E includes non-cognitive abilities and so is marked differently to the other sections. You will be awarded full marks if your response completely matches the correct answer. If your answer is close but not exactly right you will receive partial marks, and if there are no correct answers you will receive no marks. Your score is then calculated and expressed in one of four bands, band 1 being the highest and band 4 being the lowest. The band resembles how close your responses were to the assessment panel's agreed answers.

Things you MUST NOT do as a medical student:

➢ Write or sign drug charts.
➢ Sign or authorise anything that a doctor should do (operation consent forms, death certificates etc).
➢ Make any decisions that affect treatment.
➢ Change any treatment regime for any reason.
➢ Perform practical procedures without supervision.
➢ Break patient confidentiality or do anything that places confidentiality at risk.
➢ Behave dishonestly in any way.

Things you MUST do as a medical student:

➢ Raise any concerns regarding patient safety with an appropriate person.
➢ Report any inappropriate behaviour you witness to an appropriate person.
➢ Attend all scheduled teaching and training.
➢ Take responsibility for your learning and seek opportunities to learn.
➢ Dress and present yourself in a clean and smart way.

Things you CAN do as a medical student:

➢ Speak to patients.
➢ Examine patients.
➢ Write in patient notes (but must indicate your name and role).
➢ Perform simple practical procedures like taking blood, inserting cannulas or catheters (if you are trained to and with adequate supervision).
➢ Help doctors with more complex procedures according to their strict directions.
➢ Attend meetings where patients are discussed.
➢ Do things you have been trained to do.

Top tip! Always put patient safety first. If you do this, you can never go far wrong.

Question Answering Strategy

Treat every option as independent – the options may seem similar, but don't let the different options confuse you, read each option as if it is a question on its own. It is important to know that responses should **NOT** be judged as though they are the **ONLY** thing you are to do. An answer should not be judged as inappropriate because it incomplete, but only if there is some actual inappropriate action taking place. For example, if a scenario says "a patient on the ward complains she is in pain", the response "ask the patient what is causing the problem" would be very appropriate, even though any good response would also include informing the nurses and doctors about what you had been told.

There might be multiple correct responses for each scenario, so don't feel you have to answer each stem differently. Thus an answer choice may be used once, more than once or not at all for all scenarios.

If you are unsure of the answer, mark the question and move on. Avoid spending longer than 30 seconds on any question, otherwise you will fall behind the pace and not finish the section.

As with every other section, if you are completely unsure of the answers, answer the question anyway. There is no negative marking and your initial instinct may be close to the intended answer.

➢ If there are several people mentioned in the scenario make sure you are answering about the correct person.
➢ Think of what you 'should' do rather than what you necessarily would do.
➢ Always think of **patient safety** and acting in the patient's best interests.

Read "Tomorrow's Doctors"

This is a publication produced by the GMC (General Medical Council) which can be found on their website. The GMC regulate the medical profession, ensuring standards remain high. This publication can be found on their website, and it outlines the expectations of the next generation of doctors – the generation of doctors you are aspiring to join. **Reading through this will get you into a professional way of thinking** that will help you judge these questions accurately.

Step into Character

When doing this section, imagine you're there. Imagine yourself as a caring and conscientious medical student a few years from now, in each situation as it unfolds. What would you do? What do you think would be the right thing to do?

Hierarchy

The patient is of primary importance. All decisions that affect patient care should be made to benefit the patient. Of secondary importance are your work colleagues. So if there is no risk to patients, you should help out your colleagues and avoid doing anything that would undermine them or harm their reputation – but if doing so would bring detriment to any patient then the patients priorities come to the top. Finally of lowest importance is yourself. You should avoid working outside hours and strive to further your education, but not at the expense of more important or urgent priorities. Remember the key principles of professional conduct and you cannot go far wrong. **Of first and foremost importance is patient safety.** Make sure you make all judgements with this in mind.

> ***Top tip!*** Read the GMC publication "*Tomorrow's Doctors*" – this will help you think the right way.

Medical Ethics

There tend to be a few ethical questions in each SJT paper so it is well worth your time to learn medical ethics. Whilst there are huge ethical textbooks available– you only need to be familiar with the basic principles for the purposes of the UKCAT. These principles can be applied to all cases regardless what the social/ethnic background the healthcare professional or patient is from. In addition to being helpful in the UKCAT, you'll need to know them for the interview stages anyway so they're well worth learning now rather than later. The principles are:

Beneficence

The wellbeing of the patient should be the doctor's first priority. In medicine this means that one must act in the patient's best interests to ensure the best outcome is achieved for them i.e. 'Do Good'.

Non-Maleficence

This is the principle of avoiding harm to the patient (i.e. Do no harm). There can be a danger that in a willingness to treat, doctors can sometimes cause more harm to the patient than good. This can especially be the case with major interventions, such as chemotherapy or surgery. Where a course of action has both potential harms and potential benefits, non-maleficence must be balanced against beneficence.

Autonomy

The patient has the right to determine their own health care. This therefore requires the doctor to be a good communicator, so that the patient is sufficiently informed to make their own decisions. 'Informed consent' is thus a vital precursor to any treatment. A doctor must respect a patient's refusal for treatment even if they think it is not the correct choice. Note that patients cannot <u>demand</u> treatment – only refuse it, e.g. an alcoholic patient can refuse rehabilitation but cannot demand a liver transplant.

There are many situations where the application of autonomy can be quite complex, for example:

➢ **Treating Children**: Consent is required from the parents, although the autonomy of the child is taken into account increasingly as they get older.

➢ **Treating adults without the capacity** to make important decisions. The first challenge with this is in assessing whether or not a patient has the capacity to make the decisions. Just because a patient has a mental illness does not necessarily mean that they lack the capacity to make decisions about their health care. Where patients do lack capacity, the power to make decisions is transferred to the next of kin (or Legal Power of Attorney, if one has been set up).

Justice
This principle deals with the fair distribution and allocation of healthcare resources for the population.

Consent
This is an extension of Autonomy- patients must agree to a procedure or intervention. For consent to be valid, it must be **voluntary informed consent.** This means that the patient must have sufficient mental capacity to make the decision, they must be presented with all the relevant information (benefits, side effects and the likely complications) in a way they can understand and they must make the choice freely without being put under pressure.

Top tip! Remember that **consent is only valid** if it is given:

➢ On the basis of full information.
➢ With sufficient mental capacity.
➢ Freely without pressure.
➢ Communicated unambiguously.

Confidentiality
Patients expect that the information they reveal to doctors will be kept private- this is a key component in maintaining the trust between patients and doctors. You must ensure that patient details are kept confidential. Confidentiality can be broken if you suspect that a patient is a risk to themselves or to others e.g. Terrorism, suicides.

When answering a question on medical ethics, you need to ensure that you show an appreciation for the fact that there are often two sides to the argument. Where appropriate, you should outline both points of view and how they pertain to the main principles of medical ethics and then come to a reasoned judgement.

Situational Judgement Questions

Scenario 1

A conversation is taking place between a midwife Kate and the senior Dr Herbert: Jacob, the medical student, is observing. Dr Herbert is being rude to the Kate and is acting superior. When Dr Herbert leaves, Jacob overhears Kate talking to the other midwives about his behaviour, and how it happens frequently, and makes both the midwives and the patients feel uncomfortable.

How <u>appropriate</u> are the following actions from <u>Jacob</u>?

1. Tell Kate that you will help to file a complaint against Dr Herbert.
2. Make Dr Herbert aware that perhaps he should be kinder the next time he speaks to Kate and patients.
3. Ignore the situation and do nothing.
4. Alert his supervisor as to what he saw, and to get advice on what to do.
5. Tell Dr Herbert that his behaviour was making patients and midwives feel uncomfortable.

Scenario 2

A medical student, George, is sitting in a foot clinic with Dr Walker. George notices that Dr Walker hasn't been washing his hands between patients, despite examining the feet of all of his patients without gloves. In his training George was told that he must wash his hands properly before and after touching each patient to prevent the spread of infections.

How <u>appropriate</u> are each of the following responses by <u>George</u> in this situation?

6. Alert Dr Walker that he ought to wash his hands more after the current consultation has finished.
7. Wash his hands before and after each patient in the hopes that Dr Walker will follow by example.
8. Do nothing because Dr Walker is an experienced consultant.
9. Tell the nurse in charge of the foot patients after the clinic has finished.
10. Write in the patient notes that Dr Walker didn't wash his hands before examining them.

Scenario 3

A medical student, Linh, is working on a project with a small group of other students. The students have to examine real skull bones, which were provided by the medical school's museum, and are very valuable. One of the students in Linh's group accidentally drops the skull and some of the smaller delicate bones shatter.

How <u>appropriate</u> are the following responses by <u>Linh</u>?

11. Ignore what happened, throw the skull remains away, and borrow another group's skull to finish the project.
12. Alert the museum curator about what happened as a group, and write a letter of apology together.
13. Pretend that the skull was stolen.
14. Tell the museum curator in private about who dropped the skull.
15. Tell her supervisor.

Scenario 4

A medical student, Henry, is living in a set of halls with students that study many different subjects. The other students find it funny to joke about Henry's work. Henry is finding it difficult to keep up with his work, and silently takes offense every time the other students joke with him. The night before one of Henry's exams, the other students make a joke that really affects Henry, and he is unable to concentrate on finishing up his revision.

How appropriate are each of the following responses by Henry?

12. Speak to his personal tutor about how he can organise himself and tackle his work in the future.
13. Retaliate by insulting the other students.
14. Do nothing because he doesn't want to offend anyone and is embarrassed about not being able to cope with the workload.
15. Move out of the halls.
16. Speak to his medical student friends about how annoying he finds his flat mates.

Scenario 5

Mark, a medical student, is working with a group of nursing and physiotherapy students to learn about integrated care. Mark is mistaken for a junior doctor, as he is not in uniform, and is asked to test the urine of an elderly patient on the ward using a dipstick. Mark is familiar with the patient, and knows exactly how to do the test. Unfortunately, the doctor that asked him to do the test had to run off, and there are no other members of staff that are able to do the test for another 5 hours. The results of the test will determine the patient's management.

How appropriate are the following responses by Mark?

21. Get the most senior student in his study group to perform the test and write the results in the patient's notes.
22. Do the test himself and write the results in the patient's notes.
23. Bleep the doctor that is in charge of the patient to alert him about his mistake.
24. Pretend that the doctor never asked him to do the test.
25. Try to find another member of staff that would be capable of performing the test.

Scenario 6

A medical student, Adele, is studying for her first year exams. She has started to panic, and does not feel as though she will be able to complete her revision before the exams start. If Adele fails the exams she would have to resit them in her holidays, which she has come to terms with. She is embarrassed of the possibility of failing, and would rather tell her friends and family that she was ill and unable to take the exams than face the embarrassment of failure. It is against the Medical School rules to opt out of an exam without a medical reason and a Doctor's letter.

How appropriate are the following actions for Adele to take?

26. Fake an illness and postpone her exams.
27. Speak to her parents and her personal tutor about her struggle to get through the revision.
28. Speak to the other medical students to see if they all felt the same way about their work.
29. Refuse to turn up to the exams on the day and pretend that she had food poisoning.
30. Make an efficient revision plan for her remaining days before the exams and attempt to do the exams as best as she can.

Scenario 7

Rohan, a final year medical student, notices that Dijam, one of the medical students on his ward who had been drinking a lot the previous night is on call.

How <u>appropriate</u> are the following actions by <u>Rohan</u>?

31. Advise Dijam to go home.
32. Ignore the situation because Dijam wasn't actually treating any of the patients.
33. Inform the doctors that are on call with Dijam.
34. Joke with Dijam about how he managed to make it into work on time.
35. Inform the Doctor that is in charge of Dijam and Rohan's attachment about Dijam's state.

Scenario 8

Patrick is a medical student, and is working with another group of students on a project that they will receive a joint mark for. Patrick has noticed that there are a couple of loud dominating people in the group, and that the rest of the group are very shy and quiet, and rarely contribute to the conversations. Jina is one particularly loud student that is involved, however she has been making some excellent points and is happy to do a lot of the work.

How <u>appropriate</u> are the following responses by <u>Patrick</u>?

36. Ignore the situation and allow Jina to do the majority of the work.
37. Ask his personal tutor for advice on how he should tackle the situation.
38. Ask the quieter members of the team about what they think of Jina.
39. Subtly hint to everyone to try to contribute more during the sessions so that it is a more even contribution from everyone.
40. Confront Jina and tell her to be less dominating during the sessions.

Scenario 9

Nazia, a medical student, has been working on busy hospital ward. She has been writing up notes from the patient's notes into her notebook so that she can construct a presentation on the case for her study group. No-one is allowed to remove the patient's notes from the hospital. However, she has noticed that one of her friends, Joshua, has a set of patient's notes sticking out of his bag. He has an appointment to get to, and has no time to write the notes up whilst at the hospital. Joshua says that he will return the notes first thing in the morning after he completes the work at home.

How <u>appropriate </u>are the following responses from <u>Nazia</u>?

41. Tell Joshua to do the presentation the next day instead when he has more time.
42. Ignore what he is doing.
43. Tell the ward nurses after Joshua leaves with the notes.
44. Seek advice from your clinical supervisor.
45. Tell Joshua that you will write the notes for him so he doesn't have to take the notes away from the hospital.

Scenario 10

Mr. Marshall has been seeing Dr Kelly regularly for years to check up on his diabetes. Recently, Mr Marshall has been seen by a different specialist doctor, Dr O'Brien. Dr O'Brien runs a test that shows that Mr. Marshall has cancer. He is then booked to see Dr O'Brien the following week who will break the diagnosis. Mr. Marshall is currently in clinic with Dr Kelly and asks her "is everything okay?"

How <u>appropriate</u> are the following responses by <u>Dr Kelly</u>?

46. Tell Mr. Marshall that everything is fine.
47. Reassure Mr. Marshall that Dr O'Brien will be able to answer his question better.
48. Tell Mr. Marshall that she is not allowed to discuss that information with him yet.
49. Look away and say nothing to try to express the seriousness of the situation.
50. Tell Mr. Marshall that he has cancer.

Scenario 11

Mary, a patient, has been in hospital for a long time whilst she recovers from a leg wound, and is desperate to return home. One day, Dr Anil is speaking to her on the ward. He has to leave urgently to answer his bleep call. Mary is left with a junior medical student, Julia. She asks Julia why she is still in the hospital, and wants to know if she can leave that day.

How <u>appropriate</u> are the following responses by <u>Julia</u>?

51. Explain to Mary that she is unable to answer her question, and that the doctor will be back soon.
52. Tell Mary that in most cases people wouldn't be able to leave the hospital at her stage of recovery.
53. Tell Mary that she can self-discharge from hospital if she is very keen to leave, but that it might be against medical opinion.
54. Tell Mary that she will find out and let her know.
55. Answer Mary's questions directly.

Scenario 12

Daniel, a first year medical student, is visiting a hospital for the first time since he started medical school. The doctor supervising them asked Hannah, another student to let the group know that they would be having a hand washing assessment consisting of practical and theoretical aspects. Unfortunately, Daniel was not been about the assessment, and doesn't know how to wash his hands properly.

How <u>appropriate</u> are the following responses by <u>Daniel</u>?

56. Ask to have his turn once a few of his colleagues had been so he can observe.
57. Confront Hannah and ask her why she didn't tell him about the assessment.
58. Tell the doctor that it was Hannah's fault.
59. Ask the group to see how many people were prepared for the assessment.
60. Ask the doctor if he can have his assessment another day so he can learn the skill and the theory properly.

Scenario 13

Helen, a medical student, is waiting for her exam results. She was very worried because she didn't feel as though she was ready for them. When the results come out, she realises that she has to retake her exams. She had booked to go travelling with a friend in South America over the summer holidays, but the resit exams are during the holidays and she is now worried that she will be unable to go, or that if she goes she will not have enough time to revise for the exams. She is also worried that her friend will be left to travel by herself if she doesn't go.

How <u>appropriate</u> are the following responses by <u>Helen</u> in this situation?

61. Call her friend and cancel the holiday.
62. Go travelling but take her revision with her and revise every day.
63. Go for part of the holiday and come home early to revise for the exams.
64. Go travelling and cram in the revision in the few days between coming back and taking the exams.
65. Try to get another friend to replace her so she can stay at home and revise but without leaving her friend to fend for herself.

Scenario 14

Celia, a medical student, is living at home instead of at halls because she doesn't live far away from the medical school. She found it hard to make friends in first year, and wants to move out for her second year or she fears that she will be further isolated from everyone. Unfortunately, that would depend on financial support from her parents. Celia's parents are unable to provide much financial aid, and Celia doesn't have time to take up another job.

How <u>appropriate</u> are the following responses by <u>Celia</u>?

66. Confront her parents and demand the money because they are 'denying her a student experience'.
67. Live at home but join a sports team so she can meet more people and join in with the student lifestyle a little more.
68. Start spending every night at her friend's room in halls.
69. Live at home in resentment and isolate herself from her university friends.
70. Come to an agreement with her parents that if she can move out for a couple of years and then live at home for the rest of medical school.

Scenario 15

Xun, a medical student, is due to hand in an essay the following day at 8AM but is only half way to finishing it at 9PM. The essay will contribute 20% to his final grade and he is beginning to panic.

How <u>appropriate</u> are the following responses by <u>Xun</u>?

71. Stay up late and finish the essay so that he doesn't miss the deadline.
72. Call the head of the assessments and explain his situation to them, in the hope that there will be some leniency.
73. Give up and hand in the essay half-complete.
74. Copy out a similar essay that a friend has written.
75. Fake an illness and ask for an extension.

Scenario 16

Nahor, a medical student, has always enjoyed having creative hairstyles. He is starting his rotations in the hospitals next week, and is worried that he will be unable to express himself through his hair anymore.

How appropriate are the following responses by Nahor in this situation?

76. Cut his hair and get a professional looking colour and style.
77. Start his hospital rotations with his pink long hair, and refuse to change it if he is asked to.
78. Start his hospital rotations with his pink long hair, and only change it if he is asked to.
79. Keep his hair a little quirky but make it look more professional that it has previously been.
80. Request permission from the clinical dean to keep his hair as it is.

Scenario 17

Charles, a medical student, was on call with Dr Patel in a busy hospital. Dr Patel told Charles to wait for the doctor that is going to handover to arrive before he leaves. The doctor isn't due to arrive for another 30 minutes. Charles has a sports match in 15 minutes, and needs to leave before then. Unfortunately Dr Patel is busy with a patient and is not answering his bleep.

How appropriate are the following responses by Charles?

81. Leave and email Dr Patel with a letter of apology.
82. Call up the captain of the sports team to apologise, and promise that you will make the second half of the match.
83. Leave the on call room and try to find Dr Patel to talk to him in person.
84. Leave a message with one of the nurses in the on call room to tell the doctor that is meant to be taking over.
85. Try to call up the doctor that is taking over to explain the situation to him.

Scenario 18

Archie, a medical student, is in clinic with Dr Coombe. Dr Coombe explains to the patient that her medication isn't working and that will have to try something else. Dr Coombe has to take an urgent call and walks out of the room- leaving Archie and the patient in the room. The patient then starts to ask Archie lots of questions about her medication.

How appropriate are the following responses by Archie?

86. Explain that he is unable to say, but that the patient should direct her questions towards Dr Coombe when he returns.
87. Try to answer the questions to the best of his ability.
88. Tell the patient that they should 'Google' the answers.
89. Tell the patient that he will 'Google' the answers.
90. Excuse himself and walk out of the room to leave the patient in there by herself until Dr Coombe returns.

Scenario 19

Matthias, a medical student, has hurt his knee whilst playing hockey. He will need to wear a full leg brace which will prevent him from walking around the hospital. Matthias is concerned that it will affect his studies adversely. He will have to take at least 6 weeks off.

How <u>appropriate</u> are the following responses by <u>Matthias</u>?

91. Write to the medical school and his personal tutor for advice as soon as possible.
92. Try to go to the hospital for 2 days to see if he can cope.
93. Do all of his book work whilst she is unable to walk around the hospital, so that he can focus on clinical training when he is better.
94. Stop going into hospital without letting anyone know.
95. Stop going into hospital and ask his friends to let the medical school know.

Scenario 20

Jessie, a medical student, has a friend called Gemma. Jessie suspects that Gemma has an eating disorder. Gemma was very stressed at medical school, and Jessie is uncertain with how to proceed.

How <u>appropriate</u> are the following responses by <u>Jessie</u> in this situation?

96. Ignore the situation and hope that someone else will notice.
97. Try to talk to Gemma and bring up her eating disorder.
98. Chat to Gemma about her stress and ask if she is coping. Allow her to bring up the disorder on her own account.
99. Speak to Gemma's parents about it, without consulting her.
100. Speak to your personal tutor for advice.

Scenario 21

Helen, a medical student, is has to retake her end of year exams because she failed them the first time. She had booked to go travelling with a friend in South America over the summer holidays, but the resit exams are during this period. She is worried that she will be unable to go and therefore, her friend will be left to travel by herself. If she goes she won't have enough time to revise for the exams.

How <u>appropriate</u> are the following responses by <u>Helen</u> in this situation?

101. Call her friend and cancel the holiday.
102. Go travelling but take her revision with her and revise every day.
103. Go for part of the holiday and come home early to revise for the exams.
104. Go travelling and cram in the revision in the few days between coming back and taking the exams.
105. Transfer her holiday booking to another mutually good friend so she can stay at home and revise but without leaving her friend to fend for herself.

Scenario 22

Daniel and Sean are medical students who are working together on a project. They get into a heated argument in the hospital lobby because Daniel has been prioritising his social life recently which is frustrating Sean.

How <u>important</u> are the following factors for <u>Sean</u> in deciding on what to do?

106. Sean can generally produce better work than Daniel anyway.
107. The mark that they get will be recorded in their log books.
108. Daniel and Sean have to work together for the rest of the year.
109. Daniel has recently broken up with his girlfriend.
110. Sean usually does most of the work when they have to do projects together.

Scenario 23

A medical student Tanya is invited to attend a clinic with Dr Garg who is in charge of Tanya's grade for the whole term. On the morning of the clinic, Tanya realises that she has not finished her essay that is due the next day.

How <u>important</u> are the following factors for <u>Tanya</u> to consider in deciding on what to do?

111. The importance of the essay towards her final mark for the year.
112. Tanya's friend did not find the clinic very educational.
113. Tanya's reputation with Dr Garg.
114. Whether or not Tanya will be able to attend a different clinic with Dr Garg.
115. How long it will take to finish the essay.

Scenario 24

Caroline, a final year medical student, is teaching first year medical students. She notices that they frequently arrive looking untidy and has noticed that some of the doctors have started to comment on how badly dressed the first year students are. She is worried that she will offend the students if she asks them to dress more appropriately, because 2 of the students are on her sports team.

How <u>important</u> are the following factors for <u>Caroline</u> in deciding on what to do?

116. Caroline's reputation with the doctors.
117. The first year students are only in hospital for 2 hours every week.
118. The first year students have direct contact with the patients and the hospital staff.
119. 2 of the students are on her sports team.
120. The first year students don't have their professionalism exams until third year.

Scenario 25

A medical student, Albert, is in his third year and is captain of the hockey team. He has noticed that his hockey training on Wednesday afternoons always clashes with his consultant teaching sessions. The consultant will be responsible for his final grade for the year.

How <u>important</u> are the following factors for <u>Albert</u> in deciding on what to do?
121. His hockey team needs him this year to win the championships.
122. Albert is on a sports scholarship at medical school.
123. His grade will determine if he can progress to his fourth year.
124. The consultant is free on Wednesday mornings.
125. This is the only teaching he will get on this particular topic this year.

Scenario 26

A patient is in a consultation with Dr Davison and Sybil, a medical student is observing. The doctor swears a number of times during the consultation, and Sybil notices that the patient is getting uncomfortable.

How <u>important</u> are the following factors for <u>Sybil</u> in deciding on what to do?

126. Dr Davison is marking one of Sybil's assessments.
127. The patient appears to be uncomfortable with Dr Davison swearing.
128. How often Dr Davison swears during other patient consultations.
129. If other members of staff are aware of Dr Davison's swearing.
130. If the patient has seen Dr Davison before.

Scenario 27

Marco and Alex are medical students on their surgical placement. They are invited to observe surgery with Mr. Daniels and told not to touch the sterile equipment. Before the operation begins, Marco sees Alex accidentally touch the sterile trolley with the operating equipment on it. Alex doesn't tell anyone, and Marco thinks that he should inform someone.

How <u>important</u> are the following factors for <u>Marco</u> in deciding on what to do?

131. The risk to the patient who is about to have the operation.
132. The inconvenience for all of the theatre staff to have to bring out a new sterile trolley.
133. Alex would be embarrassed because he touched something that he wasn't meant to.
134. Alex only briefly touched the trolley.
135. Mr Daniels would be disappointed in Marco and Alex.

Scenario 28

A medical student, Freddie, is on a busy hospital ward. A patient is addicted to pain medication and constantly bullies staff, so that they are reluctant to see her. Freddie has noticed that the doctors and nurses have been attending to her less frequently than before. One day, after she has been reviewed by the doctors and nurses, she starts to verbally abuse Freddie. She demands that he gets her more pain medication.

How <u>important</u> are the following factors for <u>Freddie</u> in determining what he should do?

136. The patient might be in pain.
137. The patient is being avoided by staff.
138. Freddie is not authorised to administer pain medication.
139. The patient may have already had her regular pain medication.
140. The patient has recently been reviewed by the doctors and nurses.

Scenario 29

Jenny is a junior doctor who is training under Mr. Gupta. Her sister, Claire, is due to be operated on by Mr. Gupta to correct a hernia. Claire is nervous about the operation and asks Jenny what she thinks about Mr. Gupta. Jenny knows that Mr. Gupta is a very good surgeon but he is often late when seeing patients on the wards. Therefore, he always appears to be rushing, flustered, and a little sweaty when speaking to them before their operations, which can make them lose confidence in him. Jenny must decide on what to say to her sister Claire.

How <u>important</u> are the following factors for <u>Jenny</u> in deciding on what to do?

141. Mr. Gupta is very competent.
142. The surgeon is often flustered when speaking to patients.
143. Mr. Gupta recently reprimanded Jenny for filling in a drug chart incorrectly.
144. Claire is already quite anxious about having an operation.
145. Patients usually do better if they are confident and at ease before an operation.

Scenario 30

A medical student, Alex, is on the university rugby team. He has been given model answers for various written assessments from older members of the rugby team. His friend, Annabel, realises that the Medical school often repeats their questions, and that it is against the rules to pass down previous papers from year to year.

How <u>important</u> are the following factors for <u>Annabel</u> in deciding on what to do?

146. Alex and Annabel dated for the first year, until he broke up with her.
147. Alex is a hard working student.
148. In this particular year, most of the questions won't be the same as in previous years.
149. Annabel isn't part of a team where information from older members is readily available.
150. The answers are not available to all students.

Scenario 31

Matthew, a medical student, is running late for his teaching session. He missed his bus and the next one doesn't come for another hour. His class was warned yesterday that if they were late for another session without a good reason, then they would not get a good grade for professionalism at the end of the term.

How <u>important</u> are the following factors for <u>Matthew</u> in deciding on what to do?

151. His marks for professionalism are not included in his final grade for the year.
152. Public transport information updates are readily available online.
153. The rest of his class is usually late.
154. Matthew is usually on time for most classes.
155. His teacher will be involved in his studies for the next year.

Scenario 32

Michaela, a medical student, is shadowing doctors on the intensive care unit of a busy hospital. Unfortunately Michaela becomes unwell during the week. She was told on her first day to stay at home if she becomes ill to minimise the risk of spreading infection to the patients. She is reluctant to remain at home because she this is her first and only week on the intensive care unit.

How important are the following factors for Michaela in deciding on what to do?

156. Michaela cannot spend another week on the intensive care unit.
157. Michaela's illness is just a mild cold and is unlikely to cause serious harm.
158. The illness doesn't affect her ability to interact with patients.
159. Michaela was told by the doctors not to come in if she became unwell.
160. Michaela's friend told her that she would learn a lot during her time on the intensive care unit.

Scenario 33

Jenny, a 4th year medical student, has booked and paid to go on the university ski trip. Unfortunately, she finds out that she has the option to sit a set of mock practical exams during the week of the ski trip. Jenny will lose the full amount of money if she pulls out of the ski trip. One of Jenny's friends has their mock exam the day after Jenny gets back. Jenny wants to try and swap their exam dates.

How important are the following factors for Jenny in deciding on what to do?

161. How useful the mock exams will be.
162. The cost of her ski trip.
163. The mock exams are optional.
164. The university's policy on swapping dates of exams.
165. Jenny has performed well on all exams in medical school so far.

Scenario 34

Luke, a medical student, has wanted to do a particular project for months. He has already spoken with the project's supervisor and planned it with him. He has also put it as his top choice for a project, although he knows that of other people also want to do the same project. Later next week, Luke finds out that he has been allocated to his second choice project instead. His friend, Architha, has been allocated the project that he wanted even though it was her last choice. Based, on this, Luke wants to make an official appeal.

How important are the following factors for Luke in deciding whether to appeal?

166. Luke has spoken to the project supervisor.
167. Architha didn't want to have the project.
168. The project grade will count for Luke's final grade at the end of the year.
169. Luke finds it difficult to invest time in a project that he doesn't care about.
170. Luke was allocated his second choice of project.

Scenario 35

Lucinda, a medical student, has been performing very well in her exams so far. She has been in a relationship with Andy (who is also in her year) for 6 weeks. Unfortunately, Andy will need to repeat the year as he has been struggling with the workload. Lucinda is desperate to stay in his year. Andy suggests that she fail her exams on purpose so that she can stay in his year.

How <u>important</u> are the following factors for <u>Lucinda</u> in deciding on what to do?

171. If Lucinda fails her exams the mark will be on her university transcript when she graduates.
172. Jobs as a junior doctor are partially determined based on your grades at medical school.
173. Lucinda and Andy have only been in a relationship for 6 weeks.
174. Lucinda's friends are performing very well and will progress onto the next year.
175. Andy has asked her to fail her exams on purpose.

Scenario 36

Shiv, a medical student, is nearly at the end of his rotation. He really wants to go to Australia for the Christmas holidays to see his girlfriend who is on her elective there. The flights are much cheaper if he skips the final day of his rotation. Most of his medical friends have already finished for the holidays because the doctors that were in charge of them finished their final assessments early. However, Shiv has a very strict doctor who insists that their final assessments will be on the final day of term, and no sooner. The doctor is due to retire after Christmas.

How <u>important</u> are the following factors for <u>Shiv</u> in deciding on what to do?

176. Shiv must pay for his own flights with the money he has saved up.
177. Shiv's final assessment involves the doctor asking him how the term has gone for him, and then signing his log book.
178. Shiv has been punctual and has produced impressive work throughout the rotation.
179. Shiv's doctor will be retiring after Christmas.
180. Shiv's girlfriend is in Australia.

Scenario 37

Jazzmynne, a medical student, is a talented vocalist and is offered the chance to go on a prestigious singing tour for a month with her choir. Unfortunately, this would mean missing a month of classes.

How <u>important</u> are the following factors for <u>Jazzmynne</u> in deciding on what to do?

181. Her choir has never been on an international tour before and this might be Jazzmynne's only chance to go.
182. Jazzmynne would end up missing half of one of her clinical rotations.
183. Jazzmynne's parents get anxious when she misses class.
184. Jazzmynne sometimes struggles to keep up with her workload.
185. Jazzmynne's friends are also going on the tour with her.

Scenario 38

Ellen, a medical student, has been writing for the university newspaper since her first year. She likes to focus on stories that are topical for the students. Recently, the new principal of the medical school has created a ban on stories that involve student bars and social lives. Ellen wants to start a petition to change this rule.

How <u>important</u> are the following factors for <u>Ellen</u> in deciding on what to do?

186. Ellen is in her final year of medical school.
187. The university has a good reputation for responding positively to student petitions.
188. 90% of the university newspaper readers are medical students.
189. The principal wants to encourage more stories about the health press, the world, and academics, rather than gossip at the bars.
190. Ellen doesn't like the new principal very much.

Scenario 39

Guy, a medical student, works at the student bar during the week. The recent change in the university's health and safety policy imposes a maximum number of students that can enter the bar at any time. This means that on popular nights, there is usually an hour-long queue to get into the bar. Guy thinks that this is unfair, and drafts a letter to the university, asking them to expand the student bar.

How <u>important</u> are the following factors for <u>Guy</u> in deciding on what to do?

191. Students are being denied access to their own bars.
192. Guy will get more work and therefore money if the bar expands.
193. The university has dropped in student satisfaction league tables.
194. The bar is very expensive.
195. The university is having financial troubles.

Scenario 40

Olivia, a medical student, wants to run for president of the student union. She has been involved for many years, and is very dedicated to the union. Her friend, Phil, also wants to run for president. Phil is very popular, although he has not contributed as much to the union as Olivia.

How <u>important</u> are the following factors for <u>Olivia</u> in deciding on what to do?

196. Olivia and Phil were previously in a relationship.
197. Phil is in his final year but Olivia is in her penultimate year.
198. Olivia has worked for the student union for a lot longer than Phil has.
199. Neither Phil nor Olivia are happy to run for any other position on the committee.
200. Olivia gave up the presidency of the student union last year because her friend who was in his final year wanted it.

.

ANSWERS

Verbal Reasoning Answers

Question	Answer	Question	Answer	Question	Answer	Question	Answer
1	False	51	False	101	False	151	B
2	False	52	False	102	True	152	A
3	True	53	True	103	False	153	A
4	Can't tell	54	True	104	False	154	C
5	Can't tell	55	Can't tell	105	False	155	C
6	False	56	False	106	Can't tell	156	B
7	False	57	True	107	B	157	A
8	Can't tell	58	False	108	C	158	D
9	Can't tell	59	False	109	B	159	B
10	True	60	True	110	B	160	A
11	False	61	False	111	D	161	C
12	False	62	Can't tell	112	C	162	C
13	Can't tell	63	False	113	B	163	B
14	False	64	True	114	D	164	B
15	Can't tell	65	False	115	C	165	A
16	False	66	False	116	D	166	D
17	Can't tell	67	False	117	A	167	A
18	True	68	False	118	C	168	C
19	Can't tell	69	Can't tell	119	C	169	D
20	True	70	True	120	A	170	C
21	Can't tell	71	False	121	C	171	C
22	Can't tell	72	False	122	C	172	A
23	True	73	False	123	D	173	B
24	False	74	False	124	B	174	A
25	True	75	False	125	A	175	A
26	False	76	False	126	D	176	C
27	True	77	False	127	B	177	B
28	False	78	True	128	C	178	C
29	Can't tell	79	False	129	C	179	B
30	False	80	False	130	D	180	D
31	Can't tell	81	Can't tell	131	C	181	C
32	False	82	Can't tell	132	D	182	C
33	False	83	Can't tell	133	B	183	B
34	False	84	Can't tell	134	C	184	A
35	False	85	False	135	C	185	B
36	False	86	True	136	C	186	C
37	Can't tell	87	Can't tell	137	B	187	A
38	Can't tell	88	True	138	B	188	C
39	False	89	False	139	D	189	D
40	True	90	Can't tell	140	D	190	A
41	True	91	False	141	B	191	A
42	Can't tell	92	False	142	C	192	C
43	False	93	False	143	C	193	D
44	False	94	False	144	C	194	A
45	True	95	True	145	C	195	C
46	Can't tell	96	Can't tell	146	C	196	A
47	False	97	True	147	A	197	B
48	True	98	True	148	C	198	C
49	True	99	False	149	C	199	C
50	Can't tell	100	True	150	B	200	B

Set 1:

1. **False** -In paragraph 2, the passage says that only the countries that signed the protocol were legally bound.
2. False -In 2004, the condition that over 55% of emissions were accounted for was met without Australia and the US.
3. **True** -in paragraph 2: 'each country that signed the protocol agreed to reduce their emissions to their own specific target'.
4. **Can't tell** -We know this is when the Kyoto Protocol was enforced but there is no information to suggest whether emissions actually decreased.
5. **Can't tell** -Paragraph 4 says that a 60% emission reduction would have a 'significant impact', but we cannot tell if the remaining effects would be harmful or not. The passage is also talking about a global reduction of 60% - there is no mention of each individual country needing reduce their emissions by 60%.

Set 2:

6. **False** -From paragraph 1, we can see that the Soviets were mainly concerned with showing off their economic power and technological superiority.
7. **False** -Paragraph 3 says that Project Apollo was tasked with landing the first man on the moon.
8. **Can't tell** -The passage does not tell us why the Soviets did not land a man on the moon.
9. **Can't tell** -We do not know the state of the American space efforts prior to the launch of Sputnik – we just know that its launch 'prompted urgency'.
10. **True** -The Soviets had just sent Yuri Gagarin into space and it wasn't expected that the US would beat the Soviets in landing a man on the moon; therefore the US was behind the Soviets at this stage.

Set 3:

11. **False**- Paragraph 1 says Pheidippides was the fastest runner
12. **False**-Paragraph 2 says that they were standardised from 1921 but using the 1908 distance
13. **Can't tell**-Paragraph 1 says the Greeks were not expecting to beat the Persians, but we do not know if the Persians were expecting to beat the Greeks, despite their larger army
14. **False**- Paragraph 2: to be an IAAF marathon the distance must be 26.2 miles. The original route was 25 miles
15. **Can't tell** -We know that the Persian soldiers outnumbered the Greeks and had superior cavalry, but we are not told about their training

Set 4:

16. **False**- From paragraph 1, we can see that birds would not survive if they did not migrate
17. **Can't tell**-Whilst there is only mention here of migrating in flocks, nowhere does it specifically state that either all migrating birds do so or that any migrating birds do not
18. **True**- Although the leading bird does not benefit at the time, they continually change position within the flock according to paragraph 3
19. **Can't tell** -Paragraph 3 shows that the Northern bald ibis does not behave in this way so it is not known what would happen
20. **True** -Paragraph 1 states they migrate north in the spring, and south in the winter

Set 5:

21. **Can't tell** -We know the amount of wild flowers has decreased by this amount but we can't tell if the bee population fell by a proportional amount. The 50% reduction mentioned in Paragraph 1 only refers to honey bees
22. **Can't tell**-Whilst the UK have experienced a significantly greater decline than the European average, there is no data from the rest of the world.
23. True -Paragraph 2 tells us modern techniques produce more food.
24. **False** -As well as pollination, bees are also involved in complex food chains and cannot be replaced
25. **True** -From paragraph 1 we see that pesticides are one of the causes of bee population decline. Therefore, reducing pesticide usage would reduce this rate of decline.

Set 6:

26. **False** -This would affect the thinking distance, not the braking distance.
27. **True** -From paragraph 2 we see that the increased traction of winter tyres is because the softness of their material allows better traction.
28. **False**- From paragraph 4, we are told it is not safe to run the engine when the exhaust pipe is blocked because of the risk of carbon monoxide production.
29. **Can't tell**-There is not sufficient information in the passage to suggest whether the softer tyres are dangerous to use in hot conditions.
30. **False**- Paragraph 3 says it is safer to steer out of the way than to brake.

Set 7:

31. **Can't tell** -In Paragraph 1, we are told the method is named after Socrates, but we are not told whether he was the first person to use it or whether he simply adapted and/or popularised the Socratic method.
32. **False** -The Socratic method challenges the statements and opinions that a person makes, not their wisdom.
33. False -Although Socrates was trialled with these charges, the Socratic method as described was not the cause.
34. **False** -We can see from the final paragraph that he chose to die defending knowledge and wisdom, rather than fleeing in fear.
35. **False** -From paragraph 2 we see that Socrates did not provide answers to these difficult questions.

Set 8:

36. **False** -Paragraph 1 says the dialects of the Saxon, Angle and Jute tribes formed the Anglo-Saxon language.
37. **Can't tell**-Paragraph 2 says English speakers would struggle to understand Old English, but we do not know about German speakers.
38. **Can't tell**-The story of Beowulf only mentions that he kills Grendel and his mother, not about his strength compared to other warriors.
39. **False**-The Friesian dialect is similar to Old English but they are not the same.
40. **True** -The Celtic Britons were originally living in England before being forced into Wales.

Set 9:

41. **True**-Paragraph 1 says that stars in the constellation Cassiopeia are visible only in the northern hemisphere; therefore they are not visible in the southern hemisphere.
42. **Can't tell** -The passage does not tell us if Cassiopeia rises and falls in the sky or not.
43. **False**-Paragraph 3 says the star sign represents the position of the sun, not the visible constellations.
44. **False** -Paragraph 2 says Polaris is used for navigation as its position is constant in the sky.
45. **True**-Paragraph 1 mentions different constellations being visible from different places on the Earth.

Set 10:

46. **Can't tell**-The passage tells us about maple tree sap but we don't know about other trees.
47. **False** -He was angered because of the laziness of the village people.
48. **True** -Paragraph 1 says that the process is similar although different equipment is used.
49. **True**-Paragraph 1 says the sap is only harvested during March.
50. **Can't tell** -Although the laziness associated with drinking maple syrup suggests hunting is harder than syrup drinking, the people may just have not hunted because they did not need to – not because it was harder.

Set 11:

51. **False**-Paragraph 1 says Stockholm syndrome happens sometimes, not always.
52. **False** -The passage suggests that the hugging and kissing occurred due to the positive relationship formed between the captors and hostages.
53. **True** -Paragraph 4 says the FBI is willing to devote resources to understanding Stockholm syndrome in order to aid crisis negotiation.
54. **True**-The explanation given in paragraph 3 suggests that the hostages fearing for their life is a step in the development of Stockholm syndrome.

55. **Can't tell** -Although this incident is the origin of the name 'Stockholm syndrome', it is not mentioned whether this phenomenon has happened before

Set 12:

56. **False**-It is this mucous layer that offers protection from the anemone tentacles
57. **True**- Paragraph 2 mentions that the bright colour of the clownfish lures in fish which the anemone eventually stings and eats.
58. **False**-Paragraph 3 mentions that anemones increase the lifespan of clownfish but are not essential for clownfish to live.
59. **False**- Paragraphs 1 and 3 mention that only certain anemone form this mutually beneficial relationship.
60. **True** -Paragraph 2 says the anemone sting protects the clownfish from predators.

Set 13:

61. **False**-Paragraph 2 indicates he was opposed to the death penalty.
62. **Can't tell**-The passage only tells us that the guillotine was commonly used during the French Revolution, it doesn't tell us what was used for execution before the French Revolution.
63. **False** -Although it can cause death by asphyxiation, the common cause of death is snapping of the neck.
64. **True**- This was Joseph Guillotin's explanation.
65. **False** -Paragraph 1 tells us the guillotine was the common form of execution as it was the only legal method of execution.

Set 14:

66. **False** -The Gherkin is famous for its distinctive shape, and although this forms part of a cooling system it is not famous for that reason.
67. **False** -The City of London governing body wanted redevelopment to restore the old historic look – implying the Baltic Exchange had this look before the bombing.
68. **False** -The Gherkin was bought for £630m and sold for £700m, so a profit was made on the sale.
69. **Can't tell** -We are told the building is damaged by bombs, but we are not told what the intention of the attack was.
70. **True**- It is stated in paragraph 1 that Norman Foster is famous for this.

Set 15:

71. **False** -The passage tells us London is significantly more expensive.
72. **False** -There are no legal implications for paying below the living wage as it is the minimum wage that is legally binding.
73. **False**-This individual would be earning less than the living wage and so would not be able to live comfortably according to the definition in paragraph 1.
74. **False** -Some employees will be fired and others would have to work harder; some employees may already be earning more than the living wage and so would not benefit.
75. **False** -The family of that individual will also benefit from the living wage, as well as the company they work for.

Set 16:

76. **False** -Although a country with more people will likely have a greater ecological footprint, it is through their increased usage of resources, not a direct consequence of the population. There can be significant discrepancies.
77. **False**- This is the bio-productive capacity of the Earth, not the total space available.
78. **True** -The final paragraph mentions that reducing use of unsustainable resources will reduce the ecological footprint.
79. **False** -The final paragraph says that a global effort is needed.
80. **False** -The final paragraph says that we can increase the bio-productive space available.

Set 17:

81. **Can't tell** -Paragraph one states that some believe them to be 'one of the most important', which does not necessarily mean they are the most influential.
82. **Can't tell** -The passage states it started the UK punk movement, but this does not necessarily mean it began the global movement.
83. **Can't tell** -The passage states that there were lyrics written about abortion, but they do not state the moral stance these lyrics took.
84. **Can't tell** -The passage tells us that some songs attacked the music industry and that controversial topics such as the Holocaust were commented on, however we do not know if these two topics were said to be related.
85. **False** -They attacked 'blindly accepting royalty as an authority', and so attacked a royalist standpoint.
86. **True** -Not at the same time, but The Sex Pistols had two individual bassists over the course of their existence.

Set 18:

87. **Can't tell** -The passage doesn't mention what proportion of people exposed to asbestos will get mesothelioma.
88. **True** -As breast cancer is the most common cancer in the UK and very rare in men, it must be very common in women.
89. **False** -The success rates of tumour removal procedures were improved by surgical hygiene.
90. **Can't tell** -The passage doesn't mention the relative success rates between the two methods.
91. **False** -Some tumours are able to metastasise, meaning that there are also tumours that do not.

Set 19:

92. **False** -The land was claimed because the British people did not believe that anybody actually owned the land.
93. **False** -Not all of the 517,000 Aborigines are living in cities and towns.
94. **False**-They were only able to reclaim the land that they could prove they originally owned.
95. **True** -Only a few Aborigines lack the education to integrate with modern Australian life.
96. **Can't tell** -We do not know what the south-east Asian lifestyle involved.

Set 20:

97. **True** -It was discovered that chilli peppers had similar taste to black peppercorn and so became valuable around the world.
98. **True** -Paragraph 2 says that spicy food allows people to sweat.
99. **False** -Paragraph 1 says 'most' peppers are spicy, but not all.
100.**True**-The capsaicin receptor is responsible for the pain associated with spicy chillies.
101. **False** -The description of labelled line coding says these different methods of activating this receptor will cause the same sensation.

Set 21:

102. **True**- Dropping out of school will affect the level of education, which is a social determinant of health.
103. **False** -They can also be measured by the quality of life.
104. **False** -Although this would prevent the described mechanism from happening, many other mechanisms are acting at the same time. This was just one example of many possible mechanisms.
105. **False** -The final paragraph says we are reducing the gap between those more privileged and those who are more disadvantaged.
106. **Can't tell** -The life expectancy described in paragraph 2 is an average and so can't reliably be used in specific examples.

Set 22:

107. **B-** The passage suggests that the critics suppose 'human beings to be capable of no pleasures except those of which swine are capable', and so suggest the potential of higher pleasures. They do not call their critics degraded, but suggest that the critics degrade human nature, nor do they accuse critics of being either miserable or indulgent.

108. **C-** This action does not see happiness as its justification, but conforming to social norms. It does not seek to increase pleasure or reduce pain, just follow dogma, which is not according to the principle of utility.

109. **B-** Mill does not describe the religious views of his critics, or explicitly call them reactionary, and in fact describes them 'some of the most estimable in feeling and purpose'. He does mention the countries of origin for some of his critics, and they are all in Europe.

110. **B-** The passage also states 'desirable things' could be 'means' to pleasure.

111. **D-**Utility is defined as the foundation of the system, and a belief that the increasing of happiness/decreasing of happiness is good. The passage specifically states that it has not given an exhaustive definition of things that are pleasurable/painful, and it does not specifically define Epicureans, simply suggests a link between them and utilitarian's - which is not an exhaustive explanation of the term.

Set 23:

112. **C-**Though sandstone is made from sand, the passage does not state that ALL rocks are made from this material.
113. **B-**The passage discusses the valley when implementing the wall-building analogy.
114. **D-** 'Some ancient source' is all we are told, and so the source is undisclosed (Paragraph 3).
115. **C-** This rock is said in paragraph 2 to be found 'everywhere', so not 'nowhere'.
116. **D-** Paragraph 3: The grains are said to be sorted in groups 'of a size', i.e. measurements. They are all described as 'worn and rounded', and no mention is made of differentiation through age/shape.

Set 24:

117. **A-** Though the flowers smell pleasant, no mention is made of this scent being used to manufacture perfumes.
118. **C-** The passage states that the flower could bloom more than once a century, precluding 'D', but that it is thought to only do so in a century, providing evidence for 'C'.
119. **C-** The statement claims that Narcissus plants are 'prized by many' over Lilies, but this does not mean that all people - or even the majority of people - think the former is more attractive/better than the latter, or that all homeowners enjoy the plant.
120. **A-** It is actually a substance 'very similar to rum', not rum itself.
121. **C-** The genus 'belongs' to the family, as stated in paragraph 1.

Set 25:

122. **C-**Women in Illinois, not across USA, were subject to the law, and the passage does not state either a change in fashion or actual arrests, only the potential for arrests.
123. **D-** The pulling out of feathers from live birds was seen as the negative to using osprey feathers.
124. **B-** They could be possessed only 'in their proper season'.
125. **A-** The problem cited is that the article was already in use in the clothing of numerous military men. The authority of the princess/sexist politics does not feature in the passage, and 'D' is patently false
126. **D-** None of those are precluded, as only 'harmless' and 'dead' birds (in their entirety) were prohibited. Wearing a living bird was not explicitly banned.

Set 26:

127.**B-** Nothing in the above passage provides evidence for 'C', 'D' or 'A' - in fact, the 'indie' description of Pope opposes the idea of him working for a games company at all. 'B' is supported by the fact the game is available on a number of devices and system operators.

128.**C-** The immigration officer's job is to process people correctly - not to grow or limit the number of immigrants, as in 'A' and 'B'. 'D' is vague, as 'to stamp passports' does not necessarily mean to stamp them correctly, and false stamps would be counter to the purpose of the border guard's position.

129.**C-** Though the game player may perform either a body scan or finger print check when something is amiss is the candidate's documents, they will not necessarily do either of these - first, they will 'enquire', which is synonymous with 'C', 'asking...for further information'. The only one of the statements that will be universally true for discrepancies therefore is c.

130.**D-** The game-player may accept 'bribes', so 'A' is not true. The game player 'may' arrest candidates, but the passage does not state he or she must, so 'B' is false. The game-player is allowed two mistakes, so to an extent, can be forgiven - making 'C' incorrect. As further mistakes will lead to being 'pecuniarily punished', 'D' is the only accurate statement.

Set 27:

131.**C-** The head of LA NAACP is a civil rights' activist.

132.**D-** The other aspects may appear in films, but only racial slurs were cited as a 'common' element without specifying location of setting of sub-type.

133.**B-** 'Primarily' means the same as 'predominately' in this case, and the cast has been described as 'predominately' black - meaning most, but not all, cast members are black.

134.**C-** Original intended audiences were black city-dwellers: 'B' is too broad and 'A' is too narrow. 'D' is not at all supported in the passage. 'C' describes the growing audience, and how the genre is now 'not exclusive to any race' (Paragraph 2)

135.**C-** It is possible, but nothing in the statement suggests the potentially racy titles are a nod towards sexploitation genre. The innuendo may be incidental, or the choice of words completely divorced from the pornographic films of the past.

Set 28:

136.**C-** It would be a massive assumption to state that just because two characters in a book are 'vicious', all of them will be, so 'A' is not necessarily correct. 'B' also believes in a despair that is described to belong to the Comedian, but not Rorscach. The argument of the passage is that 'D', which Moore may believe, is not the case - the beloved character is not simply worshipped for his violence, but for his belief in justice. 'C' is correct, as Moore describes how he wished Rorschach not to be a favourite character, but a warning.

137.**B-** False. The fact he finds things a 'joke' is what makes him the Comedian. He may not be all that funny, but the joke is still there.

138.**B-** He does not mention madness ('D'), or invoke shame ('C'), or simply state it is good to be good ('A') - specifically, he states we must act as if the world is 'just', even when not, to attain dignity.

139.**D-** No value judgment is made comparing violent actions or on the Comedian's jokes so 'A' and 'B' are false. The passage also acknowledge Rorschach's violence, showing 'C' is wrong, but does state that his actions are due to the fact he believes he is acting in the name of justice, which lends him an ethical justification to his actions.

140.**D-** The lack of meaning in anything is what leads him to treat everything as a joke - it is not hatred, but the inability to see 'purpose' in himself or his fellow man.

Set 29:

141. **B**- The passage's explanation of The Bechdel Test does not state that the test is used to show 'sexism', so a failed film does not equate to a sexist one.

142. **C**- This is the only film that shows a female-female conversation not on a man. 'A' and 'B' only feature conversations focused on males and 'D' does not have two women speaking to one another.

143. **C**- Though of the two horror films mentioned in the extract one passes it and another one fails, the passage does not make use this to make any claims on the genre as a whole.

144. **C**- Her comment that it is 'strict' shows she has a reservation, but her general agreeing that it is a 'good idea' shows she approves of the notion. Her statement is too qualified to be described by 'A', too positive to be understood by 'B', and contains a judgement precluding 'C' as a correct statement.

145. **C**- The two women are not named within the comic strip - though two women are behind the idea (one in suggesting it, the other in illustrating it), that is not to say that the two depicted women are the same.

Set 30:

146. **C**- The possible 'idea' that repetition is funny is inherently funny is mentioned, but neither confirmed nor denied.

147. **A**- This is the only statement actually mentioned above. Laughing twice at the same joke does not make it 'twice as funny', that is a logical fallacy; it does not state that all relationships dictate that the two parties find themselves funny (this is too vague) and being 'comfortable' is not cited as encouraging laughter.

148. **C**- There is no mention of a humour requirement for the first joke.

149. **C**- Though the call-back here is described as a comic trope, this does not necessarily preclude the same device being used in something un-comic: in the same way word-play or alliteration can be used to achieve a multitude effects, not all humorous.

150. **B**- Though 'A' is a potential, it is not a requirement of the call back, and 'C' is not supported through the passage's material. At no point is the call-back named significant, compared to other tropes: it is simply one that the passage focuses on. It does however state that it can be used by a comedian, and used for comedy, so 'B' is correct.

Set 31:

151. **B**- She was the fourth, after Catherine, Mary and her namesake Harriet Elizabeth, who died as an infant.

152. **A**- He was a 'Rev', a reverend, and a 'divine'. She was born in the USA, not UK, and in the 19th century. Her town is said to be 'characteristic', and so not 'average'.

153. **A**- She is said to have 'veneration' in all who knew her.

154. **C**- It is only described as the 'most sad' and 'most tender' memory of her childhood, not her life. It is, however, described as 'the first memorable incident' and thus the earliest one of her life.

155. **C**- She wrote her Charles, so at least wrote one letter. The autobiography mentioned belonged to her brother, not her, and she had five brothers and sisters waiting for her when she was born, not only brothers. She was actually four when her mother died, as the narrator tells us, and her remembering being between 'three and four' is a false memory.

Set 32:

156. **B-** He thought it was 'a pity that only rich people could own books', and from this he 'finally determined to contrive' of a new way of printing. The passage does not state that he wished to make money, found books too expensive to get a hold of or was impatient himself when it came to the production of books.

157. **A-** The need to be careful is mentioned, as is the fact that the process takes a long time both in creating the block and due to the fact one block can only print one page. That it may tire a carver to make the block is possible, but it is not cited in the passage.

158. **D-** The statement says it is 'very likely' he was taught to read, but is not definite. That his father comes from a 'good family' does not mean he is a member of the aristocracy, necessarily. Though block printing was used as the boy grew up, it does not state this was the most popular process. The mention of Gutenberg's family's 'wealthy friends' indicates they were sociable.

159. **B-** The paper was laid on top of the block, not underneath.

160. **A-** There is nothing written in the passage praising the craftsmanship of manuscripts. The appropriateness of the titles for both book production processes is explained, and the 'wealthy friends' are described as a source to borrow books from, thus a way of expanding your reading.

Set 33:

161. **C-** In both examples given above, Apollo is the giver - but these are only two of 'several' versions, and it is possible others exist.

162. **C-** The gift of prophecy is supernatural, therefore this is the best answer. There is no evidence to suggest that she knew chastity would lead to her tragic fate, that she is 'often' seen as a home wrecker (though she is killed by Clytemnestra, this does not prove Cassandra, the slave, is perceived as a vindictive 'other woman') or that parents use the name to express hate – they may just like the sound, and not care about its history, or not know the history at all.

163. **B-** Nothing is said about the state of Cassandra's childhood, but it is mentioned that plays are written about her and that Homer has written about her, showing 'C' and 'D' are true. The fact her father was a king proves she was from a royal line.

164. **B-** The passage states the 'presentation of her character alters'.

165. **A-** It is not said that she ignores or refuses to accept the gift, or demands more presents, even in the first story, just that she refuses to sleep with him. Only the broken promise, as described in the second version of the myth, is mentioned above.

Set 34:

166. **D-** The passage attacks a generalisation, and shows an example that refutes one given to the 'musical' genre. Nothing is mentioned of Sondheim's talents, or what his role was in creating the musical, nor are their claims made to Wheeler's literary tastes (he may just like ONE penny dreadful). This musical may deal with morbid themes, but that's not to say that most do - it could be only a select few that do.

167. **A-** The pies make the crimes 'culinary' in nature, the mention of revenge shows Todd's illegal acts to be 'vengeful' and the judge's rape is a 'sexual' crime. There is nothing explicitly suggesting the crimes of any party are funny, or to be considered funny.

168. **C-** Though the original title 'A String of Pearls: A Romance' may appear to suggest a romantic relationship within the narrative, nothing in the passage states the two are a couple.

169. **D-** Is essentially synonymous is the quoted belief, 'we all deserve to die', which include both bad and good people and makes no significant reference to gender exclusion/inclusion.

170. C- There are four mentioned themes, but that does not mean there are only four themes, nor does 'legal corruption' get named as the central theme. As the entirety of Sweeney Todd is not discussed in the passage, only a central plot line, one could not exclude the potential of something positive happening in the play - even a minor incident. The themes mentioned are, however, indeed macabre.

Set 35:

171.**C**- The above passage is about WWII trains, not WWI ones.

172.**A**- The soldier makes a chair by using a tipped-up suitcase. It is a marine, not a sailor, learning on the back of a chair, and the passage states 'some', not 'many' queue for two hours to go to the diner car, whilst similarly 'some' (not necessarily 'many') go hungry.

173.**B**- The passage discourages mothers from going on trains with a baby, stating they should only do it as a necessity.

174.**A**- 'At every stop' more people come on the train.

175.**A**- The passage does not insult anyone, but it does say the railroads are doing their job 'well'.

Set 36:

176.**C** The passage states the slice of bread is an ounce, and contains 3/4 ounce of flour, making it 75% flour.

177.**B**- It says it is possible that they do, but also possible that they don't. There is no emphatic claim.

178.**C**- It is over a million loaves a day, 319 million pounds - not bushels - a year and 365,000 loaves - not over - a year.

179.**B**- False. It may seem unimportant, but the passage goes on to explain how a single slice of bread has value.

180.**D**- The government have researched waste, but not taken responsibility for it, nor is it said they should do more to combat this. The final sentence confirms that housekeepers are responsible for their own food wastage.

Set 37:

181.**C**- Fourteen women and three men are described to be arrested.

182.**C**- She was the only woman, but it does not state whether either man was brought to trial.

183.**B**- The majority ultimately rule, but Hall 'dissented', or disagreed, with the other two originally.

184.**A**- It is said that it was proved upon trial that she was informed of a right to vote and had no doubt over her entitlement at the time of voting.

185.**B**- They were charged independently.

Set 38:

186.**C**- Nowhere does it state that all European countries have similar creatures (though certain types can be found in both British Isles and Norway) nor does it state the array of animals is limited to this one nation. Sharing animals and birds does not necessitate sharing geographical features, but it is said a country with forest and moorlands is likely to have a variety of birds and animals, so one can see the link between forests and creatures.

187.**A**- There was a time when the English dreaded wolves and bears, but that indicates the past, or at least does not include the present. Norwegians being superior is not suggested here.

188.**C**- Bears are called destroyers, which is sufficient to conclude they cause damage.

189.**D**- They are ruthlessly hunted by farmers in country districts, but numerous only in the forest tracts in the Far North.

190.**A**- The word fortunately implies that it is good the wolves are no longer central. The children are under no threat, as the threat of wolves belongs to a bygone time, there is no mention of regret that such a time is gone and Norsemen are not demonstrated in the above passage to have respect for Nature, but instead they are said to interfere with it through hunting and driving wolves farther afield from their current homes.

Set 39:

191.**A-** They were seen as the 'friendly or hostile manifestation of some higher powers, demonical and Divine.' The 'manifestation' of the 'Divine' could be interpreted as a religious quality.

192.**C-** A small minority believe that dreams are not the dreamer's own psychical act, meaning the majority believe that they are.

193.**D-** There is incongruity between feelings and images, suggesting a lack of a logical link between the two. Waking thoughts are said to find some dreams repugnant, and though dreams are described as forgotten, that is not necessarily due to them being dull.

194.**A-** It asks can sense be made of each single dream.

195.**C-** A link between the psychical sleeping and waking self is suggested, but not definitively proved. Pre-scientific communities, according to the passage, had a hypothesis that left them with 'no uncertainty'. The 'origin of the dream' remains a question in Freud's writing that has been left without a satisfactory answer. That 'our reminiscences' may 'mutilate' a dream is mentioned, leaving 'C' the only statement with support from the passage.

Set 40:

196.**A-**"Most" requires over half by definition, and "most" of the people living in this area were the descendants of immigrants who moved to the country a "full century ago".

197.**B-** Hall only makes a claim for New England, not the entirety of America, being the descendants of 20,000 immigrants. The 'one million' figure comes from Franklin, not Hall. Less than 80,000 ("under" 80,000) people led to the population boom of one million. One million is over ten times (under) 80,000, so "b" is correct.

198.**C-** It is said to be "distinct" to older aristocracy "of the royal governor's courts". It is not similar to any European aristocracy. There is no specific reference to it not being a system based on lineage.

199.**C-** It says that these were the texts read by the most people, but that does not mean they were the most plentiful – other books may have outnumbered the bibles, even if they received fewer readers.

200.**B-** "A", "c" and "d" are cited in the passage (the journey took 'the better part of the year', it was 'hazardous' and 'expensive'), whereas 'B' is not referenced at all.

Quantitative Reasoning Answers

Question	Answer	Question	Answer	Question	Answer	Question	Answer
1	C	51	A	101	A	151	C
2	D	52	E	102	E	152	B
3	D	53	C	103	A	153	C
4	D	54	E	104	C	154	B
5	C	55	C	105	B	155	B
6	B	56	A	106	C	156	D
7	A	57	D	107	C	157	D
8	A	58	D	108	B	158	C
9	B	59	C	109	B	159	B
10	A	60	D	110	C	160	A
11	D	61	C	111	C	161	B
12	B	62	A	112	C	162	B
13	A	63	E	113	C	163	A
14	B	64	E	114	A	164	B
15	B	65	D	115	A	165	A
16	D	66	B	116	B	166	D
17	B	67	C	117	C	167	A
18	D	68	D	118	A	168	B
19	B	69	E	119	B	169	B
20	B	70	B	120	D	170	C
21	B	71	C	121	B	171	B
22	B	72	E	122	C	172	C
23	C	73	D	123	C	173	B
24	B	74	A	124	A	174	B
25	B	75	E	125	B	175	D
26	B	76	C	126	A	176	D
27	D	77	E	127	B	177	B
28	B	78	D	128	C	178	D
29	B	79	D	129	C	179	D
30	B	80	D	130	D	180	C
31	C	81	A	131	C	181	D
32	B	82	C	132	A	182	A
33	B	83	E	133	C	183	D
34	D	84	B	134	B	184	C
35	B	85	D	135	C	185	B
36	D	86	E	136	B	186	A
37	C	87	D	137	C	187	C
38	D	88	B	138	A	188	D
39	E	89	B	139	B	189	A
40	C	90	B	140	B	190	C
41	C	91	C	141	D	191	B
42	A	92	D	142	C	192	D
43	E	93	C	143	B	193	B
44	A	94	E	144	D	194	C
45	E	95	E	145	B	195	A
46	C	96	B	146	C	196	D
47	A	97	D	147	B	197	D
48	D	98	C	148	B	198	C
49	D	99	D	149	B	199	C
50	C	100	A	150	D	200	A

SET 1

Question 1: C
We can work out that the tax rates must fit in the following equation:
($50 x Food tax rate) + ($30 x Clothes tax rate) + $80 = $88. Only the tax rates in Casova fit correctly in this equation.

Question 2: D
To answer this question, we calculate how much the supplier will make for selling the items, by considering the tax rate in each state, and deducting it from the price accordingly.

Thus, in Bolovia, each year the supplier makes 250 x ($40/1.20 + $40/1.15 + $40/1.10 + $40/1.15) = $34,812 a year. In Asteria, each year the supplier makes 250 x ($40/1.10 + $40/1.15 + $40/1.10 + $40/1.15) = $35,572. (Note that in the case of an item being applicable to 2 tax rates, the higher rate will be charged. Thus, in Bolovia, imported clothes will be charged at the clothes tax rate of 15%, since this is higher than the imports rate.)
Thus, by moving to Asteria, the supplier will make $760 more each year. Therefore it will take 26.3 years to recover the purchase cost of $20,000.

Question 3: D
If John spends $88, he will spend £12 on tax. Thus, the tax rate is 12/88 = 13.6%.
If John shops in Asteria, the maximum tax rate he would have to pay is 10%; at Casova it would be 10%. If he spends at least $50 on food in Derivia, he pays no tax on it. Thus, he can spend a maximum of $38 on imported goods (at a maximum tax rate of 15%). This equates to a tax of $5.70 (not $12). Finally, if John spends $10 on imported goods in Bolovia – he would pay $0.50 in tax. Thus, he can spend up to $78 on clothes taxed at 15%. The tax on the clothes is therefore $11.70, giving $12.20 tax in total as the maximum. Since he pays $12 dollars tax, he shops in Bolovia.

Question 4: D
The sum of the basic prices is 100+30+10+100 = $240. Now the highest tax rate on the board is 20% (for imports to Asteria), thus the maximum tax is $240 x 1.20 = $288. However, this is impossible to attain (since if we bought everything in Asteria, the ham would be cheaper, as it is not imported and would only be taxed at the food rate). Therefore no option allows the overall price to be as high as $288, so this is the answer. Answer A) is possible if all products were bought in the state they are produced in. Answer C) is the correct answer if all products were bought in Asteria (and accounting for the reduced tax rate for the ham, which is not an import). Answer B) is possible if the ham was bought in Asteria, the caviar and orange juice were bought in Casova and the dress was bought in Bolovia.

SET 2

Question 5: C
Firstly, find the pressure it can withstand in Pascals: 200 pounds per square inch x 7,000 Pascals per pound per square inch = 1.4 million Pascals.
Then divide this by 1,000 Pa to get the depth the probe can withstand (we can see from the question that the pressure increases by 1,000 Pa for every metre depth increase):
1,400,000/1,000 = 1,400 metres into the ocean, which is 1.4 km.

Question 6: B
Calculate that the probe can drop 300,000 Pa/1,000 Pa per metre = 300 metres into the ocean before breaking.
Now rearrange the equation in the question, to make t the subject, as follows:
$2d = \sqrt{(t^3)}$
$(2d)^2 = t^3$
$t = \sqrt[3]{(2d)^2}$
Then substitute the depth into this supplied equation:
$t = \sqrt[3]{(2d)^2} = \sqrt[3]{(2 \times 300)^2} = 71$ seconds.

SET 3

Question 7: A

Calculate the amount of drug taken for each disease:

Black Trump Virus = 4 mg x 80 kg x 3 times a day x 28 days = 26.88 g

Swamp Fever = 3x80x1x7 = 1.68 g

Yellow Tick = 1x80x2x84 = 13.44 g

Red Rage = 5x80x2x21 = 16.80 g

At a quick glance, the swamp fever dosage is much lower than all the others – you can discount this and use that to save a little time if you need to.

Question 8: A

First calculate that Carol took 20.16 grams of the drug during the two courses for Yellow Tick, using the same method as for John, but using Carol's weight of 60kg. Therefore 20.16 grams (the amount left over) corresponds to the dosage for the unknown disease:

4x60x3x28 = 20.16 g, therefore the unknown disease was Black Trump Virus.

Question 9: B

The first time he takes 3 x 80 x 1 x 7 = 1.68 grams, and the second time he takes 4 x 110 x 3 x 28 = 36.96 grams. Thus the ratio is 1.68 : 36.96 = 1:22.

Question 10: A

By calculating the dose required in each of the cases, we see that the only one that is above 15.5 grams over 4 weeks is the dosage for Red Rage:

5 x 75 x 2 x 21 = 15.75 g – therefore Danny must be suffering from Red Rage.

Question 11:D

Heavier people need a higher dose. To find the maximum weight, we use the equation: 5 x weight x 2 x 21 = 10 g, where "weight" represents the maximum weight requiring a dosage of less than 10 g.

So the maximum weight to not need a dosage exceeding 10 g is = 10,000 mg/(21 days x 2 daily doses x 5 mg/kg) = 47.62 kg.

SET 4

Question 12: B

To solve this, divide the flour content by the overall mass. A quick inspection might show you that this is likely to be Madeira, which is confirmed by the calculation (250/825 = 0.3). Thus, 30% of the Madeira's total weight is flour, which is a higher percentage than for any other cake

Question 13: A

In this question, there must be one cake where: (2,600/mass of cake) = (625/mass of flour in cake). Thus, there is a number that both the mass of the cake and the mass of flour can be multiplied by, in order to get these numbers respectively.

We can see that if we multiply the mass of the sponge cake by 5, we get 2,600 g. Equally, if we multiply the mass of flour in the sponge cake recipe (125g) by 5, then we get 625 g. Thus, Sponge cake is the answer. No other cake recipe can be multiplied by a given number to get an overall weight of 2,600 g and 625 g of flour.

Question 14: B

We use 1.50+1.25+1.10+1 times the ingredients for one cake, so the wedding cake will use 4.85 times as much of the ingredients listed for one cakes. We can use this to find which of the possible answers can be the amount of sugar in the cake, i.e. the sugar called for in one recipe multiplied by 4.85.

The quickest way to do this is to divide each possible answer by 4.85, and see if the result matches the weight of sugar in any of the cakes. We see that 970 g/4.85 = 200 g, which is the amount of sugar in the chocolate cake. None of the other amounts are possible. Thus, B is the answer.

Question 15: B

A kilogram of flour costs 55 x 2/3 pence and we are using 0.25 kg, so 9.167 p worth of flour goes into a Madeira cake. For sugar, we have 0.175 kg x 70 p per kg = 12.25 p worth of sugar going into the cake. The ratio is thus 9.167:12.25 = approx 0.75:1 = 3:4

Question 16: D

As before, the flour costs: 55 p per 1.5 kg x 2/3 x 0.2 kg = 7.3 pence.
The milk costs: 44 p per kg x 150 g/1000 g per kg = 6.6 pence.
Thus the ratio is 7.3:6.6 = 1:0.9 = 10:9.

SET 5

Question 17: B

In total, 108 people out of the 200 tested have the disease; this is 108/200 = 0.54. Thus, the answer is 54%.

Question 18: D

As the infection rate is different for men and women, the infection rates must be calculated separately and combined:
(231,768 x 0.53 women x 0.63) + (231,768 x 0.47 men x 0.45) = 126,406 to the nearest whole person.

Question 19: B

There are 45 men and 63 women in the test group who have the Kryptos virus. Thus 15 of the men and 45 of the women have visited Atlantis. As we now know that 60 people have visited Atlantis, we can see that 108 – 60 = 48 have not visited. Now we simply calculate 48 as a percentage of 108. 48/108 = 0.44. Thus, 44% of people testing positive for the Virus in Test A have *not* visited Atlantis.

Question 20: B

We can see that 20/45 men testing positive in Test A have also tested positive in Test B, so we assume that the rest were false positives stemming from the inaccuracies of Test A. We are told to assume the same proportion of false positives in the women tested, so we simply apply this fraction to the number of women testing positive in Test A. Thus, we simply calculate 63 x (20/45) = 28. Thus, we expect that 28 women actually have Kryptos Virus.

Question 21: B

In total 108 people tested positive under test A, and 49 of these tested positive under test B (using the data given in the last question). Therefore the percentage of people positive in Test A also testing positive in Test B is 49 out of 108, which is 45.4%.

SET 6

Question 22: B

The cost of the plan is 190 + 600 + 140 = £930 per day

Question 23: C

Firstly we need to find the two options that save the most money, aside from the one already stated. The two best options are to send material from Plant A to Store 1, and material from plant B to store 2. We can see from the table that these 2 options will be £30 per day cheaper than sending from Plant A to store 2, and plant B to store 1 (as with the current business plan).

The new total cost is 100 + 180 + 450 = £730. Thus the saving is (930 – 730) = £200. £200 is 22% of £930, so the percentage saving is 22% (to the nearest whole number).

SET 7

Question 24: B
The shop sold 512 books outside of the visit event (sum of sales in the table), and 106 at the event. Thus the percentage at the event was 106/(512+106) = 17%.

Question 25: B
Firstly calculate the different revenues:
Non-fiction revenue = (12+30) x£10 = £420
Fiction revenue = (50+45+23+90+103+159) x£6 = £2,820
Then calculate the non-fiction percentage: 420/(2,820+420) = 13%.

Question 26: B
The weekly revenue is seven times the daily revenue.
Daily revenue from Fiction: (50+45+23+90+103+159) x£6 = £2,820.
Daily revenue from Non-fiction 2x(12+30) x£10 = £840.
Therefore weekly revenue is 7x(£28,20+£840) = £25,620.

Question 27: D
The shop's revenue is now £6 x (100+90+23+90+103+159) + £10 x (12+30) per day. This income equates to £3,810 per day and £26,670 per week.

Therefore the percentage difference is 26,670/25,620 = 1.04, giving a 4% increase on the previous week.

SET 8

Question 28: B
2 nights in Venice in a 3 star hotel, 1 room (the children are exempt) = 2x1x3 = 6 euros
2 nights in Rome in a 3 star hotel, 3 people paying (the child aged 9 is exempt)= 2x3x5 = 30 euros
2 nights in Padua in a 3 star hotel, 2 people paying (both children exempt) = 2x2x2 = 8 euros
2 nights in Siena in the high season, 3 paying (child aged 9 exempt) = 2x3x2 = 12 euros
So the entire cost is the sum of these costs = 6+30+8+12 = 56 euros.

Question 29: B
In Rome he pays 6 euros x 7 nights = 42 Euros. In Padua he pays 3 euros x 8 nights = 24 Euros. 42:24 = 7:4.

Question 30: B
A 3 star hotel in Venice for 2 days costs Alice 6 Euros. 3 days in a 4 star hotel in Padua costs 9 Euros. This is 50% more in Padua than in Venice.

Question 31: C
The maximum cost of tax in a 4 star hotel in Rome is 6 euros x 10 nights = 60 EUR. Up until this point it will always be cheaper in Padua. In Padua the cost for a 4 star hotel is 3 euros a night, therefore after 20 days the cost of the Padua hotel is equal to the cost of a stay of equivalent duration in Rome.

SET 9

Question 32: B
First find the wall length: 15m x 0.6 = 9m. Therefore, the area of the room is 9m x 9m = 81 m^2

Question 33: B
The area of the house is 100 + 4 + (10 x 20) + (3 x 10) + (15 x 15) + 81 = 640 m^2.
The area of the master bedroom is 225 m^2, so the percentage area is 225/640 = 35%.
Question 34: D
The extra wall that is needed is the amount to extend both walls plus the new end wall.

The 20m wall is extended to 25m, and it is of height 3m, thus 5 x 3 = 15 m^2 is required.
Then the same amount of wall is needed for the other side, thus 2 x 15 = 30 m^2.
Then the back wall must be rebuilt, size = 10m x 3m = 30 m^2.
Sum these areas to a total of 60 m^2.

Question 35: B
Builder 1 costs: (15 x 300) + 200 = £4,700
Builder 2 costs: (16 x 300) = £4,800.
Therefore the requested ratio is 47:48, which is 1:1.02, to 3 s.f.

SET 10

Question 36: D
200 SMSs are free, so he pays for 7. £5 monthly fee + 7 SMSs x £0.20 + 15 minutes x £0.20 = £9.40

Question 37: C
Plan A SMSs cost 10p each. Plan B minimum cost is £5 monthly fee, but then provides 200 free SMSs. 51 SMSs at £0.10 each cost £5.10, which is more than £5. Thus, sending 51 SMSs would be cheaper on Plan B (sending 50 would be the same price on each plan).

Question 38: D
To answer this question, work out the cost of each plan.
5 minutes x 30 days = 150 minutes. 150 minutes cost: 150 x £0.10 = £15 on Plan A, 150 x £0.20 = £30 on

Plan B, (150-100 free minutes) x £0.20 = £10 on Plan C and 150 x £0.00 = £0 on Plan D.
Including the monthly fee, the cost to call becomes A: £15, B: £35, C: £20 and D: £15. All SMSs cost on Plan A but not D, so D is cheapest.

Note that we did not have to calculate the cost of texts in order to get the answer. If you like, you could work out the cost of the SMSs on each plan too, but if you notice that after calculating the cost of calls and monthly fees Plan A and Plan D come out at the same price, it is apparent that Plan D will be cheaper as SMSs are free, and this will save time.

Question 39: E
They each send 223 SMSs and make no calls. Option E is cheaper for Evan than Chris: For Plan B (223 SMSs – 200 free SMSs) x £0.20 = £4.60, so with the £5 monthly fee the total cost is £9.60. For Plan C all 223 SMSs are within the free limit, but the monthly fee is £10, so Chris pays more.

In option A, Evan pays £10.80, whilst Chris pays just the £10 monthly fee.
In option B, Evan pays £10.20, whilst Chris still just pays the monthly fee of £10.
In option C, Evan pays £36.80, whilst Chris still pays only the monthly fee of £10 (this is the biggest saving Chris makes relative to Evan out of all the options).
In option D, Evan pays between £27.40 and £29.80, depending on which month (and whether there are 28, 30 or 31 days in it), whilst Chris pays between £12.40 and £14.80, again dependent on which month.

Question 40: C
100 minutes are free on Plan C. Plan D has unlimited minutes and costs £5 more than C per month. At 20p a minute, Rachel can call for 25 minutes for £5, so can exceed her free minutes by 25 %, at which point Plan D is the same price. If she exceeds the free minutes allowance by any more than this, then plan D would be cheaper.

SET 11

Question 41: C

4 tablespoons is 4 x 15 ml = 60 ml. 250 ml is 1 cup, so 4 tablespoons is 60 ml/250 ml = 0.24 cups. 2 cups + 1 cup + ½ cup + 0.24 cups = 3.74 cups.

Question 42: A

First calculate the weight of butter called for by the recipe:

4 tablespoons = 60 ml = 0.06 litres = 0.06 dm^3 (the question states that 1dm^3 = 1 litre).
Weight of butter: 950 grams/dm^3 x 0.06 dm^3 = 57 grams.

Next, calculate the weight of milk called for by the recipe:

½ cup = 1.25 dl = 0.125 litres = 0.125 dm^3.
Weight of milk: 1050 grams/dm^3 x 0.125 dm^3 = 131.25 grams.

Question 43: E

Any whole number multiple of flour, sugar or milk can be measured with a ½ cup.

4 tablespoons is 60 ml, ½ cup is 125 ml. The least common multiple of 60 and 125 is 1500, representing the smallest possible amount of butter that can be measured with half-cup measures.

1500 grams of butter makes 25 batches of muffins, which would require 25 x 2 cups = 50 cups of flour.
Thus, the weight ratio of Milk:Butter is 131.25/57:1 = 2.3:1.

Question 44: A

The recipe will have:

2 cups of milk = 500 ml = 0.5 dm^3
1 cup of sugar = 250 ml = 0.25 dm^3
½ cup of flour = 125 ml = 0.125 dm^3
4 tablespoons of butter = 60 ml = 0.06 dm^3.
Therefore the volume of the batter is 0.5 dm^3 + 0.25 dm^3 + 0.125 dm^3 + 0.06 dm^3 = 0.935 dm^3.

Now, to calculate the density of the batter, multiply the density of each ingredient by the proportion of the batter it makes up, then add up these figures, as follows:

(1050 grams/dm^3 milk x 0.5/0.935) + (850 grams/dm^3 sugar x 0.25/0.935) + (600 grams/dm^3 flour x 0.125/0.935) + (950 grams/dm^3 butter x 0.06/0.935) = 561.5 grams/dm^3 + 227.3 grams/dm^3 + 80.2 grams/dm^3 + 61.0 grams/dm^3 = 930 grams/dm^3

Question 45: E

10 muffins x 100 grams = 1,000 grams batter required.

The recipe calls for:

2 cups flour = 5 dl = 0.5 dm^3 flour. Weight of the flour is 0.5 dm^3 x 600 grams/dm^3 = 300 grams.
1 cup sugar = 2.5 dl = 0.25 dm^3 sugar. Weight of the sugar is 0.25 dm^3 x 850 grams/dm^3 = 212.5 grams.
From question 42 we remember that the weight of the milk as called for by the recipe is 131.25 grams and weight of the butter is 57 grams.

Thus the overall weight of the batter is 300 + 212.5 + 131.25 + 57 = 700.75 grams.
700.75/1,000 grams batter = 57/B grams butter, where B is the amount of butter required in 1,000g batter. B = 81.3 grams butter.

Question 46: C

700.75/1,000 grams batter = 300/F grams flour, where F is the amount of flour required to make 1,000 grams of muffin. F = 428.11 grams. 428.11 grams/1000 grams = 0.428 = 43 % to the nearest whole number.

SET 12

Question 47: A

The trend shows a 10 km^2 decrease in thickness for every 100 °C decrease in temperature. 10 km^2 thickness is 1,300 °C, so extrapolating the trend gives 0 km^2 thickness at 1,200 °C.

Question 48: D

Spreading rate is not affected by temperature, it is an independent variable. This question is designed to test your attention to detail and reinforce the importance of reading questions properly. Ensure you constantly pay attention to what the question is asking.

Question 49: D

Crustal volume per year = 20 km^2 crustal thickness x 20 mm/year spreading rate x 1 year = 20,000,000,000,000 mm^2 x 20 mm = 400,000,000,000,000 mm^3 = 400,000 m^3

Question 50: C

In answering this question, it is not necessary to use the same units for crustal thickness and spreading rate, as long as we use the same units for the crustal thickness *from both locations*, and likewise for the spreading rate.

Location A = 10 x 100 = 1,000. Location C = 30 x 150 = 4,500. A:C = 1:4,500/1,000 = 1:4.5

Question 51: A

Crustal volume per time = crustal thickness x spreading rate.
Crustal thickness at E is 10 km^2 and at F is 25 km^2.
Crustal volume per time is equal, so 10 km^2 x spreading rate E = 25 km^2 x spreading rate F. Therefore the spreading rate at E = 2.5 the spreading rate at F. Thus, it is 250 % faster.

Question 52: E

Temperature at D is 1,600 °C, decreased by 10 % it would be 1440 °C.
From the trend in temperature and crustal thickness this corresponds to a crustal thickness of 24 km^2.
Crustal volume per 3 years = 24 km^2 crustal thickness x 50 mm/year x 3 years = 24,000,000,000,000 mm^2 x 150 mm = 3,600,000,000,000,000 mm^3

SET 13

Question 53: C

A: 9/25, B: 6/23, C: 7/22, D: 8/24. (9+6+7+8)/(25+23+22+24) = 30/94 = 32 % to the nearest whole number.

Question 54: E

In Group A, drug-takers visual accuracy is 36%/27% = 33.33% improved.
In Group C, drug-takers visual accuracy is 31%/29% = 6.90% improved.
A:C = 33.33%/6.90%:1 = 4.83:1.

Question 55: C

10 women and 15 men have 45 % and unknown (P %) accuracy, respectively.
All 25 have an average of 36 % accuracy.
(10/25 x 45) + (15/25 x P) = 36.
P=30.

Question 56: A

Diabetics with vision problems correspond to Group A. In Group A, 15 of 25 volunteers reported better vision after taking the drug, but 9 of 25 volunteers taking a placebo also reported vision improvement. This suggests only 6 of 25 had reported improvements in their vision thanks to the effects of the drug.
6/25 x 100,000 people = 24,000 people.

Question 57: D

The placebo group showed no change, so only the volunteers being affected by the drug compound will see greater improvements to their vision.

15 – 9 = 6 volunteers affected by drug originally.

200% of the dose gave (18-9)/6 = 1.5 = 150 % the number of people with drug-related improvements.

300% of the dose will thus give 300 % / 200 % x 150 % = 225 % the number of people.

6 volunteers x 225% = 13.5 volunteers. (9+13.5)/25 volunteers = 22.5/25 volunteers = 90.0 % of volunteers.

Question 58: D

D is supported, because in all groups taking the placebo, there was an increase in accuracy with reading letters, suggesting better vision, and in many cases this was equivalent to the increase in those taking the drug.

The data suggest that A) and B) are incorrect. Only one group showed a higher increase in accuracy amongst the placebo group, in all other groups the people taking the drug had a larger % increase in accuracy. In healthy volunteers, there was as much of an increase in accuracy amongst those taking a placebo, suggesting the drug does not have as much of an effect in healthy volunteers. Options C) and E) are relatively meaningless statements which are not supported by the data.

SET 14

Question 59: C

5 calories x 200 pounds x 1 hour = 1000 calories running.

Cycling burns 50 calories + (5 calories x -5) for each mile = 25 calories per mile. Cycling 5 miles gives a total burn 125 calories, which is less than the amount burned running.

Thus, the maximum calorie burn comes from running, which will burn 1000 calories.

Question 60: D

Losing 10 pounds requires a 35 000 calorie deficit.

30 min run: 200 pounds x 0.5 hours x 5 calories = 500 calories.

20 mile cycle at 20 mph: 50 calories + (5 calories/mph x 10 mph) = 100 calories/mile for 20 miles = 2,000 calories. Daily burn is 2500 calories. 35,000/2,000 calories per day = 14 days taken to lose 10 pounds.

Question 61: C

Both their weight loss goal and calories burned running are linearly proportional to weight. Thus, they need to run for the same amount of time in order to achieve their goals.

Question 62: A

10% of 140 pounds is 14 pounds of weight, thus this is how much weight she wishes to lose.

At 3,500 calories/pound she needs a 14 pounds x 3500 calories/pound = 49,000 calorie deficit.

Her BMR is 1500 calories and she eats 400+500+250+200=1,350 calories per day, so her daily calorie deficit is 1,500 calories-1,350 calories = 150 calories.

It will take her 49 000 calories/150 calories per day = 326.67 days to reach her goal (327 to the nearest day).

Question 63: E

10 miles at 10 mph: 50 calories + (5 calories x 0 mph) = 50 calories/mile for 10 miles = 500 calories.

She requires a 49,000 calorie deficit, as worked out in the previous question. Previously she had a daily deficit of 150 calories, now she has a daily deficit of 650 calories. Thus, she now has a calorie deficit which is 4.33 times the previous deficit, so she will reach her goal 4.33 times faster.

Question 64: E

1 chocolate is the least she can eat, which means she eats 3 pieces of chicken and 6 bowls of cereal.

1x350 calories + 3x250 calories + 6x400 calories = 3,500 calories.

The lowest calorie arrangement of the 3 other foods is 1 lasagna, 3 vegetables and 6 apples.

1x700 calories + 3x200 calories + 6x100 calories = 1,900 calories.

She has a 3,500 calories per day – 1500 calorie BMR = 2,000 calorie surplus before and 400 calorie surplus after. 2,000 calories:400 calories = 5:1.

SET 15

Question 65: D

Price during day with single tickets is 4 coupons x £1 = £4.

Price at night with 10% off coupons is 3 coupons x £0.90 = £2.70.

Thus the saving is £1.30

Hence, the % saving is £1.30/£4.00 = 0.325 = 32.5 %.

Question 66: B

Price without a wristband is £1 per coupon x 120 % = £1.20 per coupon.

The number of coupons required is: 10 coupons entrance + 40 coupons for roller coaster + 6 coupons for candy floss + 1 coupon for the games + 4 coupons for the fun house + 3 coupons for the swings = 64 coupons.

64 coupons x £1.20 = £76.80.

Price with a wristband: £70 and 6 coupons for candy floss + 1 coupon for the games x £1.20 = £8.40. Thus the total price with a wristband is £78.40.

Therefore, the ratio is 1:£76.80/£78.40, which is 1:0.98.

Question 67: C

Andy rode the swings 20 % more times than he played games. The smallest number of times he could have gone on the swings is 6 times (since he can't have gone on the swings a non-integer number of times) so he played 5 games and went on the rollercoaster 9 times.

At night rates, rollercoaster 9 times x 3 coupons = 27 coupons and swings 6 times x 2 coupons = 12 coupons.

39 coupons at £1 each are worth £39, which is less than the £70 wristband.

If he had played 10 games, ridden the swings 12 times and rollercoaster 18 times, the wristband would have been more cost effective. This is the second cheapest possibility whilst still going on the swings an integer number of times (since 10 is the next multiple of 5). Thus, we know Andy must have played 5 games, been on the swings 6 times and the rollercoaster 9 times.

39 ride coupons + 5 game coupons + 5 entrance coupons = 49 coupons = £49.

Question 68: D

They got 69 coupons each for £69 pounds. They each must have spent 10 coupons at the entrance.

Together the roller coaster and fun house cost 6 coupons, so Anna took 59/6 = 9 rides on each and had 5 coupons left over, since the question states she went on each ride for *half* her rides, we assume she did not use any of the remaining coupons, since she could only have gone on one more ride, and thus it would not have been exactly half.

The fun house and swings cost 5 coupons together, so James took 59/5 = 11 rides on each and had 4 coupons left which he spent on 1 last ride on the swings.

Anna took 18 rides and James 23 rides. Anna: James = 1:23/18 = 1:1.28.

Question 69: E

First we calculate how much candyfloss Erik buys each weekend, using the 100% increase for the first 4 weeks, and the 50% increase thereafter as detailed in the question.

Week 1: 1, 2: 2, 3: 4, 4: 8, 5: 16, 6: 24, 7: 36, 8: 54, 9: 81, 10: 0. Thus, he bought a total of 226 lots of candy floss.

226 candy floss x 2 coupons x £1 pound each = £452.

Cost with season pass = £1000.
Cost without pass = £700 + £452 = £1,152.

SET 16

Question 70: B

2 x (£14.00 + £2.00 + 2x£2.00) + 1 x (£8.00 + 3x£1.00) + 3 x (£10.00) = £40.00 + £11.00 + £30.00 = £81.00.
50% off orders over £50 means he pays £81.00/2 = £40.50.
Ratio of cost Without:With is £1152/£1000:1 = 1.15:1.

Question 71: C

£35 is 50% of £70.
£70 buys £70/£14 = 5 large cheese pan pizzas.
Large pizzas have 10 slices: 10 slices x 5 pizzas = 50 slices.

Question 72: E

£60 is 50% off £120.
£120 is evenly divisible by all prices of plain cheese pizzas except the large pan. Dividing £120 by the price of the large pan gives 8.571. Since Joey cannot have bought a non-integer number of pizzas, he cannot have bought this type of pizza which costs £14.00.

Question 73: D

30 slices is 3 large pizzas or 5 small pizzas.
3 large pan pizzas with 2 toppings and stuffed crust cost: 3 x (£14.00 + (2x£2.00) + £2.00) = £60.00.
5 small pan pizzas with 2 toppings and stuffed crust cost: 5 x (£10.00 + 2x£0.50 + £1.00) = £60.00.
Large:Small ratio is 1:£60.00/£60.00 = 1:1.00

Question 74: A

The lowest price order over £31 is 2 small pizzas and 1 medium pizza costing £32 total. 30% off £32 = £22.40. They get 20 slices with this order, but we know that they got 25% more than they could eat. Thus, if we treat 20 slices as 125%, then 100% is the amount that they ate. 20/1.25 = 16, so this is the amount that they could eat.

SET 17

Question 75: E

1 hour at Job A = £10 starter - £5 travel + £10 per hour = £15.
1 hour at Job B = £5 starter - £0 travel + £15 per hour = £20.
1 hour at Job C = £5 starter - £10 travel + £20 per hour = £15.
A:B:C = £15:£20:£15 = 1:1.33:1.

Question 76: C

In her first 50 hours she worked 25 2-hour jobs: 25 x (£10 - £5 + 2x£10) = 25 x £25 = £625.
Her hourly wage was then increased to £10 + £5 = £15.

She then worked 4 1-hour jobs: 4 x (£10 - £5 + 1x£15) = 4 x £20 = £80.
Then she worked 1 4-hour job: 1 x (£10 - £5 + 4x£15) = 1 x £65 = £65.

Her total earnings were £625 + £80 + £65 = £770.00

Question 77: E

For Job A, for the first 50 hours she would earn £10 an hour. Thus, for the first 25 2-hour jobs she would earn 25 x (£10 - £5 +2x£10) = £625. After 50 hours, her hourly wage would increase to £15 an hour. Thus, for the second lot of 25 2-hour jobs she would earn 25 x (£10 - £5 + 2x£15) = £875. Thus, in total she would earn £1,750.

For Job B, for the 50 2-hour jobs, she would earn 50 x (£5 + 2x£15) = £1,750. She does not get the pay increase because she does not work any hours after the pay rise at 100 hours.

For Job C, for the 50 2-hour jobs, she would earn 50 x (£5 - £10 + 2x£20) = £1,750.

Thus, B and C are the same.

Question 78: D

Average job length for Job C is 4 hours.

1 4-hour job earns: £5 starter - £10 travel + 4x£20 per hour = £75 per job.

Maximum earnings £1250/£75 = 17 jobs.

17 jobs x 4 hours = 68 hours.

Question 79: D

Hourly wage has risen twice by £5 to £30 per hour (since it rises £5 for each 100 hours worked).

100 hours/4 hour jobs = 25 jobs.

For a 4 hour job she earns: £5 starter - £10 travel + 4x£30 per hour = £115 per job.

25 jobs x £115 per job = £2,875.

10% of £2,875 = £287.50. This is the amount she pays in income tax.

Question 80: D

Working 50 hours for Job B earns 50 times the hourly rate plus 50 times the fixed starter wage, as jobs average 1 hour in duration. Therefore the income = (50x£15) + (50x£5) = £1,000.00.

The extra 50 hours can be worked at either Job A, B or C (note that Jobs A and B have travel expenses).

The same calculation for Job A gives (10x50) + (10 x 25) – (5x25) = £625.00.

The same calculation for Job C gives (50x20) + (5x12.5) – (10x12.5) = £937.50.

Therefore she earns most by working 100 hours for Job B.

SET 18

Question 81: A

Monday has the 2nd highest number of passengers, so this will be the 2nd highest grossing day. On Monday the revenue is £5 x 2346 underground passengers = £11,730.00.

On Wednesday the revenue is 3,103 x 0.85 x £5 = £1,3187.75. £13,187.75 - £11,730.00 = £1,457.75

Question 82: C

Total number of weekday underground passengers = 2346 +1798 +3103 + 2118 + 1397 = 10,762

Total number of weekday car passengers = total passengers – number of drivers =

Monday: 1873-1517=356

Tusesday: 2421-1632=789

Wednesday: 1116-987=129

Thursday: 2101-1465=636

Friday: 2822-2024 =798

356+789+129+636+798 = 2708

The average ratio is 10,762 : 2,708 = 1:3.97

Question 83: E
Tuesday: 2,421/1,632= 1.48
Weekend: 1,339/478= 2.80.
Ratio of Tuesday to Saturday = 1.48/2.8 = 1:1.89

Question 84: B
This is straightforward: 2,346/576 = 4.07:1 = 1:0.25

Question 85: D
There are 4,219 commuters each day (as seen by adding the total car passengers and underground passengers on any given day). For every 1 car there are 1.7 passengers and 2 underground riders. Thus, by dividing 1.7 by 3.7 and multiplying this by the total number of passengers (4219), we can calculate how many people are in cars: 1.7/3.7 x 4,219 = 1,938 people drive (to the nearest whole number, obviously there cannot be a non-integer number of people driving).
Now, by dividing the number of people driving (1938) by the number of passengers, we can calculate the number of cars: 1938/1.7 = 1,140 cars.
1,140 cars x £4 = £4,560. £4,560 + 1,938x£1 = £6,498. 80% of £6,498 is £5,198.40.

SET 19

Question 86: E
First calculate the Superior room cost at night: 3hrs x £26.00/hr = £78.00
Now add 10%: £78 x 1.1 = £85.80

Question 87: D
Total cost minus deposit = 12hrs x £30/hr = £360
Deposit = £460 - £360 = £100

Question 88: B
Total deposit = £10 + £25 = £35
6hrs in Standard room = 6hrs x £18/hr = £108
6hrs in Basic Room = £221 – (£108 + £35) = £78
Basic room hourly rate (2-6hrs) = £78 ÷ 6hrs = £13/hr

Question 89: B
1.5hrs in Superior room (night session) = 1.5hrs x £30/hr = £45
Decreased by 5% = £45 x 0.95 = £42.75
Total cost = £50 deposit + £42.75 = £92.75

Question 90: B
Basic room all day cost = 18hrs x £8/hr = £144
All week = 7 days x £144 = £1,008
Three weeks = £1,008 x 3 = £3,024
Deducting the VAT = £3,024/1.25 = £2,419.20

SET 20

Question 91: C
Total number of people aged under 22 = sum of first two columns = 62
Number aged <22 who spotted >10 differences = 11 + 8 + 3 + 2 = 24
Percentage = 24/62 = 38.7%

Question 92: D
Valid results for 5-10 spots for ages 16-22 = 0.25 x 12 = 3
Total number of valid results for 16-22 = 10 + 3 + 8 + 2 = 23
Percentage of over 15 spots for 16-22 = 2 ÷ 23 = 8.7%

Question 93: C
Total who spotted over 10 = sum of bottom two rows = 52
25% of 52 = 13

Question 94: E
Total 48+ who spotted <5 = 15 + 19 = 34
Total aged 48+ = sum of final two columns = 66
Percentage of 48+ who spotted <5 = 34 ÷ 66 = 52% (2 s.f.)
52% of 10,000 = 0.52 x 10,000 = 5,200

Question 95: E
50% increase in 16-34s who spot 11-15 = 1.5 x (8 + 6) = 21
New total who spot 11-15 = 11 + 21 + 2 + 8 + 9 = 51
Ratio = 21:51

SET 21

Question 96: B
Number that play Football = 22% of 1300 = 286
Number that play Hockey = 8 % of 1300 = 104
Thus, the difference = 286-104 = 182 Boys + Girls; Therefore, 182/2 = 91 Boys

Question 97: D
22% of 350 = 77 students
77 ÷ 11 people per team = 7 teams

Question 98: C
Number of basketball boys = 0.05 x 1,300 = 65
80% of 65 = 52
Number of netball girls = 0.08 x1, 300 = 104
Total number of netball-players = 104 + 52 = 156
Male proportion = 52 ÷ 156 = 33% (2 s.f.)

Question 99: D
Number of *Other* students = 0.12 x 1,300 = 156
Other ball sports = 0.25 x 156 = 39
Total non-ball sports (swimming & athletics) = (0.06 + 0.03) x 1300 = 117
Total "other" non ball sports = 156 – 39 = 117
Total ball sports = 1,300 – 117 – 117 = 1,066

Question 100: A
Girls who play hockey = 0.07 x 1,300 = 91
Boys who play cricket = 0.1 x 1,300 = 130
Difference = 39. *Note the tennis info makes no difference (50:50 split)*

SET 22

Question 101: A
Total apples processed in 1998 = 1,100,547 + 2,983,411 = 4,083,958
Total apples processed in 2003 = 1,931,784 + 2,439,012 = 4,370,796
Ratio = 4,370,796 ÷ 4,083,958 = 1.07 (i.e. 7% increase)

Question 102: E
Number of No Goods in worst year = 571,221
Total number of No Goods = sum of bottom row = 2,823,732
Percentage = 571,221 ÷ 2,823,732 = 20.2% (3 s.f.)

Question 103: A
2004 total No Goods = 3 x 571,221 = 1,713,663
70% of edible apples are processed, as are all passable apples.
Difference = (0.7 x 1,931,784 + 2,439,012) – 1,713,663 = 2,077,598

Question 104: C
Total number of edibles 1998-2003 = sum of top row = 9,201,790
20% increase = 1.2 x 9,201,790 = 11,042,148
30% of these are sold as they come = 0.3 x 11,042,148 = 3,312,644

Question 105: B
Apples processed for cider = (1,931,784 x 0.7) + 2,439,012 = 3,791,260.8
Litres of cider = 3,791,260.80 ÷ 20 = 189,600 litres (4 s.f.)

SET 23

Question 106: C
Decreased average speed = 0.92 x 5 mph = 4.6 mph
Miles covered = 4.6 x (40 ÷ 60) = 3.07 miles
Km covered = 1.6 x 3.07 miles = 4.9 km

Question 107: C
Distance per session = 26 miles ÷ 4 = 6.5 miles
Time per session = 6.5 miles ÷ 5 mph = 1.3 hrs = 1hr 18mins

Question 108: B
New wet average speed = 0.92 x 4.6 mph = 4.232 mph
12 km in miles = 12 km ÷ 1.6 = 7.5 miles
Time taken = 7.5 miles ÷ 4.232 mph = 1.77 hrs = 1hr 46mins

Question 109: B
Distance of second jog = 4 km x 1.5 = 6 km
Distance of third jog = 6 km x 1.5 = 9 km
Distance of last jog = 9 km x 1.5 = 13.5 km
13.5 km in miles = 13.5 km ÷ 1.6 = 8.4375 miles
Time = 8.4375 miles ÷ 5 mph = 1.69 hrs = 1hr 41mins

Question 110: C
3hrs 42mins = 3.7 hrs
Average speed = 26 miles ÷ 3.7 hrs = 7.027 mph
7.027 mph ÷ 5 mph = 1.405 (i.e. 41% increase)

SET 24

Question 111: C
Standard price = (£325 + £100) ÷ 2 = £212.50
For two people for one week = £212.50 x 2 = £425
Deducting 20% due to discount = 0.8 x £425 = £340

Question 112: C
Four weeks rent per person = 4 x £480 = £1,920
Total group rent = 12 x £1,920 = £23,040
Booking fee per person = 0.1 x £480 = £48
Total booking fee = 12 x £48 = £576
Total cost = £23,040 + £576 = £23,616

Question 113: C
One person for 10 days = £80 x (20÷7) = £228.57
Two people for 10 days = 2 x £228.57 = £457.14
Booking fee = £492.89 - £457.14 = £35.75

Question 114: A
Total rent = £220 x 2 weeks x 4 people = £1,760
Total discount = £1,760 x 0.2 = £352
Total cost = £1,760 - £352 = £1,408

Question 115: A
Booking fee = 0.1 x £19,500 = £1,950
Total rental charge = £19,500 - £1,950 = £17,550
Number of people = £17,550 ÷ £325 = 54
Number in each palazzo = 54 ÷ 3 = 18 people.

SET 25

Question 116: B
The price of the food is £3.95 + £2.95 + £3.95 = £10.85. Orders between £10 and £15 are charged £1.50 for delivery. Including delivery, the cost is £12.35. We then add 20%, so multiply this by 1.2. Hence the cost of the takeaway is £14.82.

Question 117: C
The total price is (3 x £2.95) + (2 x £4.95) + £3.95 = £22.70. Delivery is free above £15. We then add 20%, hence the total cost is £27.24.
A promotional offer is introduced whereby customers receive a 10% discount for orders over £9 (not including delivery).

Question 118: A
The total price is (2 x £2.95) + £3.95 = £9.85
Add £3 for delivery under £10: 9.85 + 3 = 11.865
Add 20% for VAT: 11.865 x 1.2 = £15.42

Question 119: B
The total is £3.95 + (3 x £2.95) + £3.95 = £16.75
Delivery is free over £15. We then add 20% for VAT: 16.75 x 1.2 = £20.10

Question 120: D
The total price is (2 x £2.95) + (2 x £4.95) + £3.95 = £19.75 (price of only two noodles because of offer)
Delivery is free over £15. We then add 20% for VAT: 19.75 x 1.2 = £23.70

SET 26

Question 121: B

Divide the profits earned by MediCo by the total profits earned by all suppliers: (15,000 + 30,000 + 25,000 + 35,000) = £105,000. 30,000/105,000 = 28.6%.

Question 122: C

Divide the profits earned by MediCo and Lifecare combined by the total profits earned by all suppliers: (15,000 + 30,000 + 25,000 + 35,000) = £105000. (30,000 + 35,000)/105,000 = 61.9%.

Question 123: C

Increase the profit of PillPlus by 15% and use this value when calculating the new total profit earned by all suppliers: 25,000 x 1.15 = 28,750. 28,750/(15,000 + 30,000 + 28,750 + 35,000) = 26.4%.

Question 124: A

As all profits across suppliers decrease by an equal amount, this is irrelevant and cancels in the division. 0.9(35,000 + 15,000)/0.9(35,000 + 28,750 + 30,000 + 15,000) = 46%.

Question 125: B

Take account of the first fall in profits of 10% and then a further fall of 5%: (15,000 + 35,000) x 0.9 x 0.95 = £42,750.

SET 27

Question 126: A

The total value for the Stuntman is £12500 + £345 + £145 + £295 = £13,285.
Adding 20% VAT, this is £13,285 x 1.2 = £15,942.

Question 127: B

Remember to include tax in all calculations:
Saloon: (£21500 + £495 + £245 + £445) = £22,685. £22,685 x 1.2 = £27,222.
Pod: (£18000 + £445 + £395 + £495) = £19335. £19335 x 1.2 = £23,202.
£27,222 - £23,202 = £4020

Question 128: C

Racer: (£15,000 x 1.2) = £18,000.
Stuntman: (£12500 + £345 + £145 + £295) = £13,285. £13,285 x 1.2 = £15,942.
£18,000 - £15,942 = £2,058

Question 129: C

The Pod with no optional extras is £18000 x 1.2 = £21,600.
The Racer with all optional extras with a 10% discount is (£15000 + £395 + £195 + £395) x 0.9 x 1.2 = £17,263.80.
£21,600 - £17263.80 = £4,336.20

Question 130: D

Saloon with leather seats and easy-park technology = £21500 + £495 + £445 = £22440.
Add 20% = £22,440 x 1.2 = £26,928. Reduced by 20% = £26928 x 0.8 = £21,542.40.
Pod = £18,000 x 1.2 = £21600.
£21,600 - £21,542.40 = £57.60

SET 28

Question 131: C
Emissions increased by 1,000 tonnes from 1,000 to 2,000 tonnes over 5 years, therefore the rate of increase was 200 tonnes per year

Question 132: A
If there had been no crash, 2,010 emissions would have been 3,000 Tonnes, as calculated by applying an increase in emissions of 200 Tonnes/year from 2005 to 2010.
With the economic crash, 2010 emissions were 2500 Tonnes:
3,000 – 2,500 = 500 Tonnes less in 2010 due to the economic crash.

Question 133: C
Percentage increase = (new amount – old amount)/old amount x 100
= (3,000–2,000)/2,000 x 100 = 50%.
Note that you are asked for the percentage INCREASE. (New amount/old amount) x100 = percentage CHANGE.

Question 134: B
2015 – 2020 the amount would increase from 3,000 tonnes to 3,500 tonnes without any action. This equates to a rate of increase of 100 tonnes per year. With the new act, this is reduced by 50% to 50 tonnes per year, thus over 5 years: Overall saving = 50 x 5 = 250 Tonnes

Question 135: C
The emissions in 2020 = projected – rate reduction (50% of the difference between projected total and current total). Rate reduction = 50 tonnes per year. Projected rate = current emissions (3,000 tonnes) + projected increase without the act (5 x 100, which is 500).
= (3,000+500) – (5 x 50) = 3250 Tonnes

SET 29

Question 136: B
For between 10 and 100 units, single sided black and white printing costs £0.07 per page. 74 x 7p = £5.18.

Question 137: C
£100 will clearly buy more than 100 sheets as all prices are under £1, therefore use the 100+ price:
The price for double sided colour printing over 100 sheets is £0.25.
£100/0.25 = 400 sheets

Question 138: A
For over 100 sheets of double sided black and white, the cost per sheet is £0.10 each. Hence the total non-discounted price for 150 sheets is 150 x £0.10 = £15. If this is discounted by 10%, this is £15 x 0.9 = £13.50.

Question 139: B
Price for buying separately = 150 x 0.15 = £22.50
Price buying together = 150 x 0.10 x 0.9 (discount) = £13.50
Difference = £9
Number of sheets could buy with £9 = 9/0.15 = 60 sheets

Question 140: B
The price for 227 sheets of double sided black and white printing is £0.10 each, so the total is £22.70.
The price for 34 sheets of double sided colour printing is £0.30 each, so the total is £10.20.
The total for all the sheets is £32.90.
If this is discounted by 10%, this is £32.90 x 0.9 = £29.61.

SET 30

Question 141: D
We can calculate the number of people who reacted positively in each group and then add up the total:
75% of 300 is 225
65% of 300 is 195
70% of 300 is 210
55% of 300 is 165
225 + 195 + 210 + 165 = 795

Question 142: C
In group 2, 30% reacted negatively: 30% of 300 is 90.
In group 3, 15% reacted negatively: 15% of 300 is 45.
Therefore the difference is 45; 45 more people in group 2 reacted negatively than people in group 3.

Question 143: B
We can calculate the number of people who reacted negatively in each group and then add up the total:
20% of 300 is 60
30% of 300 is 90
15% of 300 is 45
25% of 300 is 75
60 + 90 + 45 + 75 = 270
270 as a percentage of the total, 1200, is 22.5%, which rounds to 23%.

Question 144: D
The overall success rate of the first four groups was = (75 + 65 + 70 + 55)/4 = 66.25%
Therefore increase in success rate = 82/66.25 = 23.77% increase.

Question 145: B
In the answer to question 143 we calculated that in the first 4 groups, 270 people reacted negatively. In group 5, 15% of 300 people, which is 45 people, reacted negatively. Hence the negative reactions total 315 people.

SET 31

Question 146: C
The total number of views of The Last Chase is 20,000 + 20,000 + 15,000 + 20,000 = 75,000.
The total number of views of The Final Frontier is 15,000 + 20,000 + 25,000 + 35,000 = 95,000.
Hence the difference is 95,000 – 75,000 = 20,000

Question 147: B
The difference in viewers is 20,000. If £2,500 is earned per 1,000 viewers, then the difference in advertising revenue will be £2,500 x 20 = £50,000.

Question 148: B
Growth rate is 5,000 per quarter between Q1 and Q3 of 2014. Therefore the total growth during 2015:
35,000 + (5,000 x 4) = 55,000

Question 149: B

Growth rate is 5,000 per quarter between Q1 and Q3 of 2014. Therefore the total growth during 2015:

Q1: 35,000 + 5,000 = 40,000

Q2: 40,000 + 5,000 = 45,000

Q3: 45,000 + 5,000 = 50,000

Q4: 50,000 + 5,000 = 55,000

Thus, the total number of views = 40,000 + 45,000 + 50,000 + 55,000 = 190,000.

Question 150: D

Without the show cancellation, there are 35,000 Final Frontier views and 20,000 Last Chase views. With the cancellation, half of the Last Chase views transfer over to Final Frontier, this equates to 10,000 views. Therefore the Final Frontier now has 45,000 views in this scenario.

SET 32

Question 151: C

55% + 25% = 80% of Scottish patients wait less than half an hour. 80% of 50,000 patients = 40,000, therefore 40,000 patients waited for less than half an hour for an appointment.

Question 152: B

We can work out how many patients had to wait more than half an hour for an appointment in each part of the UK then find the total:

In England, 10% of 100,000 patients = 10,000 patients had to wait longer than half an hour.

In Scotland, 20% of 50,000 patients = 10,000 patients had to wait longer than half an hour.

In Wales, 25% of 25,000 patients = 6,250 patients had to wait longer than half an hour.

In Northern Ireland, 15% of 25,000 patients = 3,750 patients had to wait longer than half an hour.

The total number of patients that had to wait longer than half an hour is 10,000 + 10,000 + 6,250 + 3,750 = 30,000.

30,000/200,000 = 15%

Question 153: C

In the previous question we found that 30,000 patients had to wait longer than half an hour, so 40% of 30,000 people complained = 12,000.

In England, 30% of 100,000 patients = 30,000 patients had to wait 11-30 minutes.

In Scotland, 25% of 50,000 patients = 12,500 patients had to wait 11-30 minutes.

In Wales, 25% of 25,000 patients = 6,250 patients had to wait had to wait 11-30 minutes.

In Northern Ireland, 25% of 25,000 patients = 6,250 patients had to wait 11-30 minutes.

The total number of patients that had to wait 11-30 minutes is 30,000 + 12,500 + 6,250 + 6,250 = 55,000.

If 20% of 55,000 patients complain, this is 11,000.

Hence the total number of complaints is 11,000 + 12,000 = 23,000.

Question 154: B

Use the total survey size to calculate the proportion: 23,000/200,000 = 11.5%.

Question 155: B

We worked out in question 153 that 30,000 people had to wait longer than 30 minutes and 55,000 people had to wait between 11 and 30 minutes. If the targets are met, 15,000 people will have to wait longer than 30 minutes and 41,250 will have to wait between 11 and 30 minutes. If 20% of these 41,250 people complain, this is 8,250 complaints. If 40% of the 15,000 people complain this is 6,000 complaints. Hence there are a total of 14,250 complaints. The previous number of complaints was 23,000, hence the percentage decrease is (23,000-14,250)/23,000 = 0.38 = 38%.

SET 33

Question 156: D

The decrease in the price of crude oil between January and March is $150-$100 = $50, as can be seen in the graph. This fall has occurred over a 2-month period, giving a decrease in price of $25 per month.

Question 157: D

This is a question of estimation. The average production across the year is at least 7 million barrels per day. Multiplying this by 365 gives around 2,550 million barrels per year. All other options require less than 7 million barrels daily production, and it is clear there are at least 7 million barrels per day. Therefore the answer is 2,700 million.

Alternatively, we can estimate using 30 days per month, and multiplying the amount of barrels produced per day in each month by 30 (this is more accurate but more time consuming). 6+7+7+7.5+7.5+7+7.5+8+8.5+8.5+8+9 = 91.5, multiplying by 30 gives just over 2,700 million barrels per year.

Question 158: C

Use both graphs. For July, multiply the oil price by the amount sold in the month, and then multiply by the number of days in the month.
July = 7.5 million barrels x $75 per barrel x 31 days = $17,400 million = $17.4 billion

Question 159: B

If the costs are 40%, the gross profit is 60%.
Oil sales in June 2014 totalled 7 million barrels x $100 per barrel x 30 days = £21,000 million = $21 billion.
Therefore gross profit was 0.6 x $21 billion = $12.6 billion.

Question 160: A

You are given the total sales value of $204 billion, so work with this. Work clearly in stages and this question is not hard.
The profit is 60% of this, which is $122.4 billion.
This is split 5:2 between the oil companies and the oil-producing nation. Thus, the profit for the oil companies is 5/7 of $122.4 billion is profit for the oil companies, which is $87.43 billion.
Corporation tax is then 30% of this profit, which is $26.23 billion.

SET 34

Question 161: B

Calculate the total people with no asthma, then take it away from the total number of people which is 250:
80% of the 50 people aged 0-5 have no asthma, which is 40.
75% of the 50 people aged 5-10 have no asthma, which is 37.5.
85% of the people aged 10-21 have no asthma, which is 42.5.
95% of the people aged 21-30 have no asthma, which is 47.5.
95% of the people aged 30+ have no asthma, which is 47.5.
Hence the total people who have no asthma is 215.
Hence the total people with asthma is 250 – 215 = 35.

Question 162: B

Of children aged 0-5, 15% have mild asthma which is 7.5. Hence 3.75 will develop respiratory problems.
Of children aged 0-5, 5% have severe asthma which is 2.5. Hence 2.25 will develop respiratory problems.
Of children aged 5-10, 20% have mild asthma which is 10. Hence 5 will develop respiratory problems.
Of children aged 5-10, 5% have severe asthma which is 2.5. Hence 2.25 will develop respiratory problems.
Hence 13.25 children per 100 will develop respiratory problems, so the answer is 13.25%.

Question 163: A

(15%+20%)/2 = 17.5% diagnosed. 17.5% x 0.35 = 6.125% Incorrect diagnoses.

Question 164: B

Taking into account that only 65% of children diagnosed with mild asthma were diagnosed correctly:
17.5% diagnosed (mild) ➔ 11.375% correctly diagnosed ➔ 5.69% complications
5% diagnosed (severe) ➔ 4.5% complications (all are correct diagnoses)
Therefore 5.69 + 4.5 = 10% overall respiratory complication rate.

Question 165: A

False diagnoses: (0.15x0.35x0.07x50,000,000) 0-5 year olds + (0.2x0.35x0.1x50,000,000) 5-10 year olds = 533,750
Cost per diagnosis: £50 per year = £250 over 5 years
Total money wasted: 533,750 x £250 = £133 million

SET 35

Question 166: D

Total value of company A = (price per share x number of shares) = £60 x 10 million = £600 million
Government holding = 75% of 600 million = £450 million
Disinvestment (50%) = 0.5 x 450 = £225 million
Hence £225 million is raised from the disinvestment.

Question 167: A

Total value of company B = (price per share x number of shares) = £20 x 50 million = 1,000 million
Government holding = 50% of 1,000 Million = £500 million
Disinvestment (25%) = 0.25 x 500 = £125 million

Question 168: B

Government holds 1/3 of the 30 million shares, which is 10 million shares.
It sold each share for £35, £5 less than the £40 market price. Hence the additional revenue for selling at the market price would have been £5 per share x 10 million shares = £50 million.

Question 169: B

Government holds 25% of 40 million shares, which is 10 million shares.
The price of each share fell from £30 to £35, so fell by £5 per share.
If the price of 10 million shares fell by £5, the total fall was £50 million.

Question 170: C

Government holds 12.5% of 50 million shares, which is 6.25 million.
The price has risen by £5 per share, so the total rise is £31.25 million.

Question 171: B

Total value of option A = £10 x 60 million x 75% = £450 Million
Total value of option B = £20 x 50 million x 50% = £500 Million
Hence they will fetch difference values, with B fetching more.

SET 36

Question 172: C
In 2011-2012, food grain production was 100, and this was a 25% increase on 2010-2011.
If 100 is 125%, then 100% = 80. Hence food production in tonnes in 2010-2011 was 80 tonnes.

Question 173: B
Target production (2011-12) = 60 tonnes
Actual production (2010-11) = 50/125% = 40 tonnes
Difference = 60 - 40 = 20 tonnes

Question 174: B
Difference = Target - Actual = 50 - 40 = 10 tonnes

Question 175: D
Cotton production (2010-11) = 30/120% = 25 tonnes
Jute production (2010-11) = 20/125% = 16 tonnes
Combined = 25 + 16 = 41 tonnes

Question 176: D
Food grain production (2010-11) = 100/125% = 80 tonnes
Oil seeds production (2010-11) = 50/125% = 40 tonnes
Difference = 80 - 40 = 40 tonnes

Question 177: B
Total production (2011-12) = 100+50+40+30+20 = 240 tonnes
Cotton as a percentage of total = 30/240 = 12.5%

SET 37

Question 178: D
Sales of product B in Feb = 7,000
Total sales of all products in Feb = 10,250 + 7,000 + 3,750 + 3100 = 24,100
Percentage of product B's sales = 7,000/24,100 = 29%

Question 179: D
Percentage increase:
Product A = (11,000-10,500)/10,500 = 4.76%
Product B = (7,500-7,250)/7,250 = 3.45%
Product C = (4,250-4,000)/4,000 = 6.25%
Product D = (4,000-3,500)/3,500 = 14.29%

Hence product D witnessed highest percentage growth.

However to answer this question more quickly, look at the numbers – the numbers are giving you a clue. You can visually see that product D's sales' values have gone up the equal maximum amount of £500. But it is also apparent that the absolute value of sales is the lowest, therefore you can deduce that D is the largest percentage increase without actually doing any sums!

SECTION 2: QUANTITATIVE REASONING   **ANSWERS**

Question 180: C
Sales of product C in May = 4,250 x 1.2 = 5,100
Therefore sales of product D in May = 5,100
Percentage increase in sales of D from April to May = (5,100 – 4,000)/4,000 = 27.5%

Question 181: D
Sale of products (A+C) in January = 13,000
Sale of products (A+C) in April = 15,250
Percentage increase in combined sale from January to April = (15,250 – 13,000)/13,000 = 17.31%

Question 182: A
Sale of product (A+B) in May = 1.2 x (11,000+75,00) = 22,200
Sale of product (C+D) in May = 1.3 x (4,250+4,000) = 10,725
Total sales in May = 32925

Question 183: D
Sale of product A in May = 1.2 x 11,000 = 13,200
Sale of product (B+C+D) in May = 1.1 x (7,500+4,250+4,000) = 173,25
Total sales in May = 13,200+17,325 = 30,525
Percentage of sales of A over total sales = 13,200/30,525 = 43.24%

SET 38

Question 184: C
Overall profit is 30% of revenue. Since profit = £2.5 million, overall revenue = 2.5/30 x 100 = £8.3 Million

Question 185: B
Let us assume cost per article = C; Total number of articles = N
Cost per consignment:
Rail = 25C/30N = 0.83C/N
Road = 25C/45N = 0.56C/N
Air = 50C/25N = 2C/N
Hence road has the lowest cost per consignment.
However if you look at the figures, a shortcut is apparent. Road occupies by far the greatest number of consignments, but the cost is the equal lowest in the business. Therefore at a glance you can see the answer is road, even before you open the calculator and start doing unnecessary sums.

Question 186: A
The ratio will be the same for any number of consignments as the proportions are preserved.
Ratio of total revenue to total cost = £20:£5 = 4:1

Question 187: C
From the table it is given that 50% of the total costs are associated with air transportation, so 50% of the total costs are due to air travel.
50% x £54,000 = £27,000

Question 188: D
From the table it is given that 30% are delivered by rail and 45% by road, so 75% of consignments are delivered by rail and road taken together.
75% x 17,145 = 12,859

SET 39

Question 189: A

Set the percentage of lead in alloy A to a, and the percentage of tin in alloy C to b. We can then find the percentage of copper in each as a function of a and b.

Alloy	Zinc	Tin	Lead	Copper	Nickel
A	10%	40%	a%	(40-a)%	10%
B	25%	15%	50%	5%	5%
C	15%	b%	20%	(30-b)%	35%

The key thing here is to use the composition of Alloy G. We can find the composition of Alloy G in terms of a and b and then set the amounts of tin, lead and copper equal to each other to find a and b:

For Alloy G, the percentages will be weighted according to the proportion A:B:C = 2:1:3:
$2/6 (40) + 1/6 (15) + 3/6 (b) = 2/6 (a) + 1/6 (50) + 3/6 (20) = 2/6 (40-a) + 1/6 (5) + 3/6 (30-b)$

$80 + 15 + 3b = 2a + 50 + 60 = 80 - 2a + 5 + 90 - 3b$
Solving above equation, we will get values:
$95 + 3b = 2a + 110$
$2a + 110 = 175 - 2a - 3b$
$3b = 65 - 4a$
$2a = 95 - 110 + 65 - 4a$
$6a = 50$
$a = 50/6$
$b = 95/9$
Percentage of Lead in alloy A = a = 50/6% = 25/3% = 8.33%

Question 190: C

Using our solution from the previous question, we found that the percentage of Tin in alloy C, b, was:
$b = 95/9$
Percentage of Tin in alloy C = 95/9 = 10.6%

Question 191: B

Zinc percentage in alloy X is equal to the average of the percentages of the composite alloys, as they are present in equal proportions. This can be found by adding together and dividing by 3.
$X = (10+25+15)/3 = 50/3 = 16.67\%$

Question 192: D

To solve, subtract the amounts of the known metals to find the remaining metal, which is equal to the percentage of Tin and Copper combined in alloy C. We know there are no other components as this is stated in the question.

$(100\% - 15\% - 20\% - 35\%) = 30\%$

Question 193: B

We know the percentages of tin in each of the alloys which make up Alloy G, and the composition of Alloy G. Alloy G is made up of alloys A:B:C in the ratio 2:1:3. Alloy A has 40% tin, alloy B has 15% and alloy C has 95/9% tin. Hence the percentage in Alloy G is (2/6 x 40)+(1/6 x 15)+(3/6 x 95/9) = 21.11%.

Question 194: C
Percentage of elements in alloy G:

We know that Alloy G has 21.11% Tin from the last question. We also know from the initial explanation that it has the same concentration of tin, lead and copper. This is 3 elements with the same concentration. We then need to work out how much nickel and zinc there is to check whether there is a 4th.

Alloy G is made up of alloys A:B:C in the ratio 2:1:3. Alloy A has 10% nickel, alloy B has 5% and alloy C has 35% nickel. Hence the percentage in Alloy G is ((2x10)+(1x5)+(3x35))/6, = 21.6666.

We can also work out from the fact that these 4 elements plus Zinc are 100% of the total that Zinc is 15%.

Zinc = 15%
Tin = 21.11%
Lead = 21.11%
Copper = 21.11%
Nickel = 21.67%

SET 40

Question 195: A
Number of persons who voted in favour of Hilary Clinton = 60% of 17% of 11,500 = 0.6x0.17x11,500 = 1173.

Question 196: D
We cannot find the number of people living in New York, as we do not know the proportion of citizens of New York who voted for people other than Robert Guiliani. We can only say that there was a minimum of 460 New York citizens. We cannot determine the actual number.

Question 197: D
0.39 x 11,500 = 44,85 votes for Bush.
Therefore 4,485/(11,500 x 0.8) gives the proportion of US citizens who voted for Bush.
This equals 48.8%.

Question 198: C
10% of 40% of people surveyed are in favour of Rumsfield and employees of the federal government, so 10% of 40% of 11,500 = 460 people.
Also from the table, Rumsfield has 5% of 11500 votes = 575 people who are in favour of him in total.
Hence the number of people who are in favour of Rumsfeld who are not employees of the federal government is 575-460 = 115.

Question 199: C
The number of people polled was constant. The decrease in percentage is from 16% to 2%, i.e. 14 % of 11,500 = 1,610 people.

Question 200: A
The number of people polled was constant. The decrease in percentage is from 40% to 39%, i.e. 1% of 11,500 = 115 people.

Abstract Reasoning Answers

Question	Answer	Question	Answer	Question	Answer	Question	Answer
1	B	51	Neither	101	A	151	A
2	Neither	52	B	102	A	152	Neither
3	A	53	A	103	Neither	153	A
4	A	54	Neither	104	B	154	B
5	Neither	55	B	105	Neither	155	A
6	B	56	A	106	A	156	Neither
7	A	57	Neither	107	Neither	157	A
8	A	58	B	108	A	158	A
9	Neither	59	Neither	109	B	159	Neither
10	Neither	60	A	110	B	160	B
11	A	61	A	111	B	161	B
12	B	62	A	112	Neither	162	A
13	Neither	63	B	113	Neither	163	A
14	A	64	B	114	B	164	B
15	A	65	A	115	A	165	A
16	B	66	A	116	A	166	A
17	B	67	A	117	A	167	B
18	A	68	B	118	Neither	168	Neither
19	A	69	Neither	119	B	169	A
20	A	70	Neither	120	Neither	170	B
21	A	71	B	121	Neither	171	Neither
22	A	72	A	122	Neither	172	B
23	B	73	Neither	123	A	173	B
24	B	74	Neither	124	A	174	A
25	Neither	75	A	125	B	175	Neither
26	B	76	A	126	Neither	176	B
27	A	77	A	127	A	177	Neither
28	A	78	B	128	Neither	178	B
29	B	79	A	129	Neither	179	B
30	B	80	Neither	130	B	180	A
31	B	81	B	131	Neither	181	Neither
32	Neither	82	Neither	132	Neither	182	Neither
33	Neither	83	Neither	133	Neither	183	A
34	A	84	A	134	A	184	A
35	A	85	A	135	B	185	Neither
36	B	86	B	136	A	186	Neither
37	A	87	A	137	B	187	Neither
38	Neither	88	B	138	Neither	188	A
39	A	89	Neither	139	Neither	189	B
40	Neither	90	B	140	B	190	A
41	B	91	Neither	141	A	191	Neither
42	Neither	92	A	142	Neither	192	A
43	A	93	Neither	143	B	193	Neither
44	B	94	A	144	A	194	B
45	Neither	95	A	145	B	195	Neither
46	B	96	B	146	Neither	196	B
47	Neither	97	B	147	B	197	Neither
48	A	98	A	148	Neither	198	B
49	B	99	B	149	A	199	Neither
50	Neither	100	B	150	A	200	B

	Set A Rule	**Set B Rule**
Set 1	**3** Shapes are white **2** Shapes are black	**2** Shapes are white **3** Shapes are black
Set 2	**2** Shapes are white **1** Shape is black	**1** Shape is white **2** Shapes are black
Set 3	There is always a **triangle** in the **top left corner**	There is always a **quadrilateral** in the **bottom right corner**
Set 4	There are an **even** number of rectangles	There are an **odd** number of rectangles
Set 5	Each circle has at least one tangential line.	At least one circle is **intersected** by a line.
Set 6	**None** of the shapes intersect with each other.	At least **one** of the shapes intersects with another shape/line.
Set 7	The total number of dots is **10**	The total number of dots is **9**
Set 8	The four-sided shapes are in **different** section of the box.	The four-sided shapes are in the **same** section of the box.
Set 9	All boxes have a **five-pointed star** in the **Centre**	All boxes have a **triangle** in the **bottom left corner**
Set 10	The black **circle** is always in the **bottom left corner**	The two small **dots** are always in the **top right corner**
Set 11	The circles **are all tangential to** each other	The circles **intersect** each other
Set 12	There are always **three squares, two triangles** and one circle	There are always **three triangles, two squares** and one circle
Set 13	The sum of the edges is **odd**	The sum of the edges of is **even**
Set 14	The sum of the edges is **twelve**	The sum of the edges is **fourteen**
Set 15	Each box contains **4** right angles	Each box contains **6** right angles
Set 16	Each black shape has a **larger** white counterpart	Each black shape has a **smaller** white counterpart
Set 17	Number of Dots = Number of **Stars**	Number of Dots = Number of **Diamonds**
Set 18	Even-sided polygons are **black** Odd-sided polygons are **white**	Even-sided polygons are **white** Odd-sided polygons are **black**

Set 19	Number of Stars = Number of **Triangles**	Number of Stars = Number of **Diamonds**
Set 20	There are **no** right angles	There is at least **one** right angle
Set 21	There is a **horizontal** line for each rectangle and a **vertical** line for each square	There is a **vertical** line for each rectangle and a **horizontal** line for each square
Set 22	One shape has **2** more edges than the other	One shape has **3** more edges than the other
Set 23	Even-sided polygons are **black** Odd-sided polygons are **white**	Even-sided polygons are **white** Odd-sided polygons are **black**
Set 24	The number of triangles + circles = **3**	The number of triangles + circles = **2**
Set 25	The vector sum of the arrows is **left/right**	The vector sum of the arrows is **up/down**
Set 26	There are **nine** corners in total	There are **ten** corners in total
Set 27	There is one **more** shape outside the circle than inside the circle	There is one **less** shape outside the circle than inside the circle
Set 28	The arrows only form **acute** angles	The arrows only form **obtuse** angles
Set 29	Shapes are made up of arrows all pointing at the same corner	Shapes are made up of arrows all pointing at different corners
Set 30	A central shape is intersected by an **even** number of other shapes	A central shape is intersected by an **odd** number of other shapes
Set 31	There is an **odd** number of corners in total	There is an **even** number of corners in total
Set 32	All **white** shapes are located on the left side	All **black** shapes are located on the left side
Set 33	The number of edges is a prime number	The number of edges is **not** prime number
Set 34	There are an even number of **black** shapes	There are an even number of **white** shapes
Set 35	All shapes contain right angles	All shapes **don't** contain any right angles
Set 36	Every shape is a quadrilateral	Every shape is **not** a quadrilateral
Set 37	There is always a **circle** in the top left hand corner	There is always a **triangle** in the top left hand corner

Set 38	**Two** corners are occupied by shapes	**Three** corners are occupied by shapes
Set 39	There is only **one** black shape	There are only **two** black shapes
Set 40	There are always three members of the same colour and shape, **but** different sizes	There are always three members of the same colour, shape **and** size

Decision Analysis Answers

Question	Answer	Question	Answer	Question	Answer	Question	Answer
1	B	51	C	101	B	151	B
2	D	52	A	102	D	152	D
3	D	53	D	103	A	153	B
4	D	54	B	104	D	154	C
5	B	55	B	105	E	155	E
6	A	56	B	106	C	156	A
7	B	57	C	107	C	157	D
8	B	58	A	108	C	158	A
9	C	59	B	109	B	159	B
10	A	60	D	110	E	160	C
11	C	61	C	111	B	161	E
12	A	62	A	112	D	162	D
13	D	63	B	113	A	163	D
14	A	64	D	114	A	164	A
15	B	65	B	115	B	165	C
16	B	66	C	116	C	166	D
17	D	67	D	117	E	167	B
18	C	68	B	118	A	168	D
19	B	69	A	119	D	169	E
20	A	70	A	120	B	170	B
21	B	71	C	121	C	171	C
22	C	72	D	122	D	172	D
23	D	73	B	123	B	173	A
24	B	74	A	124	C	174	B
25	A	75	D	125	E	175	C
26	B	76	C	126	A	176	E
27	C	77	C	127	B	177	E
28	A	78	A	128	B	178	D
29	D	79	C	129	D	179	E
30	B	80	D	130	A	180	A
31	A	81	A	131	E	181	D
32	C	82	C	132	E	182	D
33	D	83	C	133	D	183	B
34	A	84	B	134	A	184	C
35	D	85	C	135	B	185	C
36	C	86	D	136	D	186	B
37	B	87	A	137	C	187	E
38	C	88	B	138	E	188	C
39	B	89	C	139	A	189	A
40	B	90	B	140	B	190	D
41	A	91	C	141	D	191	C
42	D	92	B	142	C	192	C
43	C	93	B	143	E	193	E
44	A	94	A	144	B	194	A
45	B	95	B	145	A	195	D
46	B	96	D	146	C	196	E
47	C	97	C	147	D	197	B
48	D	98	B	148	D	198	C
49	C	99	B	149	B	199	D
50	A	100	D	150	E	200	D

Question 1: B

The code would read: large vehicle (opposite fast), over river, infantry, over river. The closest match is, "A tank and some soldiers have crossed the bridge." In A, the word "carrying" is not represented in the code, so although fairly close this would be a worse choice.

Question 2: D

The code would read: fast high large vehicle, over trees. A "fast high large vehicle" would be well translated as an aeroplane, especially given the context that it is travelling over trees. The closest match is therefore "A plane is flying over the forest."

Question 3: D

The code would read: many infantry, large weapon, vehicle (opposite of large), over river. An example of a vehicle that is the opposite of big in this context may well be a car. Therefore the closest match is, "A large group of infantry and a car have crossed the bridge."

Question 4: D

The code would read: many large vehicle, toward trees, opposite of many infantry, over river. The closest match is, "A formation of tanks is moving to the forest while a small group of soldiers is crossing the bridge."

Question 5: B

The code would read: many weapons, between water trees. The closest match is, "The path between the forest and river has been fortified with machine guns."

Question 6: A

The code would read: between river trees, many vehicles (opposite of large). The closest match is, "A large group of motorcycles is moving from the river to the forest."

Question 7: B

The code would read: large water vehicle (opposite of fast), over water. The closest match is, "A large boat has crossed the river." (water vehicle) would translate as boat, rather than a vehicle that is in the water, as the brackets signal a single definition. Large refers to the size of boat and not the number, as there is no mention of "many".

Question 8: B

The code would read: fast high vehicle, over river, many infantry trees. The closest match is, "A plane has crossed the river while soldiers move through the forest." The separation between the two ideas suggests that the soldiers are not in the plane but that this is a different aspect of the message.

Question 9: C.

The code would read: many infantry, opposite of toward river, many vehicles, opposite of toward river, many weapons, opposite of toward river. Because the description states that the river is between the enemy camp and your base, it could be true to say that the enemy are retreating away from the river and therefore away from your base. The message is describing the enemy as the instructions tell you that all the messages are surveillance messages regarding enemy forces. The other translations are all inaccurate so the best answer is C.

Question 10: A.

The code would read: many vehicle, many infantry, many weapon, high vehicle, toward river. Mentioning all different types of enemy equipment suggests the forces as a whole are advancing towards the river. The other translations all contain inaccuracies that are not supported by the code.

Question 11: C

The code would read: large vehicle, large vehicle, large vehicle, large vehicle, over river, infantry, opposite fast, trees. This matches the four tanks and tells us the infantry mentioned to be creeping is travelling slowly in the trees.

Question 12: A

The code would read: (water vehicle) infantry, (water vehicle) infantry, over river; (large vehicle) over river. With "water vehicle" meaning "boat" and "large vehicle" meaning "tank," this matches best with two boats with infantry and one tank crossing the river.

Question 13: D

The code would read: vehicle (infantry increase), high vehicle over. With, "high vehicle over" meaning an overhead airplane, this matches best with soldiers boarding a truck and a plane overhead.

Question 14: A

The code would read: infantry, infantry, trees; many weapons, river. This matches the soldiers in the forest and the machine-guns (large weapons) along the riverbank.

Question 15: B

The code would read: water vehicle, water vehicle, water vehicle, over river, large vehicle, large vehicle, over river. With "water vehicle" meaning boat and "large vehicle" meaning tank, this is the best match. C is close, but it suggests that the tanks and boats are simply in the river rather than actually crossing it.

Question 16: B

The code would read: (high vehicle large weapon), infantry increase; water vehicle, water vehicle, over river. With "high vehicle large weapon" meaning the heavily armed helicopter, this is the best match.

Question 17: D

The code would read: many infantry, over river, many vehicle, over river, many water vehicle, over river. This is the best match. A is close, but only implies two of each type of unit when "every available" unit is described in the question.

Question 18: C

The code would read: (water vehicle) infantry increase, vehicle (opposite of many), trees. With "opposite of many" meaning few, this is the best match.

Question 19: B

The code would read: many high vehicle, over river (fast), over trees (fast). This is the best match. C is close, but is not as clear as B

Question 20: A

The code would read: large vehicle, large vehicle, trees, many (vehicle infantry), over river. This is the best match. C. has the number of tanks and trucks switched and D has the infantry in the wrong place.

Question 21: B

Any of these words might help, but the word "rocket" would be the most helpful. With "rocket," you could send a message saying something like, "rocket over river."

Question 22: C

Having the word "destroy" would be the most helpful. The instructions say the code deals only with observations of enemy soldiers, so "enemy" would not be very useful. For bridge you already have the code (2V)/(over river) which would define the bridge accurately, and for soldier you already have the code Y/infantry.

Question 23: D

The code would read: human human, move, water. D is the best match, since C has only one human. Water and move taken together in brackets might be well translated as swimming.

Question 24: B

The code would read: breathe, human, air, cold. B is the best match. D has a cold woman instead of cold air, making no reference to air. Option C has two different translations of cold and makes no mention of breathing.

Question 25: A

The code would read: (trees fire) human human move. There is no mention of water or arrows; C introduces new ideas so A is the best match.

Question 26: B

The code would read: water, move, hill. B is the simplest and most accurate interpretation of this. A better code for this though might include (1A) "water move", being a river. Nonetheless from the options river is a better translation than the others of this concept.

Question 27: C

The code would read: (good human), home trees, (food opposite). With (good human) might mean "hero", (food opposite) mean "no food," C. is the best match.

Question 28: A

The code would read: (earth move) large, trees, (up opposite). The earth moving eliminates C and D, and B uses earth to mean soil as well as earthquake. Therefore A is the best match.

Question 29: D

The code would read: human (opposite of good), move, spear, opposite of fight, human human. Human (opposite of good) means, "villain," and opposite of fight refers to peace. D. is the best match.

Question 30: B

The code would read: human (good), move trees, tree opposite of up, up fire. Human (good) refers to a hero, "up fire" might mean lighting a fire.

Question 31: A

The code reads: large human, large home, up hill. With "large" meaning "great" or "powerful," A would be the best match.

Question 32: C

The code would read: human (opposite of good), fire, (air, opposite of good), opposite of breathe. A misses the part about breathing, D adds a lake, and B misses the point that the villain could not breathe. C is the best match.

Question 33: D

The code would read: human human, fight (large) trees. A is close, but it groups the word large with trees rather than with fight, thus it is a worse translation of the word "battle".

Question 34: A

The code reads: (large trees) fire, opposite of up, earth. B and C include the symbol for air, and D includes the symbol for breathe.

Question 35: D

The code reads: human (opposite of good), earth (opposite of good), (water + move = river) (water + opposite = dry), air (opposite of good). A misses the bad air, B misses that it is a villain, and C is unclear.

Question 36: C

These symbols are human, fight and food. The others have symbols for air, trees and hill included, which would not help to encode the message.

Question 37: B
The symbols are fight, large and human. A includes the symbol for air, C includes the symbol for opposite and D includes the symbols for breathe and fire. B is the best match for the question.

Question 38: C
You could use the symbols human and good for hero as in previous questions, human could be used for lady. It would be more useful to have a symbol for love than it would for fall or lady, as that is the key additional message.

Question 39: B
The code includes symbols for human and good/bad which could be used for villain and hero, and the symbol for fire could be used to express "burn." The most useful word would be army.

Question 40: B
A. This answer does not use the plural of 'friend'.
C. This answer uses the plural of 'I' which the code does not say to use.
D. The code says to use the opposite of 'you'.
E. This answer does not 'decrease' Queen to 'Princess'.

Question 41: A
B. This answer does not use the plural of 'ride'.
C. This answer doesn't increase scary to be 'very scary'.
D. This answer does not use the plural of 'loop'.
E. This answer uses the opposite 'scary' which the code does not say to use.

Question 42: D
A. This answer does not use the opposite of 'you'.
B. This answer does not make use the negative which is in the code.
C. This answer uses the opposite of 'this'.
F. This answer does not make use of the negative which is in the code

Question 43: C
A. This answer does not 'increase' 'wet'.
B. This answer is in the future tense; the code is in the past tense.
D. This answer does not involve the word 'us'.
E. This answer does not use the plural to make 'us'.

Question 44: A
B. This answer does not use the opposite of 'you'.
C. This answer does not include the negative mentioned in the code.
D. The code does not mention the word 'feel'.
E. This answer is in the past tense; the code uses the future tense.

Question 45: B.
The code reads: white metal beam, blue metal beam, blue screw, green wood block. A, C and D have the materials or colours wrong. By being systematic, a potentially complex question can be made much simpler.

Question 46: B
The code reads: yellow wood block, yellow wood block, yellow metal block, nail, green metal block. C is close, but it uses a screw instead of a nail.

Question 47: C
The code reads: nail black, red beam, blue wood beam, blue wood beam. A and B miss the black nail, and D adds the word "metal" when the code does not include it.

Question 48: D

The code reads: grey wood block, glue screw, red wood block. A misses the screw, B misses the glue, C has a metal block instead of a wooden block.

Question 49: C

The code reads: white blue metal beam, white blue metal beam, screw, green yellow wood block. A includes teal, which does not belong, B misses that the block is wooden, and D has white screws, which are not in the code.

Question 50: A

The code reads: white wood beam, screw, black metal beam. B, C and D do not match.

Question 51: C

The code reads: red wood block, red wood block, nail, white wood block. A and D have a screw instead of a nail, and B uses the code incorrectly.

Question 52: A

The code reads: blue green wood beam, blue green wood beam, blue green wood beam, screw, green metal block. B has grey instead of yellow, C uses the code incorrectly and D has a white and yellow beam instead of a blue and yellow beam.

Question 53: D

The code reads: red metal beam, glue, black wood block, black wood block. A and C are not specific enough, and B uses the code incorrectly.

Question 54: B

A, C and D can be implied by other words in the code, but there is no good way to express "centre" using the code as it is.

Question 55: B

C and D can be implied by the code, A can be expressed by the codes for red and white (in brackets together, they could indicate a combination colour) but there is no good way to express "end" using the code as it is. Therefore this would be the most useful addition to the code.

Question 56: B

The code reads: rock, dry unstable suitable for roads. A misses that it is unstable, C incorrectly includes "overgrown," D misses the type of construction. Therefore A is the closest translation of the code as it encodes everything within the code with no extra information introduced.

Question 57: C

The code reads: soil, stable packed, suitable for buildings. A incorrectly has rock, B incorrectly has unstable, D incorrectly has wet and the wrong type of construction.

Question 58: A

The code reads: (wet soil) overgrown, unstable. B incorrectly includes rock, C incorrectly includes stable, D incorrectly includes dry. Marsh is a good translation of (wet soil), as taken together in brackets they have a new and more complex meaning.

Question 59: B

The code reads gravel wet (loose), unstable. A incorrectly includes road construction, C incorrectly leaves out wet, D incorrectly includes soil. Although the code does not state that nothing can be built, as we gain a greater understanding of the code we can see that if things are able to be built it is encoded that the land is suitable for that purpose. But even if we neglect this assumption (which might or might not be correct) from a process of elimination we can deduce that answer B is the best response.

Question 60: D
The code reads: even rock, slippery, stable, and suitable for buildings. A has the construction type wrong, B incorrectly includes unstable, C incorrectly includes gravel. So by a process of elimination we arrive at D, the closest translation of the code.

Question 61: C
The code reads: soil, uneven packed, stable, suitable for roads. A incorrectly includes even, B incorrectly includes unstable, loose, even, D has the wrong type of construction.

Question 62: A
The code reads: soil, wet loose bare, stable, suitable for roads. B and D are wrong about the type of construction, C incorrectly includes overgrown and bog.

Question 63: B
The code reads: gravel, overgrown (loose), even (stable), suitable for buildings. C incorrectly includes paved and D is wrong about the type of construction. A has a different interpretation of the word "even" – so we have to make a decision between A and B. Now although sentence A includes all the same information as sentence B, most people would say that sentence B makes more sense, therefore it is the best option to choose.

Question 64: D
The code reads: rock, slippery loose, suitable for roads opposite. A incorrectly includes hilly, B incorrectly includes flat and is wrong about the type of construction, C incorrectly includes flat.

Question 65: B
The code reads: soil (hard stable), (uneven overgrown ground) suitable for buildings. A incorrectly includes flat, C has the wrong type of construction, D incorrectly includes a forest. An uneven overgrown area of ground could be well translated as a meadow.

Question 66: C
The code would read: (soil wet), bare even loose, suitable for buildings. A incorrectly includes overgrown and has the wrong type of construction, B is wrong about the type of construction (there is no opposite indicating construction could not take place), D incorrectly includes hilly and has the wrong type of construction. (Soil wet) together means mud

Question 67: D
These symbols are unstable, (loose rock soil). Option D translates sand as (loose rock soil). This might initially seem bizarre but it is logical when you look at it closer. Remember that we must take all the words together in brackets and look for a unifying definition. The phrase is talking about A soil-like substance made from rocks, which is loose. This is close to what sand is, so it is a good translation. But don't worry if you didn't see this, you can also use a process of elimination. A includes both stable and unstable, B incorrectly includes wet and gravel, C incorrectly includes packed and overgrown.

Question 68: B
These symbols are, (soil wet) and loose. A incorrectly includes rock, C incorrectly includes overgrown, D incorrectly includes an opposite of either wet or soil.

Question 69: A
These symbols are, (Overgrown, Wet, Ground) Wet, (Dry, Ground) (Opposite Wet). B doesn't include the fact that the forest is a rainforest, C states that deserts are dry (not that they don't get much rain), and D states that deserts get more rain than rainforests!

Question 70 A
These symbols are wet, loose, unstable. B includes both bare and overgrown, C makes no mention of wetness, a crucial feature of a bog and D incorrectly includes suitable for buildings.

Question 71: C

These symbols are (overgrown soil) rock – with the overgrown soil term referring to the grassy growth. A unnecessarily includes dry, B incorrectly includes gravel of which there is no mention, D includes both packed and loose so doesn't make good sense.

Question 72: D

These symbols are uneven, (overgrown opposite). A incorrectly includes slippery, B incorrectly includes wet, C should include bare or opposite overgrown to better translate the text.

Question 73: B

These symbols are even ground, overgrown. A includes packed soil, which isn't mentioned, C includes both even and uneven, D includes both bare and overgrown opposite, neither of which are true.

Question 74: A

These symbols are: uneven, rock, dry. B is close, but includes loose instead of dry, C incorrectly includes slippery, D is missing uneven or something to show craters.

Question 75: D

We already have a code for wet, and land would not help us translate this. Now the code for "water" could be tempting, but the word water alone could mean many different things, from a tank of water to a pond, river, lake or the sea, for example. With the word crater, we can add it to the current code to say a (wet crater) or (stable wet crater), which could be a good translation of the code.

Question 76: C

Structure is the one word here that would greatly help you write a message in this situation. By describing the land and using the word structure, you can indicate that a building is already there.

Question 77: C

Cold, snow and hard might be helpful and accurate descriptors, but ice is much more precise to translate "frozen". There is no current way to use the cold to translate this accurately.

Question 78: A

In the Spanish code, the message is stop, state purpose.

Question 79: C

In the English code, the message reads: destination, you, continue on.

Question 80: D

In the Spanish code, the message reads: stop, (merchant we), you state purpose.

Question 81: A

In the French code, the message reads: you stop, (military we), destination port, you destination.

Question 82: D

In the English code, the message reads: stop you, (military we), we you toward port. Placing the final term in brackets indicates a unifying meaning, that the ship is instructed to follow the military ship towards port.

Question 83: C

In the English code, the message reads: stop, military (we), you continue on toward (destination). This one is quite straightforward – once you translate each aspect of the code accurately, the meaning becomes clear. Option C is the only option which helps to translate this code accurately.

Question 84: B

In the Spanish code, the message reads: we military; you toward destination; state purpose. It is clear from the code you must give information to the requesting ship. There is no mention of stopping, distressed crew members or following in the code, therefore option B is the closest translation.

Question 85: C

In the French code, the message reads: state purpose you, continue on. You are not requested to stop. Option C incorporates as much of the code as possible whilst introducing nothing new, thus it is the best choice.

Question 86: D

In the French code, the message reads: (distress, we), stop, state purpose. Option D is the only option which acknowledges the distress call, so it is the best translation of the code.

Question 87: A

The symbols are stop and state purpose in the French code. In the English code, they would be toward stop, and in the Spanish code they would be military you, which are much less coherent.

Question 88: B

In the Spanish code the message reads, "merchant, we; continue on, you." In the French code it reads, "distress, destination; port, state purpose," in the English code it reads, "distress, state purpose; merchant, stop, which make less sense.

Question 89: C

The message reads "(military, we), stop, state purpose," in the English code, forming a complete message. In the French code it reads, "(toward, you), state purpose, destination," in the Spanish code it reads, "(toward, state purpose), you, we," which are much less coherent.

Question 90: B

In the Spanish code, the message reads, "stop, state purpose, you." In the French code it reads, "military, you, state purpose," and in the English code it reads, "you, we (stop)," which are much less coherent.

Question 91: C

In the French code, the message reads: merchant, we; continue on, we; toward, destination. This is the best translation. Make sure, as ever, that you are translating every aspect of the code and introducing no new information. In addition, the semi-colons here help to guide you as well – they show you how different parts of the message group together.

Question 92: B

In the Spanish code, the message reads: merchant, we; destination, port.

Question 93: B

In the French code, the message reads: continue on, you; continue on, we, toward, destination. This is the best translation.

Question 94: A

In the English code, the message reads: stop, (merchant we), state purpose, you.

Question 95: B

In the English code, the message reads: merchant, we, state purpose, you, merchant, military. This is the closest translation.

Question 96: D

In the Spanish code, the message reads: stop, distress, we. This instructs the ship to stop to help and states the reason.

Question 97: C
In the Spanish code, the message reads: you, state purpose, (destination, you).

Question 98: B
"Ship" can be implied using the code as it is, "peaceful" is more important to have than "mission," and "opposite" would not help. The concept of peace is hard to convey with the current code therefore it would be the most useful addition.

Question 99: B
"Control" would be the most useful word to have in this situation. "Follow" and "vessel" can be implied using the code as it is, and "give up" could be implied if the word "control" were included, for example by saying (control, stop).

Question 100: D
Opposite is the most useful word here, as you can say (destination, opposite) to code for the place of origin. Journey is not necessary as the (destination, opposite) implies that this relates to the current journey. Likewise the other words are unnecessary for conveying basic meaning in a simple code.

Question 101: B
A. There is no mention of the word 'visit.'
C. The code specifies the past tense of 'go' not the future.
D. This does not use the plural of 'I.'
E. This does not combine the children and parents to make 'family.'

Question 102: D
A. The code says 'increase' 'hot' so warm is not hot enough!
B. Future tense of 'day' required.
C. Sand and water should be combined to make 'beach'.
D. This sentence does not include the word 'beach'.

Question 103: A
B. No mention of 'toys'.
C. No mention of 'toys'.
D. The word 'toys' should be combined.
E. The code specifies the past tense of play.

Question 104: D
A. Does not include word 'hot'.
B. We' and 'beach' are not mentioned in the code.
C. There is no mention of the word 'restaurant.
E.   Wrong tense of 'eat'.

Question 105: E
A. No mention of the 'sea'.
B. Code specifies negative of swim – we will not swim.
C. Code requires future tense.
D. Code specifies opposite of 'good' so the weather is bad.

Question 106: C
A. This answer does not include the word 'boat'.
B. This answer does not include the word 'sea'.
D. The code specifies the plural of 'child'.
E. This answer does not include the word 'boat' or 'sea'.

Question 107: C

A. This translation uses the plural of 'day'.
B. This translation does not use the plural of sand-castle.
D. This answer does not use the plural of child.
E. This answer does not use the plural of child or sand-castle.

Question 108: C

A. The code says to increase 'old' rather than the opposite.
B. The code asks for the past tense of 'find', not the opposite.
D. Does not include the word 'wall'.
E. This is the wrong tense of 'find'.

Question109: B

A. This does not include the word 'man'.
C. This is the opposite of 'relationship' and 'love'.
D. This is in the future tense but the code specifies the past.
E. This does not include the 'relationship' element to the code.

Question 110: E

A. The code says opposite of 'queen', which is 'king'.
B. The code says to increase + opposite of 'recent'.
C. This does not include the word 'war'.
D. The code specifies the opposite of 'recent'.

Question 111: B

A. The code specifies the opposite of 'love'.
C. The code says to combine 'tribe' with the opposite of 'Queen' to make tribe chief.
D. This ignores the word 'prince' which combines with 'Queen' and opposite of 'Queen' to make royal family.
E. The words are in the wrong order – cannot assume this.

Question 112: D

A. The code specifies the opposite of 'take'.
B. War' and 'man' should be combined to make 'warrior'.
C. This is in the wrong tense, and the code specifies the opposite of 'take'.
E. The code does not say to use the opposite of 'Queen'.

Question 113: A

B. Does not include the word 'language', and the code specifies the opposite of 'hidden'.
C. The code says the stories are 'hidden' which is not included in this answer.
D. The 'secrets' should be plural.
E. The code specifies the past tense.

Question 114: A

A. This answer includes a negative which is not in the sentence.
B. This answer does not use the opposite of 'rare'.
C. This answer refers to the 'King' but not the 'royal family'.
D. This answer refers to warriors but does not include the word 'tribe'.

Question 115: B

A. The code says to decrease 'van', so 'car'.
C. The code specifies 'want' should be in the past tense.
D. The code says to use the opposite of 'black'.
E. The code says decrease + opposite of women which gives boy.

Question 116: C
A. This answer does not include the 'negative' aspect.
B. Both man and woman should be plural.
C. The code says to use the opposite of 'bad', so 'worse' is incorrect.
D. This ignores the negative in the sentence, and 'worse' is incorrect as above.

Question 117: E
A. The 'driver' should be plural.
B. This answer does not include the word 'distance'.
C. The code says to increase 'van' which could become 'lorry'.
D. The opposite of 'short' should be used

Question 118: A
A. The code says to use the past tense of 'day'.
B. This does not combine the word 'fast' with the word 'road'.
C. This answer also does not use the word 'fast'.
D. The code specifies the past tense.

Question 119: D
A. The opposite of 'find' should be used.
B. This answer does not include the use of the word 'find'.
C. The opposite of girl should be used.
E. 'Van' should be decreased which could become 'car'.

Question 120: B
A. This answer does not include the opposite of 'day' – 'night'.
C. This answer does not use the future tense.
D. This answer does not include the J(E12) section of the code.
E. 'Woman' should not be made plural.

Question 121: C
A. This answer uses the word 'find' instead of 'lost'.
B. This answer does not use the past tense.
D. This answer says the driver is going to 'school' not 'work'.
E. This answer uses the word 'road' rather than the word 'travel'.

Question122: D
A. This answer does not use the opposite of 'ice'.
B. 'Me' + 'You' does not = 'many'.
C. This answer does not use the opposite of 'ice'.
E. 'Me' + 'You' does not = 'the people.

Question 123: B
A. The code says to use the opposite of 'woman' so 'Queen' does not fit.
C. The code says to use the opposite of 'common'.
D. The code says to use the opposite of 'woman' so 'Queen' does not fit.
E. The code does not include the use of the word 'young' so 'Princess' does not fit.

Question 124: C
A. The code says 'woman' and opposite of 'woman' but does not refer to 'young'.
B. The code does not use the negative or opposite of 'party'.
D. The code uses the opposite of 'loss'.
E. This answer does not include the use of the word 'noble'.

Question 125: E
A. The code requires the plural of man.
B. This answer is in the wrong order.
C. The code uses the opposite of 'women.
D. There is no negative in the code.

Question 126: A
A. There is no negative in the code.
B. The code specifies the opposite of 'noble'.
C. The code does not refer to the word 'met.
D. This answer uses the opposite genders to the code.

Question 127: B
A. The answer should use the plural of astronaut.
C. This answer does not combine 'space' and 'man'.
D. The code uses the opposite of 'heavy' and does not use the opposite of 'slow'.
E. The code uses the opposite of 'heavy'.

Question 128: B
A. This answer does not include the word 'moon'.
C. The code specifies the opposite of 'day' so 'today' is incorrect.
D. This is in the wrong order.
E. This answer does not include the word 'return'.

Question 129: D
A. This does not combine 'Earth' with 'star'.
B. The code does not use the plural of 'star'.
C. The code uses the opposite of 'cold' and 'dark'.
E. The code does not refer to 'space'.

Question 130: A
B. The negative of 'understood' should be used.
C. The opposite of 'small' should be used.
D. The opposite of 'small' and 'understood' should be used.
E. The negative of 'understood' is not 'misunderstanding'.

Question 131: E
A. 'Scientist' should be plural.
B. This answer does not combine 'science' with 'man'.
C. This answer does not use the word 'question'.
D. This answer does not include the word 'science'.

Question 132: E
A. This answer does not include 'lighter'.
B. This answer has 'Earth' and 'Mars' the wrong way round.
C. Heavier' and 'lighter' are the wrong way around in this answer.
D. This answer does not include the word 'heavy'.

Question 133: D
A. This answer does not use the plural of 'woman'.
B. This answer does not use the word 'danger'.
C. This answer does not refer to the word 'building'.
E. This answer does not use the word 'trap'.

Question 134: A

B. This answer does not combine 'emergency' and 'service', and does not use the word 'question'.
C. This answer does not use the word 'emergency' or 'service' or 'police'.
D. This answer uses the opposite of 'question'.
E. This answer does not use the word 'crime'.

Question 135: B

A. This answer does not combine 'fire' and 'man'.
C. This answer uses a negative which is not in the code.
D. This answer does not use the opposite of 'sad'.
E. This answer does not use the plural of fireman.

Question 136: D

A. The code refers to 'local' men.
B. This answer does not use the word 'fire'.
C. The code specifies 'men' not 'women'.
E. This answer uses a negative not present in the code.

Question 137: C

A. This answer uses the future tense.
B. This code refers to a 'vehicle' not used in this answer.
D. This answer uses the opposite of 'fast'.
E. This answer does not show that the building was on fire.

Question 138: E

A. The code includes the word 'pretty'.
B. The code says to decrease 'dress' which could translate to 'skirt'.
C. The code uses the opposite of 'long'.
D. The code uses the opposite of 'boy'.

Question 139: A

B. This answer does not involve the word 'adult'.
C. This answer does not involve the word 'music'.
D. The code does not use the negative seen in this answer.
E. This answer does not combine 'music', 'teach' and 'adult'.

Question 140: B

A. The code identifies the book is for the opposite of writing
C. The code specifies the opposite of 'love'.
D. This answer does not combine reading and book.
E. The code uses the opposite of 'boys'.

Question 141: D

A. This answer does not use the opposite of 'nice'.
B. This answer has the younger girls being mean to the older girls.
C. This answer does not use the opposite of 'boys'.
E. This answer refers to individual girls, whereas the sentence talks about 'girls' plural.

Question 142: C

A. The code asks for the future tense.
B. The code specifies the trip is during the day.
D. This answer is in the past tense and the trip is during the day.
E. The code says 'plus' parents – there is no negative.

Question 143: E

A. The code does not include a negative, it says to increase 'patient.
B. This answer uses the past tense for winter.
C. This answer involves a negative not in the code.
D. This answer involves a negative not in the code and is in the wrong tense.

Question 144: B

A. Code asks for opposite of 'remember'.
C. Code asks for opposite of 'eat.
D. This answer does not involve the word 'water'.
E. This answer is in the wrong tense.

Question 145: A

B. The code specifies the opposite of 'cold'.
C. The code does not use the word 'I' and uses a negative not in the code.
D. This answer is in the wrong tense.
E. This answer uses a negative not in the code and is in the wrong tense.

Question 146: C

A. This is the opposite answer, translating to 'The hospital has plenty of beds because there is more money'.
B. This answer does not specify 'less' money, it just says 'money'.
D. This answer is talking about hospitals plural, but the sentence talks about one specifically.
E. This answer translates into the patients having no beds, not the hospital.

Question 147: D

A. The code specifies drugs plural.
B. This ignores the increase on 'asks for' and ignores the word 'student'.
C. This answer separates the words 'student' and 'nurse'.
E. This answer ignores the word 'nurse'.

Question 148: D

A. This sentence in the wrong order.
B. This sentence is in the wrong order.
C. This sentence does not use the opposite of 'safe'.
E. The word 'angry' is not in the code.

Question 149: B

A. The code uses the opposite of 'excess'.
C. The code specifies an increase in patients.
D. The code uses the word 'cold' to describe the weather – there is no use of opposite.
E. There are increased numbers of patients.

Question 150: E

A. This answer is in the past tense, the code specifies the future.
B. This answer does not include 'hospital' and 'doctors' and is in the wrong tense.
C. This answer does not include the word 'nurses' and is in the wrong tense.
D. This answer does not include the word 'nurses'.

Question 151: B

A. The code specifies the opposite of 'evening' which is 'morning'.
C. The code says to increase 'busy'.
D. This answer does not use the opposite of 'above' when describing the train.
E. This answer includes a negative not used in the code.

Question 152: D
A. This answer does not combine 'train' and 'compartment', and the use of 'full' and 'empty' are the wrong way round.
B. In this answer the use of 'empty' and opposite of 'empty' are the wrong way round.
E. This answer does not combine 'train' with 'compartment' to make 'carriage'.
F. In this answer, the use of 'this' and the opposite of 'this', 'that', are the wrong way round.

Question 153: B
A. This answer uses 'from' rather than 'towards', and does not use the future tense of delayed.
C. This answer uses 'from' rather than 'towards'.
D. This answer uses the past tense of delayed instead of the future.
E. This answer does not use the opposite of 'above'-ground train.

Question 154: C
A. The code uses a negative not included in this answer.
B. The code uses a negative, and the opposite of 'evening'.
D. This answer is in the wrong tense – the code specifies the 'future' of 'this'+'day'.
E. This answer does not use the opposite of 'evening'.

Question 155: E
A. This answer does not include the word 'emergency'.
B. This answer does not use the code that translates as 'future' 'this' which could be 'next'.
C. This answer does not include the word 'driver'.
D. The code specifies the past tense.

Question 156: A
B. This answer does not increase the word 'stations' so does not translate into 'many stations'.
C. This answer has a negative in it which is not in the sentence.
D. This answer translates into 'over-ground' rather than underground.
E. This answer does not use the plural of 'station'.

Question 157: D
A. This answer does not make use of the word 'angry'.
B. This answer does not include 'angry' or 'conversation', nor combine them as the code specifies.
C. This answer does not use the word 'conversation'.
E. This does not combine 'boy' or 'girl' with 'friend'.

Question 158: A
B. This answer does not combine 'party' with 'exercise' to make 'dance'.
C. This answer does not use the word 'party'.
D. The code does not use the word 'I'.
E. Again, the code does not use the word 'I', nor does it use the word 'party' on its own.

Question 159: B
A. The code says to use the future tense – this answer is in the past tense.
C. The code says to use the opposite of 'day' which is 'night'.
D. The code says to combine 'blue' and 'yellow' – this makes 'green'.
E. This uses the wrong combination of colours.

Question 160: C
A. The code includes the word 'I', when combined with 'friends' this could be used to make 'my friends', which is not used in this answer
B. This answer is in the wrong tense
D. This answer includes a negative not used in the code.
E. This answer includes a negative not in the code, and is in the wrong tense.

Question 161: E
A. The code says to use the opposite of 'that' which could be 'this'.
B. This answer uses a negative not used in the code.
C. This answer uses the plural of I, and a negative not used in the code.
D. This answer uses the plural of 'I' which the code does not say to use.

Question 162: D
A. The code says to use the opposite of 'dark'.
B. The code says to use the past tense, this answer is in the present.
C. The code says to use the opposite of 'dark'.
E. This answer does not increase 'bright' to 'very bright' or 'too bright'.

Question 163: D
A. The code says to use the opposite of 'day'.
B. There is no mention of light or dark in the code.
C. This answer is in the past tense which is not specified in the code.
E. Wrong tense and uses day instead of night

Question 164: A
B. This answer does not use 'every' or 'year' which are in the code.
C. This answer does not combine 'parents' and 'children'.
D. This answer does not combine 'parents' and 'children'.
E. This answer includes a negative which is not in the code.

Question 165: C
A. This answer is in the past tense, but the code says to use the future.
B. This answer does not use the plural of 'I'.
D. This answer does not use the plural of 'I' and is in the wrong tense.
E. This answer does not use the opposite of 'far away'.

Question 166: D
A. The code says to use the future of 'day', so 'tomorrow' is more appropriate.
B. The code specifies to increase 'walk; which this answer does not do.
C. This answer does not use the plural of mountain.
E. This answer does not use the opposite of 'down'.

Question 167: B
A. This answer does not use the opposite of 'down'.
C. This answer is in the wrong tense – the code says to use the past tense
D. This answer is not in the right tense, and does not use the opposite of 'down'.
E. This answer does not include the negative which is in the code.

Question 168: D
A. This answer is in the future tense – the code is in the present tense.
B. This answer does not use the plural of 'tree'.
C. This answer does not use the opposite of 'down'.
E. This answer is in the wrong tense and does not use the opposite of 'down'.

Question 169: E
A. This answer does not use the plural/opposite of 'I'.
B. This answer does not use the opposite of 'we' or the future of 'tonight'.
C. This answer does not use the opposite of 'outside'.
D. The code says to use the opposite of 'outside' and the future tense of tonight.

Question 170: B
A. This answer involves a negative which is not in the code.
C. This answer does not combine 'lights' and 'sky' to make 'star's.
D. This answer does not use the plural of 'star'.
E. This answer does not use the word 'night', or opposite of 'day'.

Question 171: C
A. This answer is in the future tense, and this answer does not use the opposite of 'land'.
B. This answer is in the future tense, the code uses the past tense.
D. This answer does not combine 'plane' and 'road' to give 'runway'.
E. This answer is in the present tense.

Question 172: D
A. The code says to use 'you' first.
B. This answer is not a question.
C. The code says to use the opposite of 'your', so 'my' passport.
E. This answer is not a question, and 'I' and 'you' are the wrong way round.

Question 173: A
A. The code says to use the negative of 'look' which this answer does not use.
B. The negative in this sentence is in the wrong place.
C. This answer uses two negatives which the code does not.
D. This answer does not use the opposite of 'in' to make 'out' of the window.

Question 174: B
A. This answer uses the opposite of 'smooth' which the code does not say to do.
C. This answer does not combine 'plane' and 'driver' to make 'pilot'.
D. This answer uses the opposite of 'land'.
E. This answer is in the future tense which the code does not say to use.

Question 175: C
A. This answer is in the future tense; the code specifies the past tense.
B. This answer does not combine 'plane' and 'worker' to give air hostess.
D. The code says to increase 'big' to give 'bigger' or 'very big'.
E. This answer combines the wrong words.

Question 176: E
A. This answer is in the future tense; the code specifies the past.
B. The code says to use the opposite of 'light'.
C. The code says to use the opposite of 'your'.
D. This answer does not combine 'bag' with 'holiday' and 'big'.

Question 177: E
A. There is no mention of the word 'like' in the code.
B. This answer is in the wrong tense.
C. The code says to use the opposite of 'trust'.
D. This answer uses the opposite of 'your'.

Question 178: D
A. This answer does not combine 'staff' with 'meeting'.
B. This answer is in the past tense – the code specifies the future.
C. This answer is in the past tense – the code specifies the future.
E. This answer does not combine 'staff' with 'meeting'.

Question 179: E
A. This answer does not increase 'casual' to very casual.
B. This answer does not use the opposite of 'smart'.
C. This answer is in the wrong tense.
D. This answer is in the wrong tense.

Question 180: A
B. This answer does not increase 'hot'.
C. This answer does not use the past of 'day'.
D. This answer does not use the opposite of 'cold'.
E. This answer is in the future tense – the code uses the past tense.

Question 181: D
A. This answer does not combine 'work' and 'room' to give 'office.
B. This answer does not make use of the word 'inside'.
C. The code does not mention any people, and this answer does not combine words to give 'office'.
E. This answer uses the opposite of 'tall'.

Question 182: D
A. This answer does not use the opposite of 'large'.
B. The code does not use the word 'your', it says the desk is a '(personal+belonging)', or 'my'.
C. This answer does not combine 'belonging' with 'personal' to give 'my'.
E. This answer does not increase 'small'.

Question 183: B
A. This answer uses the word 'staff', whereas the sentence specifies the bosses or 'leaders'.
C. This answer does not use the opposite of 'before' work.
D. This answer describes a 'staff' party rather than an 'office' party.
E. This answer uses the future tense.

Question 184: C
A. The code does not say to use plural for both animals.
B. This answer does not use the plural of 'lion'.
D. This answer uses plural of 'zebra' rather than 'lion'.
E. This answer is in the wrong tense – code specifies past.

Question 185: C
A. This answer does not increase 'dog' to 'wolf'.
B. This answer is in the present tense – the code uses the past tense.
D. This answer is in the future tense.
E. This answer does not use the negative mentioned in the code.

Question 186: B
A. This answer does not combine 'stripy' with 'horse' to make 'zebra'.
C. The code says to use the opposite of 'lost'.
D. The code says to use the opposite of 'father'.
E. This answer is in the future tense, which the code does not say to use.

Question 187: E
  A. This answer would combine 'stripy' with big cat, the code uses 'spotty'.
  B. This answer does not use the plural of 'big cat' at the end of the sentence.
  C. There is no mention of big or small in the code.
  D. This answer does not use the word 'runs'.

Question 188: C
  A. This answer uses the future tense, the code specifies the past.
  B. The code combines 'throughout' and 'day' – there is no mention of it being yesterday.
  D. This answer includes a negative not in the code.
  E. This answer does not combine 'mother' and 'father' with 'children' to make 'family'.

Question 189: A
  B. This answer does not use the opposite of 'far from'.
  C. This answer is in the future tense which is not specified in the code.
  D. This answer does not use the plural of 'animal'.
  E. This answer does not combine 'cats' with 'dogs' and 'horses' to make 'animals'.

Question 190: D
  A. This answer does not increase 'hot' to 'very hot'.
  B. This answer does not use the plural of 'tree'.
  C. This answer does not make use of the word 'sun'.
  E. This answer does not use the plural of 'animal'.

Question 191: C
  A. This answer does not use the plural of lion.
  B. In this answer, 'female' and 'male' are the wrong way round.
  D. This answer does not use the plural of male lion.
  E. This answer does not use the plural of female lion.

Question 192: C
  A. The code uses the past tense, this answer is in the future tense.
  B. This answer uses the present tense.
  D. In this answer the negative is in the wrong place, which changes the meaning of the sentence.
  E. This answer includes another negative which is not in the code.

Question 193: E
  A. There is no mention of the word 'year' in the code, it uses the word 'season'.
  B. This answer does not increase 'tall' to be 'very tall'.
  C. This answer includes a negative not in the code.
  D. This answer does not use the plural of 'tree'.

Question 194: A
  B. This answer does not combine 'parents' with 'children' to make 'family'.
  C. This answer uses the future tense – the code specifies the past.
  D. This answer uses the present tense – the code specifies the past.
  E. This answer includes a negative not in the code.

Question 195: D
  A. There is no mention of stealing in the code.
  B. This answer uses the future tense.
  C. This answer does not combine 'university' with 'worker'.
  E. This answer includes a negative not in the code.

Question 196: E

A. This answer uses the present tense – the code uses the future tense.
B. This answer includes a negative not in the code.
C. This answer uses the past tense.
D. This answer does not increase the word 'money'.

Question 197: B

A. This answer does not combine 'bank' with 'worker'.
C. This answer does not use the plural of 'banker'.
D. This answer does not increase the word 'money'.
E. This answer includes a negative not in the code.

Question 198: C

A. The code uses the opposite of 'old'.
B. This answer does not increase the word 'good'.
D. This answer does not combine 'bank' with 'boss'.
E. This answer includes a negative not in the code.

Question 199: D

A. This answer does not use the opposite of 'take out'.
B. This answer uses the past tense instead of the future.
C. The code specifies 'child' rather than 'parent'.
E. This answer does not use the opposite of 'take out'.

Question 200: D

A. This answer uses 'family' instead of 'parents'.
B. This answer includes two negatives – the code only uses one.
C. This answer does not include the negative mentioned in the code.
E. In this answer, the negative is in the wrong place.

Situational Judgement Answers

Question	Answer	Question	Answer	Question	Answer	Question	Answer
1	D	51	A	101	C	151	C
2	B	52	D	102	B	152	B
3	D	53	C	103	A	153	D
4	A	54	A	104	D	154	A
5	B	55	C	105	A	155	A
6	A	56	A	106	C	156	A
7	B	57	C	107	B	157	C
8	D	58	D	108	B	158	D
9	C	59	A	109	C	159	A
10	D	60	B	110	A	160	B
11	D	61	D	111	A	161	A
12	A	62	C	112	D	162	C
13	D	63	A	113	C	163	B
14	C	64	D	114	A	164	A
15	B	65	A	115	A	165	C
16	A	66	D	116	B	166	A
17	D	67	A	117	D	167	A
18	D	68	C	118	A	168	D
19	C	69	A	119	C	169	C
20	C	70	A	120	D	170	A
21	D	71	A	121	D	171	A
22	B	72	B	122	A	172	A
23	A	73	D	123	A	173	B
24	D	74	D	124	B	174	C
25	D	75	D	125	A	175	C
26	D	76	A	126	D	176	A
27	A	77	D	127	B	177	D
28	A	78	C	128	B	178	B
29	D	79	A	129	C	179	D
30	A	80	B	130	A	180	C
31	A	81	D	131	A	181	A
32	D	82	A	132	D	182	A
33	B	83	A	133	C	183	C
34	D	84	C	134	C	184	A
35	B	85	A	135	C	185	D
36	C	86	A	136	B	186	C
37	A	87	D	137	D	187	A
38	B	88	C	138	A	188	A
39	B	89	D	139	A	189	C
40	C	90	C	140	A	190	D
41	A	91	A	141	A	191	A
42	D	92	C	142	B	192	C
43	B	93	A	143	D	193	A
44	A	94	D	144	A	194	D
45	B	95	C	145	A	195	B
46	D	96	D	146	C	196	D
47	A	97	B	147	B	197	A
48	B	98	A	148	B	198	B
49	D	99	B	149	D	199	A
50	C	100	D	150	A	200	A

Scenario 1:

1. **Very inappropriate** because Jacob didn't know the entire story and this could be resolved by having a simple conversation instead. There is no need at his stage to get more people involved, especially as the doctor's behaviour has not directly affected the patient's safety or treatment.

2. **Appropriate but not ideal**, because the medical student would not be telling the doctor anything specific.

3. **Very inappropriate** because as a medical student you are a member of the health care team as well, so if there is something that is affecting the rest of the staff and patients, then it should not be ignored.

4. **Very appropriate** because the supervisor would be able to advise the student as to what they should do.

5. **Appropriate but not ideal**, whilst it makes Dr Herbert aware of the issue, it is quite confrontational and Dr Herbert may become defensive.

Scenario 2:

6. **Very appropriate**, because Dr Walker could have gotten into a bad habit and may be unaware that he hasn't been washing his hands.

7. **Appropriate but not ideal,** because Dr Walker may not pick up on the hint, although it might save George some awkwardness in having to ask Dr Walker directly.

8. **Very inappropriate** because hospitals function as a team. If George is aware of something that could potentially cause patients harm, he must try to solve the issue.

9. **Inappropriate but not awful**, because it is not addressing the situation and could make it a bigger problem than it actually is. In general, problems with doctors should be escalated to more senior doctors; problems with nurses should be escalated to more senior nurses.

10. **Very inappropriate** because Dr Walker would not have been informed and the fact that George would have witnessed it without trying to correct the problem could back fire onto him and get him into trouble if any harm were to arise.

Scenario 3:

11. **Very inappropriate** because the medical school museum would have to account for the missing bones. The bones are very valuable, and even the remains of bones could be useful as they would make them into slides or as cut sections.

12. **Very appropriate** because it acknowledges the respect to both the bones and the museum. The bones came from a real human, so cannot be treated as though they are any old piece of waste.

13. **Very inappropriate** because this would prompt an investigation and would waste a lot of money from the medical school. It would also mean that future classes may be banned from performing such projects, hindering their educational experience.

14. **Inappropriate but not awful,** because despite the fact that the curator would be informed of what occurred, it could get your colleague into trouble that could have been avoided.

15. **Appropriate but not ideal,** because the supervisor can give advice as to what to do, but it does not directly address the problem.

Scenario 4:

16. **Very appropriate** because his tutor can give him proper advice and will also be aware of any reasons behind a potentially disappointing exam mark.

17. **Very inappropriate** because it will increase tensions and result in a more stressful environment, which would hinder his progress even more.

18. **Very inappropriate** because he will end up feeling very isolated and lonely and anxious, which will also ruin both his friendships and his work progress.

19. **Inappropriate but not awful,** because he will lose out on friendships as well as go through the difficulty of finding another place to live. This could end up as a lonely option with no support network.

20. **Appropriate but not ideal** because he may find that everyone is having similar problems. It doesn't directly address the problems but Henry might find it helpful to discuss the situation with someone else.

Scenario 5:

21. **Very inappropriate** because Mark was only asked because he was mistaken for a doctor. Therefore exchanging one student for another would be an inappropriate action. Also, the other student wasn't asked.

22. **Appropriate but not ideal,** because Mark could document the results as a student and write exactly who he was. Students are allowed to perform tests, just not to administer medication.

23. **Very appropriate** because it will alert the doctor as to his mistake, and the student can be advised appropriately.

24. **Very inappropriate** because the test needs to be done, and the doctor would assume that the test had been done. Therefore the patient could be left waiting for a long time.

25. **Very appropriate** because they might be better qualified to do the test.

Scenario 6:

26. **Very inappropriate** because it is dishonest and if the truth were to emerge, she could be expelled from the medical school for such an act.

27. **Very appropriate** because they can support her and help her organise the rest of her revision.

28. **Very appropriate** because it can reassure her and give her more confidence as most people would probably feel similar.

29. **Very inappropriate** because this is also dishonest and therefore, unprofessional.

30. **Very appropriate** because she might just pass her exams and surprise herself.

Scenario 7:

31. **Very appropriate** because Dijam should not be in the hospital and is not employed to be in the hospital so can go home to recuperate.

32. **Very inappropriate** because Dijam still has contact with the patients and it is against the rules to be hungover or have alcohol in your system as a student on the wards. Dijam could get asked to do certain tasks and must make sure that he is mentally and physically competent.

33. **Appropriate** because they might send Dijam home as well, or could allow him to stay but restrict what he was allowed to do for the day.

34. **Very inappropriate** because this is a very serious violation of professionalism and joking about it is not addressing the problem.

35. **Appropriate but not ideal** because Dijam could get into more trouble than he probably ought to. That doctor also may not have witnessed Dijam in his state anyway, so it is better to inform the doctors that Dijam is shadowing than the one that is in charge.

Scenario 8:

36. **Inappropriate but not awful** as the work should be a joint effort from everyone but it won't be confrontational.

37. **Very appropriate** because Patrick's personal tutor can advise him accordingly.

38. **Appropriate but not ideal** because it will allow them to speak up but the conversation would not involve Jina.

39. **Appropriate but not ideal** because the group members may not pick up on the hinting.

40. **Inappropriate** because the confrontational approach could offend Jina and not achieve what Patrick was hoping for.

Scenario 9:

41. **Very appropriate** because Joshua should never be allowed to breach confidentiality and take the patient's notes away from the hospital.

42. **Very inappropriate** because Nazia has a duty to not allow any serious breaches of confidentiality if she is aware of them.

43. **Appropriate but not ideal** because although people have been made aware, the notes have already left the hospital.

44. **Very appropriate** because your clinical advisor can give you the best advice when it is unclear what is best to do.

45. **Appropriate but not ideal** because it prevents Joshua from taking the notes away from the hospital but will cost Megan her time.

Scenario 10:

46. **Very inappropriate** as this is a clear lie and therefore grossly unprofessional.

47. **Very appropriate** because Dr Kelly cannot really explain much to Mr. Marshall without breaking the bad news to him.

48. **Appropriate but not ideal** because this may damage their relationship.

49. **Very inappropriate** because this may create confusion and being unnecessarily cryptic.

50. **Inappropriate but not awful** because although it will address his concerns, Dr Kelly is not the best person to break the news.

Scenario 11:

51. **Very appropriate** because Julia is unable to advise Mary.

52. **Very inappropriate** because Julia isn't experienced enough to assess when Mary will be able to go home.

53. **Inappropriate but not awful** because whilst technically true, it is not Julia's responsibility to advise Mary on anything without the permission of her doctor.

54. **Very appropriate** as she would then be giving correct information and also addressing Mary's concerns.

55. **Inappropriate** because Julia is not qualified and cannot answer Mary's questions.

Scenario 12:

56. **Very appropriate** because it shows that Daniel is trying his best to learn the skill with minimal fuss.

57. **Inappropriate but not awful** because Hannah needs to know that she missed someone out, but it won't solve the immediate problem.

58. **Very inappropriate** because it could have been a genuine mistake on Hannah's part, and will not make the current situation better.

59. **Very appropriate** because it might have been an issue that affected lots of people, instead of just Daniel.

60. **Appropriate but not ideal.** This shows that Daniel cares about his assessment but also means extra hassle for the doctor.

Scenario 13:

61. **Very inappropriate** because her friend will have spent a lot of money on the flights and will be left to fend for herself or not be able to go.

62. **Inappropriate but not awful** because the holiday will not be enjoyable for Helen's friend, and Helen will also not benefit from having a fun experience.

63. **Very appropriate** because Helen also needs a break and being able to go for part of the holiday will be rewarding without having to miss out completely, and will leave enough time to prepare for the exams too.

64. **Very inappropriate** because Helen will be jeopardizing her chances of remaining in medical school.

65. **Very appropriate** because she will not be disappointing her friend as much, and will still be able to do her revision.

Scenario 14:

66. **Very inappropriate** because Celia's parents have not chosen to isolate her on purpose.

67. **Very appropriate** because Celia can meet new people without having to worry about insulting her parents.

68. **Inappropriate but not awful** as although she will be closer to her friends, she may turn into an unwelcome guest quite quickly.

69. **Very inappropriate** because this will affect her mental health and her relationships, and will probably lead to underperformance in her studies as well

70. **Very appropriate** because it shows that she understands her family's situation whilst attempting to address her own predicaments.

Scenario 15:

71. **Very appropriate** – Xun should try to do it to the best of his ability in the remaining time.

72. **Appropriate but not ideal**– it is unlikely that the deadline will be unchanged but there is always space for honesty and he might just be lucky.

73. **Very inappropriate** because this action will affect his final grade.

74. **Very inappropriate** because this is plagiarism and both Xun and his friend would be penalised for it.

75. Very inappropriate because he would be lying to the assessment office and could get into a lot of trouble for it.

Scenario 16:

76. **Very appropriate** because he will be showing that he respects the hospital, infection control, and the patients.

77. **Very inappropriate** because this will set a bad first impression to his patients and colleagues – made worse by his refusal.

78. **Inappropriate but not awful.** Nahor may set a bad first impression but there is a small chance that he might be allowed to keep it.

79. **Very appropriate** because he can still enjoy keeping his hair in an individual style without looking unprofessional.

80. **Appropriate but not ideal.** Whilst this is a proactive approach, it is such a minor issue that it is not worth wasting the dean's time about. In addition, the answer is very likely to be 'no'.

Scenario 17:

81. **Very inappropriate** because Dr Patel will not receive the email until he has handed over to the doctor that they are waiting for and it could affect patient safety if Charles leaves.

82. **Very appropriate** because Charles knew he was going to be on call. If the doctor was running late then it would be different, but as this was planned Charles should wait for his commitment to finish first.

83. **Very appropriate** because it addresses the problem directly and Dr Patel would then know that Charles was leaving.

84. **Inappropriate but not awful** because Charles should not rely on messengers as they aren't as reliable as telling Dr Patel himself.

85. **Very appropriate** because the doctor that is taking over will be aware of the situation and can brief Dr Patel appropriately.

Scenario 18:

86. **Very appropriate** because Archie is being truthful and professional without ignoring the patient and still addresses her concerns.

87. **Very inappropriate** because Archie is not qualified to answer questions regarding management from a patient.

88. **Inappropriate but not awful** because whilst Archie is not giving any harmful information directly, the patient is unlikely to find his advice useful and it doesn't really address the problem.

89. **Very inappropriate** because Archie doesn't have the expertise necessary to give medical advice – with or without the use of Google.

90. **Inappropriate but not awful** because it is doesn't address the problem directly but at least isn't going to make the situation worse.

Scenario 19:

91. **Very appropriate** because they can advise Matthias on the best possible care.

92. **Inappropriate but not awful** because it may slow his recovery and may be dangerous. However, he would at least know if he was able to cope with the activity.

93. **Very appropriate** because it shows that he is being proactive and does not want to waste time.

94. **Very inappropriate** because the medical school might assume that he is being lazy and not going to hospital as he isn't committed.

95. **Inappropriate but not awful** because the medical school should find out from Matthias- not his friends.

Scenario 20:

96. **Very inappropriate** because Jessie may be the only person who notices this and is therefore in a position to address it. If nothing is done, Gemma may become very isolated.

97. **Appropriate** but not ideal because Gemma will probably not want to talk about her eating disorder and avoid the topic in the future.

98. **Very appropriate** because it shows that Jessie can be trusted and is there for Gemma, without being confrontational.

99. **Appropriate but not ideal** as whilst it may make Gemma's parents aware – it is likely to strain their friendship.

100. **Very appropriate** because they will have seen this scenario before, and will know how to respond to it.

Scenario 21:

101. **Inappropriate, but no awful** – although this will allow her to revise for her exams, her friend will have spent a lot of money on the flights and will be left to fend for herself or not be able to go.

102. **Appropriate but not ideal-** Helen would be addressing both issues but given the circumstances, her revision may suffer or her friend may not enjoy the holiday as much.

103. **Very appropriate** because Helen also needs a break and being able to go for part of the holiday would be rewarding and shouldn't affect her revision as long as she comes back early enough.

104. **Very inappropriate** because Helen will be jeopardizing her chances of remaining in medical school.

105. **Very appropriate** because she will not be disappointing her friend as much, and will still be able to do her revision.

Scenario 22:

106. **Of minor importance** because the task should be joint effort.

107. **Important,** because this means that their grade is significant, and Sean will want to do as well as possible.

108. **Important** because they should learn how to work together to prevent future problems with their group work.

109. **Of minor importance-** although this might be troubling Daniel, he shouldn't let his social life affect his work life.

110. **Very important** because Daniel maybe used to not pulling his weight, and will have to be informed that he needs to contribute more.

Scenario 23:

111. **Very important,** because if the essay counts towards Tanya's final mark for the year then she would want to do very well.

112. **Not important at all** – different people learn in different ways and every clinic is different.

113. **Of minor importance,** because Dr Garg will be assessing her at the end of the term.

114. **Very important,** because if this opportunity is available at another time, then missing this particular clinic is not particularly disastrous for Tanya's learning.

115. **Very important,** because Tanya can complete the essay in time for the clinic, then she would not be compromising her learning.

Scenario 24:

116. **Important**, because the doctors that will be assessing Caroline will associate her with the dishevelled looking first year students and it may look unprofessional.

117. **Not important at all**, because they will still be representing the medical school and as such have a duty towards acting properly.

118. **Very important,** because the first year students are therefore expected to dress appropriately and professionally.

119. **Of minor importance,** because if she needs to ask them to dress more appropriately, they shouldn't get offended.

120. **Not important at all** – the students are representing the medical profession and must appear appropriately presentable regardless of when their examinations are.

Scenario 25:

121. **Not important at all** – timetabled clinical commitments should always come first (without extenuating circumstances).

122. **Very important**, because he may have to show a sports contribution to the medical school if he is on a scholarship. If this is the case, his firm head might understand, and rearrange the teaching sessions.

123. **Very important,** because he may not be allowed to finish his degree if he chooses to miss the sessions and not inform the consultant.

124. **Important** because this might allow him to rearrange the teaching sessions.

125. **Very important** because if he is missing invaluable teaching then this will affect his training and disadvantage him in the long run.

Scenario 26:

126. **Not important at all** – patient satisfaction in important and challenging bad practice does not reflect badly on students.

127. **Important** because the patient might be reluctant to ask questions or comply with the treatment if they are uncomfortable.

128. **Important** because if it is not a regular thing, then perhaps it is because Dr Davison is particularly stressed one day and might not be aware that he is swearing.

129. **Of minor importance** because whether or not they are aware of his swearing, it still makes the patient feel uncomfortable.

130. **Very important** because that means that the patient was either comfortable with the doctor previously, or that they were uncomfortable from before.

Scenario 27:

131. **Very important** because the patient could be subjected to avoidable infections, which could be life threatening.

132. **Not important at all** because the risk of the patient receiving an infection is worth the time required for the theatre staff to get more equipment ready.

133. **Of minor importance,** because he is only a medical student so can be forgiven for making mistakes. The repercussions of not saying anything could be far more serious.

134. **Of minor importance** because there is still a risk of infection if he is not sterile but the trolley is. He could still transmit infections.

135. **Of minor importance** because it is still important to protect the patient first and foremost.

Scenario 28:

136. **Important** because if the patient really is in pain then action should be taken. However, given that the patient is addicted to pain medication, it becomes less important.
137. **Not important at all** because her demands for pain medication are irrelevant to the staff, especially since she has just been reviewed by the doctors and nurses.
138. **Very important** because Freddie cannot administer any medications.
139. **Very important** because this means that the pain medication is not working or she is asking for it unnecessarily.
140. **Very important** because the patient has been reviewed and is therefore unlikely to need anything else so soon.

Scenario 29:

141. **Very important** because this is the key issue and the most important one for patient outcomes.
142. **Important** because letting Claire know this would put Claire at ease but it is not an essential piece of information to convey.
143. **Not important at all** as it is irrelevant to Claire's operation.
144. **Very important,** because her anxiety could affect her recovery if she is not completely comfortable with the surgeon.
145. **Very important** because if this is true, it will help Claire's recovery.

Scenario 30:

146. **Of minor importance** because Annabel should respond according to the situation, not because of who is involved. However, she should be wary that her actions are not in revenge.
147. **Important** because it will show that he usually works hard, whether or not he receives the help.
148. **Important** because the help from his rugby friends would not count as cheating.
149. **Not important at all** – Annabel might be jealous that she doesn't have this support network, but that should not influence her actions.
150. **Very important** because it severely disadvantages students who don't have access to the answers.

Scenario 31:

151. **Of minor importance** – whilst it won't stop him progressing with his degree, professionalism is a very important thing, and the medical school might want to investigate it further.
152. **Important,** because Matthew would have evidence of the public transport being delayed.
153. **Not important at all,** because the punctuality of the rest of his class does not reflect on Matthew at all.
154. **Very important,** because if Matthew can prove that his punctuality is usually satisfactory, then he can be more readily forgiven or excused for being late on the one occasion.
155. **Very important,** because Matthew should maintain a good rapport with his teacher if they are to see each other regularly for the next year.

Scenario 32:

156. **Very important,** because the week will be a vital part of her learning experience, and she will miss out if she misses the opportunity.
157. **Of minor importance** because whilst it may not cause seriously harm healthy people, it could seriously harm ill patients.
158. **Not important at all** because the issue here is of infection control – not if Michaela can function in the hospital.
159. **Very important** because if a patient became ill, Michaela would be unable to say that she had not been instructed appropriately.
160. **Important,** as it would be a useful opportunity but not very important because the information is just her friend's opinion.

Scenario 33:

161. **Very important,** as this may be Jenny's only attempt to see what the exams are going to be like.

162. **Of minor importance** – Jenny's education is more important than losing out on money for a ski trip. However, it is still important, especially depending on what her financial situation is, but is not as relevant when deciding on how important the exams are.

163. **Important,** as Jenny would not have to worry about missing them or swapping her exam dates.

164. **Very important,** because if the university agrees to swap their exam dates then the issue would be resolved.

165. **Of minor importance,** although she has done well on exams so far, there is no guarantee that it would be the same for this set of mocks. It is still something to bear in mind whilst making her choice.

Scenario 34:

166. **Very important**, because it shows that he was very interested and proactive in the subject. It can also be used as evidence that Luke should be reconsidered for the project.

167. **Very important** because Architha may be willing to help Luke in his appeal as she could also gain from it.

168. **Not important at all,** because Luke should try to achieve the best grade possible with whichever project he was given.

169. **Of minor importance,** although Luke will find it difficult to concentrate on the project that he was allocated, personal preferences should not hinder his overall performance.

170. **Very important,** because the medical school can show that took his preferences into account.

Scenario 35:

171. **Very important,** because the mark will reflect on her ability for the rest of her life.

172. **Very important,** because this act might prevent Lucinda from getting the job she wants later on in her medical career.

173. **Important,** because it is a short period of time and if their relationship ends then Lucinda would have waster a year.

174. **Of minor importance**- although she is used to being with people that do well, they shouldn't affect her decision.

175. **Of minor importance,** although they are in a relationship, she needs to make the decision herself rather than be pressured into it.

Scenario 36:

176. **Very important,** because Shiv will save a lot of money if he skips the last day.

177. **Not important at all**, because the content of the assessment is not the issue but rather its timing.

178. **Important,** because this shows that Shiv is a good student. It also means that the doctor may have already formed an opinion for Shiv, and might be more likely to be lenient if he misses the final assessment.

179. **Not important at all,** because it will have no impact on Shiv's grade.

180. **Of minor importance** – although Shiv would like to meet with his girlfriend, he will be able to see her eventually so this isn't important in deciding **when** to leave.

Scenario 37:

181. **Very important** because if Jazzmynne won't get another chance to go on tour then it may be worth considering if she can miss classes.

182. **Very important,** because her learning is also important, and if she misses this rotation then she may not necessarily get the chance to catch up again.

183. **Of minor importance,** because Jazzmynne is an adult and if she feels as though she can handle the workload then she should be able to make her decisions herself. However, she should still keep her parent's concerns in mind.

184. **Very important**, because if Jazzmynne sometimes struggles to keep up with her workload without having any help, then with the extra stress of missing lots of work, she might struggle a lot.

185. **Not important at all** as Jazzmynne should not make the decision based on how much she would gain from the tour not because of what her friends decide.

Scenario 38:

186. **Of minor importance.** The changes may not come into action for Ellen to see but if she still feels strongly about the paper then it shouldn't change her actions.

187. **Very important**, as this shows that the university will take the opinions of the students into account.

188. **Very important,** because if the general stories are changed completely, then the majority of student readers may stop reading the papers. This could impact the newspaper's finances adversely.

189. **Of minor importance,** because the principal's stories can still be incorporated into the newspapers without abolishing the papers on the students' social lives.

190. **Not important at all** as this isn't a personal issue and should be handled professionally instead.

Scenario 39:

191. **Very important,** because the student bars should be safe, controlled spaces for the students to enjoy themselves.

192. **Of minor importance** – whilst extra money would be useful, the decision to appeal should be based on the needs of the student body rather than serving a selfish agenda.

193. **Very important**, because this is another factor that could bring their satisfaction ratings down further.

194. **Not important at all** – the issue is not about the cost but about the waiting times.

195. **Important,** because expanding the bar could bring in more money for the university.

Scenario 40:

196. **Not important at all,** because this should be handled amiably rather than making it personal.

197. **Very important,** because Phil does not have a chance of running again, but Olivia does.

198. **Important,** because it shows that Olivia is dedicated to the student union. It is not very important as there will be other factors that will differentiate Olivia and Phil.

199. **Very important,** because this excludes any chance of compromise with position allocation.

200. **Very important,** because it shows that Olivia has already compromised with the position previously, and will be unlikely to want to compromise again

Arrive well rested, well fed and well hydrated

UKCAT is an intensive test, so make sure you're ready for it! Unfortunately you can't take water into the test, so be well hydrated before you go in. Make sure you're well rested and fed in order to be at your best!

Ask for extra whiteboards

If you're running short of whiteboard space and need another, **plan ahead and put up your hand in good time**. You don't want to be stuck with nowhere to write, waiting for someone to notice and come to help you! Act early.

Move On

If you're struggling, move on. Every question has equal weighting and there is no negative marking. In the time it takes to answer on hard question, you could gain three times the marks by answering the easier ones. Be smart to score points

Using your UKCAT Score

Different medical schools use UKCAT in different ways – so use this to your advantage! If you score well on UKCAT, you may help your chances of success by choosing medical schools which use it as a major component of the application process. On the other hand, if your score isn't so good, you may prefer to opt for universities that don't look at your UKCAT score, or ones that use it as a more minor consideration.

By making choices after finding out your score, you can increase your chance of getting a place.

Afterword

Remember that the route to a high score is your approach and practice. Don't fall into the trap that "*you can't prepare for the UKCAT*"– this could not be further from the truth. With knowledge of the test, some useful time-saving techniques and plenty of practice you can dramatically boost your score.

Work hard, never give up and do yourself justice.

Good luck!

Acknowledgements

I would like to express my gratitude to everyone who helped make this book a reality, especially the 20 Medical Tutors who shared their expertise in compiling this huge collection of questions and answers. Special thanks go to my friends and family for their endless care and emotional support. Lastly, this would be complete without thanking Rohan, whose tireless work and good humour has made everything possible.

David Salt

About UniAdmissions

UniAdmissions is the UK's number one university admissions company, specialising in supporting **applications to Medical School and to Oxbridge**.

Every year, *UniAdmissions* works with hundreds of applicants and schools across the UK. From free resources to these *Ultimate Guide Books* and from intensive courses to bespoke individual tuition, *UniAdmissions* boasts a team of **300 Expert Tutors** and a proven track record of producing great results.

We also run an **access scheme** that provides disadvantaged students with free support. To find out more about our support like intensive **UKCAT courses** and **UKCAT tuition**, check out our website **www.uniadmissions.co.uk/ukcat**

THE ULTIMATE BMAT GUIDE

600

PRACTICE QUESTIONS

- ✓ Fully Worked Solutions
- ✓ Time Saving Techniques
- ✓ 10 Annotated Essays
- ✓ Score Boosting Strategies

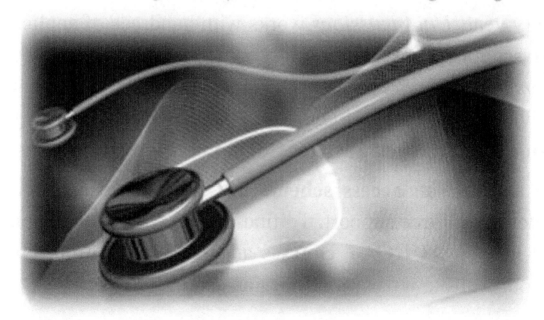

2016 ENTRY

Rohan Agarwal

UniAdmissions

www.uniadmissions.co.uk/bmat-book

BMAT
PAST PAPER
WORKED SOLUTIONS

- ✓ 2003 - 2014
- ✓ Detailed Essay Plans
- ✓ Fully Worked Answers
- ✓ 600+ Questions Explained

2015/16 ENTRY

Rohan Agarwal

UniAdmissions

www.uniadmissions.co.uk/bmat-past-papers

THE ULTIMATE OXBRIDGE INTERVIEW GUIDE

✓ Worked Answers   ✓ 18 Subjects
✓ 900 Past Questions   ✓ Expert Advice

2016 ENTRY

Rohan Agarwal

UniAdmissions

www.uniadmissions.co.uk/oxbridge-interview-book

UKCAT INTENSIVE COURSE

If you're looking to improve your UKCAT score in a short space of time, our **UKCAT intensive course** is perfect for you. It's a fully interactive seminar that guides you through all 5 sections of the UKCAT.

You are taught by our experienced UKCAT experts, who are Doctors or senior Oxbridge medical tutors who excelled in the UKCAT. The aim is to teach you powerful time-saving techniques and strategies to help you succeed for test day.

➢ Full Day intensive Course
➢ Guaranteed Small Groups
➢ 2 Full Practice Papers (Worth £ 50)
➢ Ongoing Tutor Support until Test date – never be alone again.

Timetable:

➢ **1030 - 1200:** Section 1
➢ **1200 - 1300:** Section 2
➢ **1300 - 1330:** Lunch
➢ **1330 - 1415:** Section 2

➢ **1415 - 1445:** Section 3
➢ **1500 - 1700:** Mock Test
➢ **1710 - 1750:** Mock Test Debrief
➢ **1750 - 1800:** Questions

Bookings for 2015 open on 15th April and courses are held in *London, Birmingham, Manchester and Leeds* throughout June - September.

The course is normally £175 but you can get £25 off by using the code *"UKCATUG25"* at checkout.

www.uniadmissions.co.uk/ukcat-crash-course

MEDICINE INTERVIEW COURSE

If you've got an upcoming interview for medical school – this is the perfect course for you. You get individual attention throughout the day and are taught by Oxbridge tutors + senior doctors on how to approach the medical interview.

- ➤ Full Day intensive Course
- ➤ Guaranteed Small Groups
- ➤ 4 Hours of Small group teaching
- ➤ 2 x 30 minute individual Mock Interviews + Written Feedback
- ➤ Full MMI interview circuit with written feedback
- ➤ Ongoing Tutor Support until your interview – never be alone again

Timetable:

- ➤ **1000 - 1015:** Registration
- ➤ **1015 - 1030:** Talk: Key to interview Success
- ➤ **1030 - 1130:** Tutorial: Common Interview Questions
- ➤ **1145 - 1245:** 2 x Individual Mock Interviews
- ➤ **1245 - 1330:** Lunch
- ➤ **1330 - 1430:** Medical Ethics Workshop
- ➤ **1445 - 1545:** MMI Circuit
- ➤ **1600 - 1645:** Situational Judgement Workshop
- ➤ **1645 - 1730:** Debrief and Finish

Bookings for 2015 open on 15th September and courses are held in *London,* throughout November + December.

The course is normally £295 but you can get £35 off by using the code *"UKCATUG35"* at checkout.

www.uniadmissions.co.uk/medical-school-interview-course

NOTES

NOTES

CPSIA information can be obtained
at www.ICGtesting.com
Printed in the USA
LVOW03s1919230516

489548LV00013B/590/P

9 780993 231117